Apple Pro Training Series

The Craft of Editing with Final Cut Pro

Michael Wohl

Apple
Certified

Apple Pro Training Series: The Craft of Editing with Final Cut Pro
Michael Wohl
Copyright © 2008 by Michael Wohl

Published by Peachpit Press. For information on Peachpit Press books, contact:

Peachpit Press
1249 Eighth Street
Berkeley, CA 94710
(510) 524-2178
Fax: (510) 524-2221
http://www.peachpit.com
To report errors, please send a note to errata@peachpit.com
Peachpit Press is a division of Pearson Education

Editor: Bob Lindstrom
Apple Series Editor: Serena Herr
Production Coordinator: Laurie Stewart, Happenstance Type-O-Rama
Technical Editor and Reviewer: K.D. Gulko
Copy Editor: Darren Meiss
Compositor: Happenstance Type-O-Rama
Indexer: Karin Arrigoni
Cover Illustration: Kent Oberheu
Cover Production: Happenstance Type-O-Rama
Media Reviewer: Eric Geoffroy

ISBN 10: 0-321-52036-X
ISBN 13: 978-0-321-52036-4

9 8 7 6 5 4 3 2 1
Printed and bound in the United States of America

Contents at a Glance

Table of Contents

Getting Started

Welcome to the official training course for learning the craft of editing with Final Cut Pro 6, Apple's dynamic and powerful nonlinear editing software. The goal of this book is to build upon your technical knowledge of editing with Final Cut Pro by introducing you to the aesthetic and structural challenges you will face as you sit down to edit.

This book assumes that you're comfortable with the basic operation of Final Cut Pro and aims to take you to the next level: transforming you from a technician into an artist. Just as knowing how to use a pencil doesn't make you a writer, knowing how to operate Final Cut Pro doesn't make you an editor.

Like the pencil, Final Cut Pro 6 is an incredibly versatile tool. The pencil can produce a technical manual or a poem, a carrot cake recipe or the notes of Beethoven's Fifth Symphony. Similarly, Final Cut Pro can turn out instructional videos or action scenes, dramatic dialogue sequences or sports documentaries.

This book teaches methods of editing projects just like those and will help you develop your creative skills while increasing your Final Cut Pro skills.

Furthermore, each type of project also requires a different mental approach. The lessons in this book explore *why* editors make the decisions they do, and those lessons will get you to think about your own editing in a new light.

Section One begins with a simple dialogue scene from the short film *Hope*, in which you'll learn the fundamentals of dramatic action and narrative storytelling. Later, you'll explore action scenes, including fight and chase scenes from the films *Broken Fists* and *Slapdash*.

Section Two covers editing nonfiction material such as interviews, music videos, and event documentaries. You'll cut scenes from a behind-the-scenes featurette, a documentary travel show, and a real-world music video.

Section Three explores the audio side of the post-production process, dealing extensively with sound design, sweetening dialogue tracks, conceiving and constructing ambiances and sound effects, and adding and editing music. Then, you'll create a final mix in which all your tracks are combined and finessed into a cohesive masterpiece.

The book concludes with a chapter on "putting it all together" that discusses techniques and considerations at the macro level of completing a long-form show. From scene-cuts and transitions to eliminating possible redundancies, you'll acquire a deeper understanding of the entire editing process for a wide variety of program types.

Each of the projects on the DVD contains copious extra media associated with the lesson. All of it is real-world footage gleaned from actual projects. After completing the exercises in each lesson, you are strongly encouraged to continue working with the project, exploring various ways to implement the concepts. You can try different ways of editing each scene to understand how your choices affect your audience's understanding of the material.

Throughout the book, you'll learn advanced Final Cut Pro tips and tricks, such as dynamic trimming, slipping and sliding, and subframe audio editing. You'll also learn what makes an effective montage, and how to use split edits to tell better stories.

This book is unique in its approach, in that it is much more than a guide to improving your expertise with Final Cut Pro software. It immerses that software into real-world scenarios that editors face every day. And learning how to handle those scenarios will not only teach you how to make the most of Final Cut Pro, it will also teach you how to be a great editor.

The Methodology

The emphasis of this book is hands-on training. Each exercise was designed to help you start editing at a professional level in Final Cut Pro as quickly as possible. The book assumes a basic level of familiarity with the Final Cut Pro interface and with the fundamentals of postproduction. If you are new to video editing, it would be helpful for you to start at the beginning and progress through each lesson in order. However, every section (and every lesson) is self-contained, so if you are familiar with basic editing techniques, you can start with any section and focus on that topic.

Course Structure

This book was designed to help you master the most critical professional-level editing and postproduction techniques in Final Cut Pro. Each lesson expands on the basic concepts of digital video editing, giving you the tools to customize your project workflows and use the program for your own purposes. The book delves into features that are not frequently touched on, including a special section about using Compressor to transcode and export files to a variety of formats.

The lessons fall into the following sections:

▶   Lessons 1–5: Cutting Dramatic Material

You will learn the secrets of cutting narrative scenes, including both simple and complex dialogue scenes, basic action scenes, and complex action scenes such as fights and chases. Plus, the section includes a special lesson on editing comedy.

▶   Lessons 6–9: Cutting Nonfiction Material

This section covers interviews and associated B-roll footage, documenting an event such as a wedding or trade show, and cutting a music video.

▶   Lessons 10–11: Working with Audio

You'll focus on the concepts and processes of audio editing, sound design, sound mixing, and other audio finishing techniques.

▶   Lesson 12: The Big Picture

The final lesson addresses unique concerns for combining multiple scenes into a single show.

System Requirements

Before beginning this book, you should have a working knowledge of your computer and its operating system, as well as a basic level of proficiency with Final Cut Pro.

Basic system requirements for Final Cut Pro 6 include:

- ▶ A Macintosh computer with a 1.25 GHz or faster PowerPC G4, PowerPC G5, Intel Core Duo, or Intel Xeon processor
- ▶ Mac OS X version v10.4.9 or later
- ▶ 1 GB of RAM or more
- ▶ An AGP or PCI Express Quartz Extreme graphics card
- ▶ A DVD drive
- ▶ A separate hard drive for media (recommended)

Consult the Final Cut Studio 2 technical specifications page (www.apple.com/finalcutstudio/specs.html) for complete details on specific system requirements and qualified third-party devices such as cameras, capture cards, and other peripherals.

Copying the Lesson Files

All the files you need to complete the lessons are found on the two DVD-ROM discs that come with this book.

Installing the Lesson Files

1   Insert the *APTS Craft Of Editing DVD 1* into your DVD drive.

2   For best results, drag the entire Craft_of_Editing_Book_Files folder from DVD 1 to the top level of your computer's hard drive or an attached media drive.

3   Remove *APTS Craft of Editing DVD 1* from your DVD drive and insert *APTS Craft of Editing DVD 2*.

4   Select the entire contents of DVD 2 and copy them into the Media folder on your hard drive inside the Craft_of_Editing_Book_Files folder you copied from DVD 1.

There is a total of approximately 17 GB of data on both discs.

NOTE ▶ When you keep all the lesson files and media files from the disc together in one single Craft_of_Editing_Book_Files folder on your hard drive, just as you find them on the DVD, you will ensure that the tutorial project files for each lesson will open with their media files all correctly linked and ready for you to begin the lesson.

5   To begin each lesson, launch Final Cut Pro and then open the project file listed at the beginning of each lesson.

Reconnecting Broken Media Links

For any number of reasons, you may need to separate the lesson files from the media files when you install and use them. For instance, you may choose to keep the project files in a user home directory and the media files on a dedicated media drive. In this case, when you open a project file, a window will appear asking you to reconnect the project files to their source media files.

Reconnecting files is a simple process. Just follow these steps:

1   When you first open a lesson's project file, a Final Cut Pro dialog will appear listing one or more files that are offline. Click the Reconnect button.

A Final Cut Pro Reconnect Files window appears.

2   Click Search.

Final Cut Pro will search any attached hard disks looking for the missing files. When it finds the first file, a Mac OS X Reconnect dialog will appear.

3   Select the highlighted file and click Choose.

In the Final Cut Pro Reconnect Files dialog, all of the offline files will be moved to the lower Files Located pane.

4   Click Connect.

5   Be sure to save the newly reconnected project file, or you will have to perform the reconnect operation every time you open it.

About the Apple Pro Training Series

The Craft of Editing with Final Cut Pro is part of the official training series for Apple Pro applications, developed by experts in the field and certified by Apple, Inc. The series is the course curriculum used by Apple Authorized Training Centers worldwide, and offers complete training in all Apple Pro products. The lessons are designed to let you learn at your own pace. Although each lesson provides step-by-step instructions for creating specific projects, there's room for exploration and experimentation. Each lesson concludes with review questions and answers summarizing what you've learned, which can be used to help you prepare for the Apple Pro Certification Exam.

For a complete list of Apple Pro Training Series books, see the course catalog at the end of this book, or visit www.peachpit.com/applebooklet.

Apple Pro Certification Program

The Apple Pro Training and Certification Program is designed to keep you at the forefront of Apple's digital media technology while giving you a competitive edge in today's ever-changing job market. Whether you're an editor, graphic designer, sound designer, special effects artist, or teacher, these training tools are meant to help you expand your skills.

Upon completing the course material in this book, you can become a certified Apple Pro by taking the certification exam at an Apple Authorized Training Center. Successful certification as an Apple Pro gives you official recognition of your knowledge of Apple's professional applications while allowing you to market yourself to employers and clients as a skilled, pro-level user of Apple products.

For those who prefer to learn in an instructor-led setting, Apple offers training courses at Apple Authorized Training Centers worldwide. These courses, which use the Apple Pro Training Series books as their curriculum, are taught by Apple Certified Trainers and balance concepts and lectures with hands-on labs and exercises. Apple Authorized Training Centers have been carefully selected and have met Apple's highest standards in all areas, including facilities, instructors, course delivery, and infrastructure. The goal of the program is to offer Apple customers, from beginners to the most seasoned professionals, the highest-quality training experience.

For more information or to find an Authorized Training Center near you, go to www.apple.com/software/pro/training.

Resources

This book is not intended as a comprehensive reference manual, nor does it replace the documentation that comes with the application. For comprehensive information about program features, refer to these resources:

► The Reference Guide. Accessed through the Final Cut Pro Help menu, the Reference Guide contains a complete description of all features.

► Apple's website: www.apple.com.

► Peachpit's website: As Final Cut Pro 6 is updated, Peachpit may choose to update lessons or post additional exercises as necessary on this book's companion web page. Please check www.peachpit.com/title/032152036X for revised lessons.

Cutting Dramatic Material

1

Lesson Files	Lesson Files > Lesson 01 > Basic Dialogue
Media	Media > Hope Dialogue
Time	This lesson takes approximately 120 minutes to complete.
Goals	Apply the fundamentals of storytelling to editing
	Identify the essential question that each shot answers
	Organize footage based on the needs of each scene
	Master the basic structure shared by all dialogue scenes
	Control dramatic focus to inspire edits
	Use action in a scene to guide edit decisions
	Efficiently move back out to a wider shot
	Split audio and video to hide edits

Editing Dialogue

The craft of editing requires a variety of skills and talents, ranging from understanding rhythm and timing to recognizing effective performances. You do need to know how to use Final Cut Pro (or a similar editing program) but a skilled editor also needs to know the medium inside and out. She must distill each bit of visual and audio information down to its elemental core and meaning; intuitively grasp the subtle difference between a close-up and a medium close-up; hear ten distinct sounds in a single ambience; and know how a fifth of a second can be the difference between suspense and comedy.

This volume is an advanced book, and assumes you already have a basic understanding of the tools and commands of Final Cut Pro. While this book will improve your mastery of the software and familiarize you with some of its more advanced and subtle features, the book's true purpose is to get you thinking more about why you make certain editing decisions rather than just how or which buttons to press. In many ways this book will serve as a sort of primer on the language of editing, familiarizing you with common words and turns of phrase as well as identifying the grammatical rules and trends.

Editing is a creative expression, so those rules may often beg to be broken. However, your communication will be most effective if you understand why the rules work, even if you choose to ignore them.

Learning the Language of Film

To be a film editor, you must learn to speak a new language, and to communicate effectively you must be fluent in that language. As a dutiful consumer of media, you almost certainly understand what you watch on TV, but that doesn't make you *literate*. Literacy requires the ability to read and write the language; to disassemble it and then reassemble it; to understand not only what a film means, but *why* it means what it does.

Such literacy takes time and effort. While you can teach yourself through experimentation and trial and error, the best way to learn is by pursuing both formal training and guided exercises. This book and its corresponding Apple Certification Program provide both.

Obviously, training is just a starting point. The exercises provided here are just examples of the types of situations and editorial challenges you might encounter. Every project is unique, and every show provides nearly infinite possibilities for telling its particular story. Your skill will grow the more you practice, and eventually your editing will become completely intuitive, just like reading and writing any language in which you are truly fluent.

Using Cinematic Language

The language of cinema combines images and sounds, but otherwise it is just like any other language. This is not a metaphor. A language is any systematic means of communicating information. By choosing different words, or phrasing something differently, subtle differences in meaning are conveyed. The more deftly you choose your words, and the more creatively you arrange your phrases, the more precisely and accurately you control how the story is told.

As with any language, to master this language of film you need to learn the system and syntax. Shots and sequences are just like words and phrases. Cuts and transitions serve as punctuation, controlling the flow and pacing of meaning and message. Grammatical rules such as "starting on a master shot" or "matching similar angles" help your viewer understand what type of story you are telling. The same "words" can construct poetry or prose, novels or training manuals.

Understanding these rules is fundamental to successful editing. Remember, the purpose of editing is to communicate. If your idea or point isn't clear to the viewer, you haven't communicated successfully. Of course, like any language this one is constantly evolving and growing. New ideas and techniques are forever emerging. Idioms and trends arise and fall out of fashion.

Understanding the Editor as Storyteller

Who is a film's storyteller? The writer conceives the world and the structure of the story. The director and the production crew realize that world, capturing its sounds and images. But it is the editor who *tells* the story. It is his "voice" that actually reaches the audience.

Everyone knows someone who's a great storyteller; someone who can captivate you even when describing something mundane. Conversely, everyone knows someone who can hardly tell a joke. Have you ever stopped to think about what makes that first person so fascinating? Or what ruins a joke? If you want to be an editor, you need to think about those questions. You need to understand the mechanics of *story*.

What is a story? A story is way of packaging information so it's easy to understand. In part, a story is a collection of facts constructed in a way that our brains find easy to remember. But stories are more than that. They have a magical quality, and engage us in a special way. Stories resonate in a way that tickles us, terrifies us, makes us laugh, and moves us to tears. But stories are not just fantasy. They are, in fact, how we make sense of the world. Our brains are specifically programmed to understand the world in terms of stories.

Who, what, why, when, where, and how. Are these questions familiar? Of course they are. In fact, they are possibly the six most important words in the language. Those simple questions are the tools for taking apart and understanding a story and, by extension, for understanding the world. They are also the tools for assembling a story.

Good stories are constructed by revealing the answers to those six one-word questions in a thoughtful and deliberate way. The answers must be disclosed just as the listener is ready for them and not before or after. If a storyteller spends too much time explaining *where* something took place, the listener might lose track of *who* the story was about. If the teller spends too much time explaining *why* the three men walked into the bar and doesn't get around to explaining *what* they were doing there, the listener loses interest and the joke is spoiled.

Okay, but how does this relate to video editing? It is absolutely fundamental. Every sequence you construct is a story that answers those six questions. As an editor, you must thoughtfully and deliberately answer each one, and must reveal them just as the viewer is anticipating them. Furthermore, every shot in your film answers one of those questions. One shot might identify the *who*. Another shot might clarify the *where* or even the *why*. In fact, you can nearly count on the fact that different shot types reliably answer different questions.

Close-ups tell us *who* the story is about.

Long shots illustrate *where* a scene is taking place.

Extreme close-ups put the audience inside a character's head, revealing (often with the help of sound) *why* the character is acting a certain way.

And so on. Sometimes a shot will answer more than one question, and many shots, such as over the shoulder or two-shots, focus on defining the relationships between characters, answering the question *with whom*. The editor's job is to carefully craft each scene by revealing the answers to each of those basic questions at the precise moment that they will most effectively communicate with the audience.

For example, in the most common scene-opening technique, the first shot is a master wide shot. The *where* and sometimes the *what* questions are answered, but the audience quickly begins to wonder *who* the scene is about. If the editor waits too long to cut to a close-up (CU) to answer the audience's implicit question, the scene will likely lose energy and lose its audience.

Conversely, if you begin a scene on a CU and continue to cut back and forth on CUs without ever backing out to a wider shot, the *who* of the scene remains perfectly clear, but the audience will begin to lose a sense of the *where*, the environment in which the scene is taking place. The reality of the scene will evaporate. At best, viewers will be confused; at worst, they'll change the channel.

Wielding the Secret Weapon

There is one more fundamental component of an effective story that the editor must be fully aware of in order to edit effectively: What is the story about?

The theme or main idea of the story ought to be present in every single shot in the movie. Ideally, the choices of camera angles, the lighting, the production design, and, most of all, the content of the shots will reinforce the theme. Whether they do or not, it is the editor's job to find those shots that illuminate the theme and discard the shots that cloud it.

All the magic of story, all the techniques of teasing the audience with the answers to those six questions—leading them along and engaging their emotions—are just tricks to entice them to listen to the underlying theme. Story is the spoonful of sugar that helps the medicine of theme go down.

Theme doesn't have to be heady or abstract. In advertisements, the theme is usually just the merits of the product being hawked. In many nonfiction films, the theme or purpose is expressly stated. But it's no coincidence that dramatic films are often the most effective and moving expressions of a theme, precisely because the themes are persuasively threaded into the twine of story rather than explicitly stated.

If the editor doesn't know what the theme is, or doesn't understand it clearly, it's unlikely he will be able to edit a scene in the most effective manner.

Pursuing the Invisible Art

Among the most important aspects of the editor's job is the ability to stay out of the way. It's hard for an audience to stare at a two-dimensional movie or television screen and suspend their disbelief long enough to become engaged in the story you're telling. Every time you cut, you potentially make it that much harder. Every edit is a small interruption in the flow of the story; an opportunity for the viewer to disengage and start wondering where her car is parked or if that show she likes on that other channel has started yet. It's a chance to become distracted by a growling stomach or a full bladder. Once that happens, you've lost your viewer, and that precious theme you'd been hoping to communicate is lost with her.

Your editing must strive at all times to hide the artifice of filmmaking. Your goal is to distract the viewer from the edits that keep the story moving forward; to make the action within the scene appear perfectly smooth and realistic; to stitch together the dozen or more individual shots that were recorded over many hours into 2 minutes of seamless storytelling. And you must make it look effortless.

If you have done your job properly, in fact, the film should look like there was no editing at all. Never mind the hours you have to spend finessing one edit in which a door was slammed in one shot and was gently pushed shut in another. Good editing is invisible.

If you crave the limelight, become an actor (or maybe a director). An editor's job is to make those people look good and then to quietly step back into the wings and disappear.

But don't confuse this with thinking that an editor's role is unimportant. Making those invisible edits, controlling the viewer's focus, *telling* the story the writer conceived and the production crew realized is absolutely vital to effective filmmaking.

Of course, there are exceptions to the invisible edit rule. Sometimes edits are deliberately highlighted. Sometimes sound design or other elements of your job are best brought to the fore. Indeed, a whole school of filmmakers believe that the more the artifice of film is exposed, the more effective and moving a film will be. But don't be fooled into thinking that you don't need to master your craft. Even the most glaring jump cut must be made deliberately and with the conscious intention of conveying an underlying meaning and controlling the audience's focus.

Editing the Basic Dialogue Sequence

Enough theory, it's time to start editing!

Not all projects include narrative-style dialogue, but this sequence type is so basic, and incorporates so many of the fundamental tenets of editing technique, that it's an ideal place to start. The techniques described here are the foundation of nearly every other kind of scene you will encounter, in both dramatic and nondramatic projects.

The first step is to get familiar with the footage available to you.

1   Start Final Cut Pro and open the **Basic Dialogue** project.

This project contains a dialogue scene set in a diner from the film "Hope."

2   Double-click shot **1-2** and play it in the Viewer.

This shot is a master full shot that shows the entire scene. While it does a great job of answering the where question, once the main dialogue begins, it's too far away and too far *off-axis* to answer much of the who, why, or how.

3 Scroll the Browser columns until the Description and comment fields are visible.

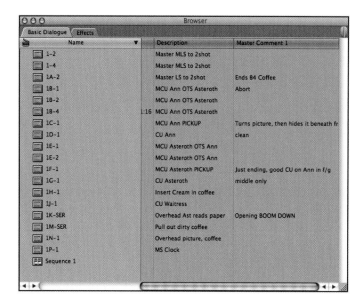

Dialogue scenes almost always contain the same standard coverage: a master shot that shows both parties, usually from a neutral angle; a pair of matching over-the-shoulder (OTS) singles; and a pair of matching clean singles.

That's it. Five shots. And it's all you need.

> **NOTE ▶** A *single* is any shot of one person, usually a close-up or medium close-up. A *dirty single* is an over-the-shoulder shot where just a little of the person in the foreground is visible. A *clean single* is one where the person in the foreground is completely out of the shot, leaving an unobstructed, or clean, view of the subject.

You might think cutting a dialogue scene is boring, or perhaps deceptively easy, but it's not true. Every day, hundreds of scenes just like this are cut, and each one is unique—guided by the nuances of the performances, and the actions and reactions within the scene.

At best, the coverage also includes a few *cutaways* and *inserts* to give you some editorial flexibility, and occasionally there'll be a *special*: a shot intended for a transition into or out of the scene. Most of the time, however, you'll work with those five main shots.

But don't worry. There's infinite room for creativity, even with such limited and predictable coverage. Think how many simple dialogue scenes there are in every film or television show. Even though the vast majority of those scenes follow this same pattern, every one feels fresh and unique. Why? Because it works. It keeps the focus on the content, not the camerawork, and it gives the editor everything needed to tell the story.

Organizing Your Clips

It's absolutely critical that you become intimately familiar with all of the available footage before you begin to cut a scene. Get in the habit of watching every take of every shot. Use markers or take notes to identify interesting and important moments.

Usually, this footage analysis begins during logging, when you can also incorporate notes from the director and information from the camera log. But if an assistant logged the footage for you, you must take some time to study the footage before diving into the scene.

One easy way to build this step into your process is to begin every scene by identifying and categorizing all of your shots. You can do this by moving clips into different bins or by making notes in one of the many comment fields. Presumably the shots have already been grouped according to scene, but now you can further categorize them by shot type, angle, or other pertinent information.

In the next example, you will use Final Cut Pro's colored labels to identify which characters appear in which shots.

1   Select all of the **1B** shots, as well as **1C-1** and **1D-1**.

These are all of the shots that favor the character Ann.

2 Control-click the selected clips and from the shortcut menu choose Label > Best Take to turn the clips red.

Right now, it's easy to remember that for this sequence, "Best Take" simply means "Shots of Ann." However, this might prove to be confusing if you are sharing this project with another editor, or if you put it down and return to it several months from now. To prevent any such confusion, you can change the text associated with the labels.

3 Choose Final Cut Pro > User Preferences and click the Labels tab.

4 Change the text next to the red color to *Ann*, change the blue label to *Asteroth*, and change purple to *Both Ann & Asteroth*.

	Good Take
■	Ann
	Asteroth
■	Both Ann & Asteroth
	B Roll

The color purple is a good visual clue, since purple is a combination of red and blue. If you prefer, you can set the labels however you like. Rather than ignore the two remaining labels, you can put them to good use, too.

5   Change the text for the color orange to *Cutaways* and the text for green to *Inserts*.

	Cutaways
■	Ann
	Asteroth
■	Both Ann & Asteroth
	Inserts

Don't worry if you don't know exactly what cutaways and inserts are. You'll learn that in a moment.

6   Click OK to close the window.

7   In the Browser, select the **1E**, **1F**, **1G**, and **1K** shots. Choose Modify > Label > Asteroth.

Name	Description	Master Commer
1-2	Master MLS to 2shot	
1-4	Master MLS to 2shot	
1A-2	Master LS to 2shot	Ends B4 Coffee
1B-1	MCU Ann OTS Asteroth	Abort
1B-2	MCU Ann OTS Asteroth	
1B-4	6 MCU Ann OTS Asteroth	
1C-1	MCU Ann PICKUP	Turns picture, th
1D-1	CU Ann	clean
1E-1	MCU Asteroth OTS Ann	
1E-2	MCU Asteroth OTS Ann	
1F-1	MCU Asteroth PICKUP	Just ending, goc
1G-1	CU Asteroth	middle only
1H-1	Insert Cream in coffee	
1J-1	CU Waitress	
1K-SER	Overhead Ast reads paper	Opening BOOM i
1M-SER	Pull out dirty coffee	
1N-1	Overhead picture, coffee	
1P-1	MS Clock	
Sequence 1		

1K is a *special* that doesn't fit into the standard coverage categories, but because it's a shot of Asteroth, it is helpful to label it with his color.

8 Scenes **1** and **1A** are both versions of the master scene, so make them purple.

That covers the basic coverage of the two actors, but a few clips are still unaccounted for.

9 Double-click **1H-1** and play it in the Viewer.

This is an insert shot of Ann pouring cream into her coffee. An *insert* is any shot that focuses on an action that occurs within other shots.

10 Double-click **1N-1** and play it in the Viewer.

The subject of this shot is the photograph. This is clearly another insert. These inserts are a bit wider than typical inserts. A more traditional insert of the photo probably would have been an extreme close-up (ECU) from Asteroth's point of view (POV). Still, they serve the classic purpose of an insert: to draw attention to a detail within the scene, and to provide options for the editor.

11 Select **1N-1** and **1H-1** and label them as Inserts (green).

Alternately, a shot of something in the environment but not visible in the other shots (such as a shot of the jukebox or the rotating pie display) would not be an insert but a *cutaway*. Cutaways are typically more flexible than inserts. Inserts must be used at the precise moment when the action occurs in the scene or not at all, but a cutaway can be used almost any time in the scene.

12 Double-click **1P-1** and play it in the Viewer.

This is a classic example of a cutaway.

13 Label **1P-1** as Cutaways (orange).

All that remain unlabeled are shots **1J-1** and **1M-SER**.

14 Open and play shot **1J-1**.

Shot **1J-1** is a CU of the waitress pouring coffee. Technically, this is neither an insert nor a cutaway, but it serves similar purposes. The scene could play perfectly well without ever showing the face of the waitress, but it gives the opportunity to provide an outside perspective on the conversation between Ann and Asteroth. It also provides further editorial flexibility. Leave this shot unlabeled.

15 Open and play shot **1M-SER**.

This shot is not really of Ann, and the pullout makes it not just an insert of the coffee. In fact, it's another special that mirrors the overhead shot of Asteroth, and is designed specifically to end the sequence.

The director carefully chose these overhead bookend shots to lend uniqueness and style to the scene. Since the movie overall is about heaven and hell, this overhead POV offers a subtle reference to an omniscience that will be reflected later in the film. Leave shot **1M-SER** unlabeled.

Although this bin only contains 18 clips, doing this sort of organization before beginning your edit is great practice. It allows you to instantly access exactly the shots you need, exactly when you need them.

Remember that good cutting requires that you keep a sense of rhythm and stay engaged in the detailed nuance of a scene. If, in the middle of editing, you have to stop and audition a number of clips to look for the right shot, or manually shuttle through a long piece of media to find the correct section, you can lose the momentum and excitement of the moment.

Part of what makes Final Cut Pro unique, and part of what makes it so popular, is the attention it pays to the subtle but critical need for the operator to sustain focus while editing. By taking advantage of features designed to speed your work and remove obstacles and extraneous steps in the process, you can remain focused on the heat and passion of the edit, and groove to the rhythm of the scene.

Begin with the Master Shot

The easiest and most sensible way to begin editing a typical scene is to start with the master shot. The master shot by definition includes the entire scene and, while it may not be the optimal framing for every moment, it provides a framework for you to lean on as you experiment with other shots.

Beginning with the master doesn't mean the sequence ultimately needs to open with it. Precocious young editors automatically frown at the idea of beginning so traditionally, pre-ferring to open a scene on an insert or a close-up. You'll have plenty of time to change the opening shot of the sequence; but to untangle the various shots and weave the story together, it helps to understand the original structure put forth on the set.

1   Double-click *Sequence 1* to open it into the Canvas and Timeline.

2   Open clip 1-2.

3   Set an In point after the director calls "action" and before Ann enters the diner (around 01:00:36:00). Set an Out point at the end of the scene, after she pushes the coffee away and before the director calls "cut" (approximately 03:15:15).

4   Edit the clip into the sequence.

▶ Watch for Performance

Remember that the most important things an editor should be observing are the actors' performances. Even a brief moment of less-than-optimum performance can destroy a scene's illusion of truth. It is your responsibility to the director, to the actors, and to the project to find the best performances for each line, each moment, and each beat of the scene and try to incorporate them. Inevitably, there will be trade-offs; there might be a camera error that undermines a great moment, or a car horn that might spoil an otherwise perfect shot.

Sometimes the compromises will be more editorial. A change of screen direction or a bit of business might not match from one shot to the next, so you have to use a less-than-perfect take in which the action does match. In another situation, a scene could be too long and you need to trim a few lines of dialogue, or just pull out some of the "air" between lines, thereby changing the nature of the performance.

Don't worry, there are tricks: using those cutaways and inserts, stealing the audio from an alternate take, trimming out a word or a whole line by going to the OTS where you can't see the actor's lips, and so on. In some ways, maintaining the performance quality is the single most important part of your job.

A New Shot Means New Information

If the performances are flawless in the master shot, and no technical elements require cutting, there may be absolutely no reason to even touch a scene. Just drop it in and move on to the next scene. Unfortunately, this is rarely the case, and it is not the case in this scene.

But how do you know when to change the angle? And what to change it to? These are perhaps the most fundamental questions an editor faces. The answer to both is that you should cut to a new shot when doing so will provide new information that will propel the story forward. Every new cut *must provide new information.*

A new shot must answer another of the six basic questions. The shot could be a CU of an actor's reaction that reveals an inner conflict or emotion *(why* or *what)*. It could be a wider shot that gives context to the events in the previous shot *(where* or *when)*. Or it could be a new shot that shows a simple mechanical detail such as a loaded gun *(how)*. No matter what, the new shot must provide new information that will propel the story forward.

So you've answered what the new shot must be, but you haven't answered when the new shot must occur. That is revealed by constantly asking yourself, "What is the audience's point of focus?" If the point of focus moves offscreen, or becomes unclear due to staging or a camera movement, you had better cut to a new shot where the point of focus is clear, and serves the story.

That's exactly what happens around 16 seconds into the diner scene.

When Ann reaches the booth, you can see the top of Asteroth's hat, but you don't know who is wearing the hat. Even if you add a shot to the beginning of the sequence identifying him, this moment is still ambiguous in terms of point of focus. Ann speaks to some man, specifically guiding the viewer's focus to him, but this particular angle doesn't allow us to see him.

Remember those basic rules of storytelling. If the audience is dying to know something, you'd better give it to them or risk losing their interest. In this case, the scene is begging for a shot of Asteroth.

1   In the sequence, set an In point after Ann says "Mr. Roth?" at 01:00:16:10.

2   Double-click shot **1E-1** and in the Viewer set an In point right before he says, "Yeah" (around 01:16:42:00). Set an Out point just as Ann crosses into the frame as she sits down (around 01:16:46:15).

Always try to make edits while action is happening in the frame: someone sitting down, lifting an arm, banging on a wall, opening a door, and so on. You'll focus on this concept in more detail in a later lesson, but it applies in any type of sequence.

Setting the Out point as Ann is sitting down allows you to "hide" the edit underneath the movement going on in the frame. That movement in the frame pulls the viewer's attention, and when you continue the action on the other side of the cut, the audience is so focused on that movement that they completely ignore the disruption that the cut might otherwise cause.

3   Perform an overwrite edit to add **1E-1** to the sequence.

4   Press \ (backslash) to play around the edit.

The In point works fine, but the Out point doesn't match up properly. She sits down in the medium close-up (MCU) and then sits down again in the master.

This happened because the pacing was different in the two shots, and also because when choosing the In point you eliminated an unnecessary pause between her question and his reply.

This is not a mistake. It's a natural part of the editing process. Every new shot potentially messes up the sync or timing of the scene. Finish the job by cleaning up the edit.

5 In the sequence, set an In point at the end of the second clip and play forward until Ann is halfway seated in the master (approximately 01:00:22:25). Set an Out point there.

NOTE ▶ The timecode numbers here refer to sequence time, not the burned-in time-code visible in the Canvas.

6 Press Command-Shift-A to deselect all, and press Shift-Delete to ripple delete the marked section and correct the edit.

7 Press \ to play around the edit again.

Don't worry if the timing of the edit isn't perfect. You'll come back and finesse it later—if you even need to.

The truth is, once you move from a wide master into a tighter shot, it's fairly jarring to jump back out unless you have a good reason to do so. The general rule is that once you go in, stay in.

Also, since there's no new information in the master at this point, there's no reason to go back to it. The idea of ending the MCU of Asteroth as Ann sits down is a good one, since there is something new going on (she sits), and that angle wasn't the best place to see it, but neither is the master. The best place to see the action is in the MCU of Ann.

8   Open **1B-2** and set an In point just as Ann is sitting down (01:08:36:00).

▶ Whose Scene Is It?

Just as all of your edit choices must be informed by the show's overall theme, for each scene you must also keep track of which character dominates the focus: whose scene it is. Inevitably, one character or another is going to be more important than the others. That character demands control of the point of focus. If you shift the focus somewhere else, the scene, and ultimately the whole show, may become muddled and boring.

The dominant character is not always obvious. Often, a scene does not feature the main character. If you're ever in doubt, ask yourself this simple question: Who has the main action in this scene? Does the main action belong to Asteroth, who is providing some crucial information? Does it belong to the waitress, who is actually a spy? Or does it belong to Ann making her request? If you know who's got the main action, you know which character's actions and reactions are going to be essential for the scene to work. Remember, this doesn't apply only to dramatic scenes. Every scene in every show must have a clear point of focus. It must have a single dominant element or character whose actions command the audience's attention.

9   In the Viewer, play the **1B-2** clip forward until something happens that inspires you to cut. That will be the Out point you set for this new clip.

You might have been tempted to cut when Asteroth lifts his head and responds to Ann, but since he immediately looks back down—and you already know that in his MCU his face is completely in shadow—there wouldn't be very much new information. Plus, you would lose her reaction, which is also important. However, if you play forward a few more seconds, something happens that again begs for a new shot.

The waitress walks up and Ann suddenly looks up and offscreen. Doesn't this compel you to show what it is she's looking at?

10   Set your Out point there (around 01:08:52:25).

11   In the sequence, position the playhead on the edit between **1E-1** and **1-2**.

12   Perform an overwrite edit to add the MCU of Ann to the sequence.

What comes next? If you look through your coverage, there are only two shots you could choose that would provide new information about what Ann is looking at. There's the master shot, where you can see the back of the waitress and see Ann looking up at her as she arrives, or there's the CU of the waitress.

Remember that there are no wrong answers. You could justify either shot, since both have strengths and weaknesses. Of course, you could lament that you really want a shot that shows the waitress over Ann's shoulder, or just a CU on the coffeepot. Sometimes you can make such requests and the production crew will go and pick them up. More often you have to live with the shots you're handed, and here you have to choose between the master and the CU. Or do you?

13 Open **1J-1**.

In and Out marks have already been set around the line "Need a menu?"

14 Press Shift-\ to play from In to Out points.

15 In the sequence, set an In point just after the waitress says, "Evening," and Ann looks up. Set the point before she says, "Need a menu?" (01:00:37:03).

16 Overwrite **1J-1** into the sequence and play the whole sequence.

Although some of your edits may need finessing, the scene should be taking shape. When **1J** ends, it cuts back to the master, and both shots work fine *together*!

This is the best of both worlds, because the CU of the waitress satisfies the audience's longing to know what Ann is looking at, and the master reveals the physical relationship of the waitress to the couple (which is the one important detail absent in the CU).

Furthermore, if you stay on the long shot until after the waitress leaves, you are left with a great two-shot of Ann and Asteroth.

This shot is perfect because it provides more new information. It illustrates the nature of their relationship in a way we haven't yet seen. We see the contrast between his darkness and her lightness. (You don't know the rest of the story, but he is a devil and she is an angel.) It also reveals that, perhaps surprisingly, they are on equal footing. He is not towering over her, or crowding her out of the frame. This subtle detail of their relationship (which becomes very important in a later scene) is only made visible in this long shot.

Remember the rule that once you move in, you shouldn't move back out? Well, here's an exception. You can move back out if something in the shot *provokes* the cut. In this case, the waitress's entrance and exit provides an opportunity to step back from the MCUs. Without the waitress's action, cutting back to this long shot would be very jarring and could have pulled the viewer out of the story. In fact, when you back out from tighter shots to wider ones, it usually signifies that the scene is over. The audience unconsciously disengages from the scene and prepares for a change to the next scene.

Instead, with the waitress to guide us, backing out to the master happens subtly, without activating the audience's "end of scene" trigger. So now, you're free to move back in. And if you play the scene forward another few seconds, the motivation for the next cut should be obvious. Ann takes out the picture, and every single person watching the scene is going to be wondering the same thing: What is she holding in her hand?

17 Open **1C-1** and play it.

In all the **1B** shots, you can't see the picture. The director realized that on set, and so he did this *pickup* of just this one part of the scene to make sure you could see the picture.

This is a case when the editor sends flowers and a thank-you note to the director. Without this pickup, it would have been very difficult to cut this moment of the scene and, since it's such an important moment, the whole scene would have suffered. But fortunately, you have **1C**.

18 Set the In point in both the sequence and the Viewer to the frame where Ann is turning the picture around to show to Asteroth. (See the timecode numbers in the illustration.)

Again, you are using action within the frame to hide the edit. The viewers' eyes will be riveted to the picture in the long shot and, when the cut happens, they will follow the movement of the picture across the cut, never noticing that an edit even took place.

19 Set an Out point in the Viewer after Ann says, "Six years old next week" (at approximately 01:14:52:00).

20 Perform an overwrite edit and press \ to play around the edit.

You may have to finesse the edit to smooth the movement of the picture turn, but don't worry about it now. You'll have time to go back and trim every edit once the rough cut is assembled.

NOTE ▶ In this case, the director specifically instructed the actor to move the picture out of frame after she turns it around. This was his way of controlling the point of focus within the shot. Sure, the picture pulled us in from the wide shot back to the MCU, but once we get there, it turns out that the picture is not important, Ann is. The audience grasps that it's a Polaroid, but quickly learns that it's not the image on the photo that's significant. In this case, you must follow the director's lead.

Matching Angles

Once you get to the heart of a two-person dialogue scene, it is usually a back-and-forth exchange between the two characters. How and when you choose to cut between shots defines the tone and style of the scene. One thing to keep in mind is that to keep the edits as invisible as possible, you must cut between angles that match one another as much as possible. MCUs should be cut against MCUs, CUs against CUs, and so on.

But not all matching shots are created equal. If one was shot with a long lens and the reverse shot made with a wide-angle lens, they will have different visual qualities and won't cut together very well. Similarly, if one shot is perfectly centered and another is dramatically off-center, cutting between them will draw unwanted attention to the difference between them, and highlight the edit, rather than the content.

Also, in the case of the singles commonly employed in a simple dialogue scene like this one, you ideally want to match *dirty* shots to dirty and *clean* to clean.

Dirty single shot

Clean single shot

Part of the reason this is important is aesthetic. The closer the geometry of the two shots is, the gentler their juxtaposition. The other important reason for shot matching involves the content. When you deliberately cut a clean single against a dirty one, or a slightly wider shot of one person with a closer shot of the other, it changes the relationship between the characters. This can be a great tool when used deliberately, but otherwise, it is an unwanted distraction.

You can hope that your production crew understood the importance of this, and designed all their shots in matching pairs, but it is still up to you to use them.

21   Open **1E-2** and set an In point just before Asteroth says, "What am I supposed to do? Bake a cake?" (at approximately 01:19:36:00).

22   Set the Out point a bit farther into the clip, around 20:07:00.

23 Edit the clip into the sequence directly after **1C-1**.

It should be pretty obvious that you'll want to cut back to Ann during the middle of this shot—not just because she has lines, but because her delivery of those lines is compelling and tells much more of the story than Asteroth's reaction does.

TIP Don't assume that you should always cut to show whomever happens to be talking. In many cases, the reaction of the other person is where the story is really happening.

24 Set an In point in the sequence just after the sound of Ann putting down the creamer (01:01:05:25) and set an Out point in the middle of the movement when Asteroth sits back and before he speaks (14:05).

NOTE ▶ Throughout this book, timecode numbers will be abbreviated to only the relevant digits. If no hours or minutes values are given, they are identical to the hours or minutes of the previous timecode citing.

25 Open **1B-4** and set an Out point in the middle of Asteroth's movement as he sits back (01:12:58:20).

26 Press Option-I to clear the In point, if one exists.

In this case, you can use the movement of Asteroth's hat to hide the edit. By matching the two Out points to occur in the middle of that action, the In point is calculated automatically or *back-timed*.

27 Overwrite the clip into the sequence and play it.

The ending of the edit, hidden by the movement of Asteroth's hat, is fairly well placed; but the beginning feels a little random, or worse, it feels like you deliberately cut to see Ann because you knew she was about to speak.

Anticipating an action like this is a perfect example of a terrible edit. You should never cut to something just *before* it happens. This indicates to the audience that something is about to happen. Rather than feeling immersed in the story, they've suddenly been warned to look out for something.

It is generally preferable to cut just after someone begins talking rather than just before. This gives the viewer the experience that they "turned their head" because they heard the person begin to speak. The same is true for any action or reaction. Let the action motivate the cut, not the other way around.

This can be easily remedied by rolling the edit slightly to the right so the cut happens a moment later.

28 Option-click the edit at the head of **1B-4** on track V1. Be sure to select only the video track.

29 Press R to select the Roll tool and type *+10*.

The edit is rolled ten frames to the right.

30 Press \ to play around the edit.

That improves the edit dramatically. Later, you will go through every edit in the sequence and perform a similar adjustment to split the video and audio in a similar manner.

Use Gang Sync

Because dialogue sequences like this are so common, Final Cut Pro provides a number of tools that are specifically designed for these cases. One of those tools is the Gang Sync mode.

Ganging the Viewer and sequence together means that whenever you move the playhead in either, the other follows along for the ride. This means that if the clip in the Viewer is in sync with the sequence at one point, you can move the playhead to a different point and the clip in the Viewer will remain in sync.

1   Position the sequence playhead anywhere over the **1B-4** clip.

2   Press F or choose View > Match Frame > Master Clip.

The original clip is loaded into the Viewer, cued up to the same frame, as the sequence shows.

3   Click the Playhead Sync pop-up menu button and choose Gang.

Now the playheads are locked together.

4   Play the sequence forward until just after Asteroth says, "A social worker or something?" but before he says, "Why do you care?" (01:01:26:00).

This is an appropriate edit point because the audience is likely to want to see Ann's reaction to Asteroth's accusation. It also allows you to cut to her for her next action (her confession) without appearing to anticipate that action.

5   In the Viewer, set an In point. Don't bother setting an Out point.

6   Perform an overwrite edit and play the sequence.

Asteroth's audio gets cut off by the new edit, but that is easily remedied.

7   Option-click to select just the audio of **1E-2** and Shift-drag it to track **A2**.

8   Zoom in, then Option-click to select the right edge of just the audio clip and extend it about 1 second.

NOTE ▶ Extending the audio clip will be much easier if you don't skip the "zoom in" instruction. Also, you may need to turn off snapping in order to resize the clip to the desired length.

▶ **Eliminating Pauses**

It is generally frowned upon for an editor to modify the timing of an actor's line readings by adding or eliminating the natural pauses that are part of their performance. Sometimes such changes are unavoidable, but you should be careful of distorting the natural pacing of the reading.

However, this warning does not apply to controlling the pacing of the back and forth between characters during a conversation. Onscreen, everything seems slower than it does in reality, so ironically, in order to make dialogue sound more natural, you will almost always need to tighten the pacing of the lines, and often overlap lines that were performed with gaps between them.

In fact, in a scene where dialogue does naturally overlap, when shooting the singles, it is common practice to instruct the actors to deliberately not overlap. This allows the editor to control the pacing of the conversation, just as you did in this last edit.

9   Press \ to play around the edit.

The two tracks are now overlapping, which is perfect because Ann is hemming and hawing while Asteroth is still berating her. This eliminates the awkward pause between their lines.

Delaying the Close-up

The standard coverage provides five basic shots, but so far you've only used three of them. In addition to the OTS MCUs, you have a pair of close-ups, but don't rush to use them too soon. While you can move in at almost any point, once you do, you can't easily move back out without some sort of motivation (such as the waitress appearing).

While close-ups provide the most emotional power, OTS shots have the added benefit of reinforcing the posture and physical relationship between the characters. For example, think about how different this scene would play if the two were sitting side by side at barstools facing forward instead of facing off in the booth. In that case, the OTS shots would show that they weren't looking at each other, but the close-up singles would omit that information.

Save your close-ups for the emotional heart of the scene. It may have been tempting to use Asteroth's close-up for the speech he gave asking Ann about her relation to the child, or her subsequent confession, though at that point you'd be stuck in close-ups for the remainder of the scene. Still, this is one possible editorial interpretation of the scene.

You'll need to determine for yourself what is the essence of each scene. One helpful technique is to identify the "hinge," or turning point, of a scene. Every scene should have a purpose (or it doesn't belong in the show), and that purpose can usually be recognized as a moment where something happens that changes the dynamic of the story, a point from which the story cannot go back. This is the essence of what it means to "move the story forward." In this scene, is the turning point Ann's confession, or is it Asteroth's decision to take on the case? Your answer tells you the moment you should probably save for your close-ups.

Another seemingly practical reason to stay on the MCUs a bit longer is that the action of Asteroth snatching the picture would barely be visible in the tighter close-ups. That action is the hinge of the scene and is the perfect time to move from MCU to CU.

1 Find the frame in the sequence where Asteroth grabs the picture and set an In point in the middle of the action (01:01:49:26).

2 Open **1G-1** (Asteroth's CU) and find the matching frame in the middle of the action as he grabs the picture (01:20:29:23). Set an In point there.

There's not much reason to set an Out point because, as you move toward the end of the scene, you're going to replace all the shots.

3 Perform an overwrite edit and play around the edit to see how well the action matches.

You should always try to match angles. So now that you've introduced Asteroth's CU, you should support it with Ann's CU.

4 Open **1D-1** and play the whole clip.

One of the great secrets of selecting nonverbal reaction shots is that there's no reason you can't choose a shot that might have happened at a different point in the scene. Many directors will set up a close-up camera position and then just direct the actor through a variety of different nonverbal reactions, one after another. This gives the editor a wide range of choices that can be used anywhere in the scene.

There is a moment in this shot where Ann slowly looks up at Asteroth, presumably gauging his reaction to the picture. Since this is exactly what the audience is doing (wondering what he's going to do), it's a perfect choice for the next edit.

5 Set an In and Out point around Ann's look (In: 01:15:51:15, Out: 54:15).

6   In the sequence, watch the **1G-1** shot, and make a determination about how long you should let it play before cutting to Ann's reaction.

Technically, there's no right or wrong answer, but the more accurately you can judge your typical viewer's attention span, the better an editor you will be. Of course, this time will vary depending on the audience you are serving. A good editor should intuitively gauge this sort of timing.

7   Position the playhead where you want Ann's reaction to begin and perform an overwrite edit. (In the illustration, the edit was made at 01:01:56:25.)

There is still a long pause before Asteroth makes his decision and says his line. This is another subtle timing decision to determine just how long you can string the audience along without losing their attention. In this case, there are probably a few seconds of suspense that can be extracted.

8 In the sequence, set an In point at the edit at the end of Ann's reaction shot and set an Out point just before Asteroth purses his lips and looks up (01:02:02:14).

9 Press Command-Shift-A to deselect all (as a safety precaution), and press Shift-Delete to ripple delete those 2 and a half seconds.

One more reaction shot from Ann is required in response to his line, "I'll ask some questions."

If you watch Ann's CU, she makes a subtle nod when he says his line, but makes a more pronounced expression of hope a moment later when he says, "Be here tomorrow." There's no reason not to use the second expression, even though it will go in the place of the first.

10 In the Viewer, find Ann's second reaction and mark it (In: 01:16:01:17, Out: 03:26).

11 In the sequence, place the playhead just after Asteroth says, "Nothing more."

12 Disable the target for track A1, so only the V1 track will be used.

13 Perform an overwrite edit to put the second reaction in the sequence.

End the Scene Quickly

You might expect that the hinge of a scene would naturally fall in the middle, but that's rarely the case. Once the key moment of a scene has occurred, that scene has served its purpose and should be ended. Often, writers will overwrite scenes, extending them long after their purpose has been accomplished. It's your job as editor to recognize this and find an elegant way to exit the scene once it has done its job.

In this case, the scene has been well crafted in that regard, and the physical action of the actor getting up gives you a perfect excuse to cut back out to the wide shot.

1   Place the playhead anywhere over the last clip in the sequence (**1-2**) and press F to load that clip in the Viewer.

   There are many ways to open this clip in the Viewer. This just happens to be a quick and easy one.

2   In the Viewer, find the frame midway through the action of Asteroth getting up from the booth and set an In point there (01:03:02:10).

3   Set an Out point after Ann turns back around, and looks at her coffee, and begins to push it away (13:18).

4   Find the frame in the sequence midway through the action of Asteroth standing up (01:02:11:15).

5   Leave A1 untargeted, and perform an overwrite edit.

   Now all that remains to complete the rough cut is to add the ending shot of the coffee.

6   Open **1M-SER** into the Viewer.

This clip is labeled SER for "series" instead of an ordinary take number. This sort of shot is common when there is a short shot, usually *MOS* (without sound), that the director wants to run several times quickly without starting and stopping the camera each time. Technically there are three takes of this shot, but they are all grouped together. As expected, this shot is MOS so you don't need to worry about the audio tracks.

While notes about numbered takes are usually reported on the camera log, in the case of a series like this one, you may not have any information to indicate which was the best version. You'll have to watch them all and choose for yourself. Here's a tip for that situation: Start at the end and go backwards. This only makes sense since once they got it right, they likely stopped repeating the shot.

7   In the Viewer, set an In point at the beginning of the third take, just before Ann pushes the coffee cup away (around 01:33:59:05), and set the Out point at the end of the take (around 34:11:00).

8   In the sequence, place the playhead at the end of shot **1-2**.

9   Perform an overwrite edit.

There are still two extraneous audio clips left over at the end of the sequence from earlier edits.

10 Select the audio from **1-2** at the end, as well as from **1B-4**, and press Delete.

11 Press Home and play the whole sequence.

Refining the Cut

Great work. You've successfully assembled the scene, thought long and hard about each of the edits, and created a version of the scene that stays true to the script. Now, you're going to start all over again and make it your own.

First, remember that regardless of how important the script may have been in getting through production, by the time you are editing the show, it really doesn't matter anymore. That doesn't mean you can't use the script as a guide, but if the footage is pulling you in a different direction, you are wise to heed its call.

Many great films are rewritten in the editing room. This is especially true for documentaries, but it can prove equally true for any type of show. It's far more important to create a sequence that makes sense and serves a deliberate purpose than to stubbornly stick to a structure that isn't working, or to insist on including passages or lines of dialogue that are redundant or irrelevant, or that confuse the scene. Don't be afraid to cut, even if it changes the script.

For example in this scene, the coffee gag (where the milk becomes curdled) is fairly important. It provides the transition to the next scene, as well as serving as a broader overarching metaphor; the white cream represents Ann (the angel) being corrupted by mixing with the black coffee (underworld). It's a clever metaphor, subtly integrated into the plot, but there's a minor technical problem. We never see Ann pour the cream into the coffee.

Fortunately, the director realized this and included an insert of Ann pouring the cream (shot **1H**). However, you have to decide how to include this shot in the scene, if at all. If you watch the scene, she does pour the cream, right around minute one. It's just that it happens mostly off-camera.

It would be relatively painless to drop in the insert shot, thereby clarifying how the cream got there, but there is a bigger problem. That long moment when she pours the cream is one of the longest *dead spots* in the scene. When you watch the sequence, it's when the viewer's focus is most likely to stray from the story. We don't know the characters, we don't even know why Ann is here yet, and now we're supposed to sit around and watch while she pours cream in her coffee? What do we care?

Dropping in the insert puts a lot of emphasis on that moment. At best, it spoils the subtlety of the metaphor and, at worst, it pulls the focus in the wrong direction. So what to do?

There's a more radical solution—but it requires some courage (at least when it comes time to explain it to the director). Cut the whole beat. Is this moment necessary? How is that moment propelling the story forward? In this case, since it appears to be harming the scene, you at least owe it to yourself to give it a try.

1   In the sequence, set an In point right after Asteroth says, "Bake a cake" (around 01:01:00:00), and set an Out point at the end of that shot.

Because you previously split this edit, the audio and video edits don't line up. Since you don't want to cut off the beginning of Ann's line (which starts before the picture cut), be sure to set the Out point at the end of the audio edit instead of the video edit.

2   Deselect all and Shift-Delete the section.

Before you can view the edit, you must clean up that bit of the clip left over from the split.

3   Press R to select the Roll tool and select the edit (V1 track only).

4   Drag the edit to the right to roll over the old piece of the clip.

5   Press A to return to the Selection tool, then back up and play this section of the sequence.

Is this an improvement? If you're unsure, play the whole sequence and see how it flows. Do you miss the frames you cut? Does the scene still work? Are you perplexed at the end as to how the cream got in the coffee? Not likely.

Does that feel good? Hopefully it does. Now it's time to attack the rest of the scene with the same ruthless fervor.

If you remember from reviewing the footage in the bin, there's a shot specifically designed to open the scene. Shot **1K** is a slow boom down showing Asteroth sitting alone in the booth. The vertical move parallels the ending shot, providing nice bookends to the scene and, since this is a story about heaven and hell, showing the scene moving down toward the earth is another reference to the broader theme. Perhaps most importantly (though very subtly), it signifies Ann's descent from heaven, which is really the opening event of the scene. With the right sound design, that concept could be enhanced or downplayed. No matter what, it's a satisfying way to introduce this dark, mysterious character without revealing his face, not to mention a fun, fancy camera move that looks cool.

6 Load **1K-SER** into the Viewer.

Knowing this is a series, you should automatically jump to the end of the clip and watch the takes in reverse.

7 Mark the last take, beginning just after the camera move begins and ending when the coffee cup on the left just reaches the edge of the frame (In: 01:32:20:15, Out: 32:30:00).

8 In the sequence, press Home to move the playhead to the head of the scene.

9 Perform an insert edit.

Making It Shorter

Next, look for more places where the scene can be tightened. Are there any lines that are redundant or extraneous? Are there actions that can be simplified or eliminated? Scenes need to play out in their own time, but shorter is almost always better. If a scene plays well at 2 minutes, it will play even better at 1:45. You can go too far, but you are so much more likely to err in the other direction that you shouldn't worry too much about making a scene too short.

Start at the beginning and look for places to trim the overall length of the scene.

1 Play the scene from the beginning.

Assuming the opening shot is going to have a sound effect tied to the camera move, you can leave it alone, but the second clip (**1-2**) does feel a little slow. Does Ann have to pause so long at the door?

It might pay to take a look at the other takes and see if they're shorter. You don't want to trade a better performance for a merely faster one, but it's worth a look. To assist in judging the length, it will help to know exactly how long the current shot is.

2   Position the playhead anywhere over the **1-2** shot and press X to mark the clip.

The Duration field in the Canvas indicates how long that In to Out is (16:10 in this case).

3   Load shot **1-4** and watch it for performance quality.

Unfortunately, even though the actors did fine in this take, the camera operator fumbled the end of the move. He panned too far, so when Ann stops at the booth, she is almost off the edge of the frame.

What else have you got?

4   Load shot **1A-2** and watch it.

This one is more promising. It looks as if it was shot with a different lens. Ann appears smaller at the top of the shot, but the ending frame is almost exactly the same as in **1-2**. This actually is a more dynamic shot, since she appears to make a more dramatic move. The performance is equally good, and the framing at the end of the shot is even better than **1-2** was. But is it shorter?

5   Set an In point just before Ann enters the diner and set the Out just after she says, "Mr. Roth?" (at approximately In: 01:07:15:08, Out: 29:05).

The Duration field says it all: 13:28. That's more than 3 seconds shorter than **1-2**. It looks like you have a winner. Just to be safe, watch both shots one more time to see if there's anything you're overlooking. Once you're satisfied it's the right thing to do, make the switch.

6   In the sequence, press Option-O to clear the Out point. Be sure that track A1 is targeted, and perform an overwrite edit.

7   Select the little piece of **1-2** still in the Timeline and press Shift-Delete to ripple delete it.

It's looking good! On to the next trouble spot.

8   Play the sequence, looking specifically for shots that seem too long.

What did you find? Perhaps you wondered about the length of the master shot after the CU of the waitress. While all the reasons for including that shot still apply, there's no reason it has to be so long!

Previously, you waited for Ann to pull out the picture to motivate the cut, but this time around, that seems to take an awfully long time. Is there any way to cut out of this shot earlier?

Not really. You could investigate using Ann's movement when she goes for the picture, but for that to match the action in shot **1C**, it would take even longer, and you would be leading the audience to the picture before they knew they cared.

But what about the head of the shot? It takes almost 10 seconds before the waitress leaves the frame. There must be a way to shorten that! The trouble is that Ann has a line ("Just coffee, please") that takes up a lot of that time. However, you can't see her face while she says the line. That means you can move the line forward and shorten the shot.

9   Zoom well into this part of the Timeline and press Command-Option-W to turn on audio waveforms.

10   Stretch the audio track to make it large enough that you can see the audio waveforms clearly.

Despite the earlier warning not to mess with the pacing of line readings, all rules are meant to be broken. You need to find a way to tighten this beat. Begin by cutting out the pauses.

11   Press B to select the Razor Blade tool and, while pressing Option (to affect only the audio track), add edits on both sides of the words.

12 Delete the sections that don't contain the words. (Option-click to select just the audio.)

Don't forget about the great sound effect of the coffee cup, but don't think you have to keep it where it is.

13 Add an edit after the coffee cup sound, too.

14 Play the sequence and find the last frame before you can see Ann's face (approximately 01:00:48:20).

15 Zoom out in the Timeline and press A to return to the Selection tool.

16 Drag the coffee cup sound to track A2 to get it out of the way.

17 Drag the "Please" audio so it ends at the frame before Ann's face becomes visible.

18 Drag the "Just coffee" audio so it occurs right before the "Please."

19 Set an Out point at the beginning of the "Just coffee" audio (01:00:47:22).

20 Set an In point at the beginning of the **1-2** clip.

This marked area is the portion of the clip you will remove to shorten the clip. You've cut more than 2 seconds. Not bad!

21 Make sure that the coffee cup sound is to the right of the marked area.

22 Press Command-Shift-A to deselect all, then press Shift-Delete to ripple delete the unwanted portion of the clip.

23 Press Home and play the entire sequence.

Amazing, huh? You'd hardly know it wasn't shot that way! This is a trick you can employ in a variety of circumstances.

Split Every Edit

One of the best ways to make your edits invisible is to separate the audio and video edits so they happen at different times. When both audio and video change on the same frame, the audience is twice as likely to notice the edit and be pulled out of the narrative. Scenes of all types benefit from splitting the edits this way, but it's essential for dialogue.

Final Cut Pro has a variety of features designed to accelerate or ease the creation of split edits. One of these is the Extend Edit command.

1 Press Shift-Z to zoom your Timeline to fit the whole sequence.

2 Zoom back in on the second edit, between **1A-2** and **1E-1**.

3 Option-click to select just the video edit.

4 Position the playhead about halfway through Ann's line (visible in the audio waveform).

5 Press E to perform an extend edit.

Extend edit is a quick way to perform a roll edit. It automatically moves the selected edit to the current playhead position. It can work to the right or to the left of the edit point.

6   Play around the edit (\) to see how the split improved the edit.

The next edit to address is between **1C-1** and **1E-2** around 01:01:02:21.

7   Play around this edit, and think about how it could be improved.

For starters, there's a pause between the end of Ann's line and the beginning of Asteroth's line. Tightening that space, so that his response appears as more of a snap, is consistent with his character.

8   Zoom in on that edit and, using the audio waveforms as a guide, set In and Out points around the quiet section at the end of the first clip and the beginning of the second.

TIP If you're ever in doubt that the area you marked contains the end of a word or something you don't want to delete, press Shift-\ to play from In to Out.

9   Deselect all and press Shift-Delete to remove the marked region.

That improves the timing, but now the edit is begging to be split, since the cut happens just as the other character begins talking.

There are two kinds of split edits. If the video leads the audio, it's called an *L-cut*, and if the audio leads the video, it's called a *J-cut*. J-cuts are far more common than L-cuts because they support the sound triggering the picture cut. Remember the audience members "turning their heads" because they heard something? Using a J-cut is a very natural and effective way to hide an edit.

10 Press R to select the Roll tool and Option-click to select the edit on track V1.

11 Roll the edit to the right by about 10 frames until it's located just past Asteroth's first couple of words.

12 Play around the edit.

The next edit is already split as the result of work you did earlier in the lesson. You should repeat steps 8 through 11 on the edit between clips **1B-4** and **1E-2** around 01:01:13:00.

Watch Out for Screen Direction Errors

If you play back the whole scene, it's mostly working very well. However, there is one more edit that still needs adjusting.

13 Play across the third edit (between **1E-1** and **1B-2**) when Ann sits down in the booth.

Does anything about this edit bother you? Something should. There's a screen direction error in it. In the outgoing shot, she's moving from left to right, but in the incoming shot she's moving right to left.

There will be more time spent on screen direction errors in later lessons, but here's a quick preview of one way to solve them.

The geography of the diner isn't in doubt, so it's not a huge error. No one is going to be confused about where she is sitting, but it is a jarring edit and there's no reason to live with it. The easiest way to solve a problem like this is to find another shot where the screen direction is correct. If you can find a shot where she is moving directly on axis with the camera, rather than moving either right to left or left to right, it could easily cut with either shot.

Fortunately, you have that shot in the master.

14 Load **1A-2** into the Viewer.

15 Find and mark the area when Ann begins to sit down, but before she completely settles in her seat (In: 01:07:35:00 Out: 36:00).

16 In the sequence, position the playhead directly on the edit. Untarget the audio track and perform an overwrite edit.

17 Play across the new edit.

While not as smooth as a simple two-shot cut, the screen direction problem is solved and her movement successfully hides both edits.

18 Save and close the project.

The Basis for All Editing

The tools and techniques covered in this first lesson are not limited to dialogue scenes. They are the same basic rules you will use (and sometimes deliberately break) in every scene you cut. Everything is built on these fundamentals.

Dialogue scenes are especially good practice. Because the standard editing pattern is fairly rigid, it's like writing haiku: You must learn to be creative and identify the specific details of the scene that make it strong and unique despite the formal rules that constrict you.

Lesson Review

1. What are the three components of story?

2. What question does a long shot frequently answer?

3. What must editors be aware of above all else?

4. What are the five basic shots common to most dialogue scenes?

5. What are three other shot categories common to dialogue scenes?

6. How should you begin editing a scene?

7. How can you create a split edit?

8. How do you label and color-code clips?

9. Describe an extend edit.

10. What does Gang Sync do, and how do you enable it?

Answers

1. First, the six questions; (who, what, where, when, why, and how); second, the order and pacing of how they are conveyed; and third, the theme or purpose.

2. A long shot typically identifies *where* an event is taking place.

3. The theme or main idea of the show they're cutting.

4. Master shot, OTS of person 1, OTS of person 2, CU of person 1, CU of person 2.

5. Inserts, cutaways, and specials.

6. Review and organize your footage in Final Cut Pro bins; then begin editing with a master shot that covers the whole duration of the scene.

7. Use the Roll tool to make the picture and sound edits occur at different times.

8. Select the clips, then Control-click and choose Label from the shortcut menu.

9. An extend edit is a roll edit that moves the selected edit to the current position of the playhead.

10. Gang Sync locks the playhead in the Viewer with the playhead in the sequence. Click the Playhead Sync pop-up and choose Gang.

2

Lesson Files   Lesson Files > Lesson 02 > Complex Dialogue

Media   Media > FBI Guys Dialogue

Time   This lesson takes approximately 90 minutes to complete.

Goals   Edit complex dialogue scenes with more than two people

Tackle scenes that combine dialogue and action

Manage dialogue scenes that occur in more than one location within a single scene

Use head turns and eyelines to clarify room geometry

Control scene pacing

Editing Complex Dialogue

By this point, you should feel confident to tackle another dialogue scene similar to the diner scene, but what happens when there are more than two people in the scene? Also, what happens when the subjects move to new positions during the scene? These elements complicate the scene, and require modifications to your editing practices.

Editing Complex Scenes

As with any scene, you are dependent on the wit and competence of the director and the crew. Complex scenes require well-thought-out coverage. In a scene where the actors move during the scene, a crew will often shoot standard coverage for each of the blocking positions. Additionally, transitional elements and little moments that require special attention will receive their own shots, or series of shots. This can quickly add up to a giant slough of footage that you must wade through and make sense of.

1   Open project Lesson 02 > **Complex Dialogue**.

2   Double-click the Unorganized Clips bin to open it in its own window.

Name	Duration	In	Out
43A_2 Agents & Wright Outside Door	00:00:36:21	Not Set	Not Set
43B_4 LS Blithers OTS Phil&Bob	00:02:15:19	Not Set	Not Set
43C_2 MLS 3shot Ending	00:00:12:14	Not Set	Not Set
43D_4 MLS Kenny Crosses	00:00:41:01	Not Set	Not Set
43E_2 MCU Kenny	00:00:40:07	Not Set	Not Set
43F_2a MCU Kenny & Vinegar	00:00:45:13	Not Set	Not Set
43G_3 MCU Blithers	00:02:29:02	Not Set	Not Set
43H_1 MS Wright	00:01:54:08	Not Set	Not Set
43J_3 CU Vinegar Bottle	00:00:53:12	Not Set	Not Set
43K_1 MCU Blithers Ending	00:00:58:11	Not Set	Not Set
43L_4 MS 3shot Ending	00:01:30:00	Not Set	Not Set
43Ma_2 MS Agents at table Entrance	00:00:35:09	Not Set	Not Set
43Mb_3 MS Agents at Table	00:02:48:04	Not Set	Not Set
43Mc_1 MS Agents at table Ending	00:00:25:21	Not Set	Not Set
43N_2 MCU Darren (Blithers POV)	00:01:25:06	Not Set	Not Set
43P_1 MCU Phil	00:02:11:04	Not Set	Not Set
43Q_2 MCU Bob	00:02:13:19	Not Set	Not Set
43R_1_MLS Agents at Door (ending)	00:01:11:18	Not Set	Not Set
43S_5 Darren jumps to MS agents	00:01:26:14	Not Set	Not Set
43T_2 CU agents at door Tilt Up	00:00:12:18	Not Set	Not Set
43U_1 MS Agents sitting (Darren's POV)	00:00:59:01	Not Set	Not Set
43V_2 MS agents (Darren's POV)	00:00:14:10	Not Set	Not Set
43W_2 MS Darren enters (Agents POV)	00:00:21:20	Not Set	Not Set
43X_3 Blithers Ending From button	00:00:17:00	Not Set	Not Set
43Y_4 LS Agents end of table OTS Blithers	00:03:01:03	Not Set	Not Set

This scene from the film "FBI Guys" is a simple boardroom scene, in which the two desk agents must face their boss after overstepping their jobs and cracking a field case. Although it is a simple scene, it contains several sections. The agents enter the room and sit down; they have a brief exchange with a jealous co-worker; the boss enters and chews them out; another agent explains how their work was helpful; and finally, after they get up to leave, they get up the nerve to ask for a promotion.

The scene contains 25 clips, labeled **43A** through **43Y**.

NOTE ▶ When naming and numbering scenes, the letters I and O are always skipped as they can too easily be confused with 1 (one) and 0 (zero).

Although the scenes are labeled in the order they were shot, that doesn't mean that they are arranged in a way that is useful to the editor. It's up to you to group and organize them so you have a solid understanding of the available options for each section of the scene.

In fact, because different parts of this scene take place in slightly different locations in the conference room, you have to keep track at all times of where the people are in the room. Even though you might have a close-up of Phil sitting at the table performing a perfect reaction, you can't use it during a part of the scene where he's supposed to be standing at the door.

3   Close the Unorganized Clips bin.

4   Click the disclosure triangle to expand the Organized Clips bin.

This bin already has been organized into three sections in which the main characters are in different positions. Additionally, two of the sections have been subdivided into shots of the agents and shots of the bosses. Since the majority of the scene is a dialogue between the two agents and the three bosses, this allows you to think of those two parties as two individuals (like Ann and Asteroth) instead of five different people.

5   Click the disclosure triangle to expand the Agents bin in the 2 Main Scene bin and double-click shot **43Y_4 LS Master OTS Blithers**.

6   Watch the clip to get a sense of the scene.

Due to the size of the room and the complexity of the scene, there is not one single master that gives a sense of the whole sequence. This shot gives a good sense of half of the room and runs almost to the end of the scene.

7   Expand the Bosses bin in the 2 Main Scene bin and double-click shot **43B_4 LS Blithers OTS Phil&Bob**.

8   Press Shift-\ (backslash) to play In to Out.

This clip shows the other half of the room.

Both of these long shots are helpful to get a sense of the scene and, because they are staged as OTS shots, they might prove useful during the edit. But because they are so wide, you should already be thinking that they're likely to get only minimal usage in the final scene. Still, they can be helpful as a foundation to the scene, upon which you can build using the tighter coverage.

Finding the First Event

The way to approach a large, multiple-event scene like this is to lay out the overall structure of the scene, and then tackle each event individually.

9   Double-click the Rough Start sequence to open it into the Canvas and Timeline.

10 Play the scene.

The structure of the scene has already been assembled for you. With a complex scene like this, it's very helpful to lay out a rough assembly of the whole sequence using your masters, even though almost all of it will eventually be replaced with tighter shots. This helps you keep the big picture of the scene in focus as you work on building out the beats one by one.

The first event you'll address is Darren's entrance. When Darren (in the dark red shirt) enters the conference room, he has a brief exchange with the two agents. This is covered in two matching medium shots, **43U** and **43W**.

11 From the Entrance bin, open **43W_2 MS Darren enters (Agents POV)** and play it.

Darren enters, says his line, then sits down and makes a series of mocking gestures. Obviously, the intention was not to use all these gestures; the actor was providing a series of choices for you.

12 Set an In on the first frame just as Darren enters the shot (around 02:51:31:18) and set an Out after he sits down (approximately 38:00).

By now you're probably thinking that you're going to want a reaction from the agents before Darren sits down, so why are you keeping this shot so long? It's still a good idea to lay in Darren's whole action so you will have a consistent sound track covering his sitting.

13 In the sequence, look for a frame to approximate Darren's position at the beginning of **43W**.

Because **43W** is from the agents' POV, the correct matching frame should be just as Darren passes where they're sitting. Fortunately, due to the master shot's compressed geometry, it's very hard to tell exactly when he passes them. (It could be anywhere from 45:15 to 47:10.) This gives you plenty of flexibility in choosing where to drop in the MS.

14   Set an In point in the sequence at approximately 46:00.

15   Overwrite **43W** into the sequence.

16   Open **43U_1 MS Agents sitting (Darren's POV)** and play it.

You are looking for a moment that sells the idea that they're reacting to Darren. But where is the best place to begin? Always start by looking for a physical movement. Performances are made up of physical actions. Sometimes they are obvious—jumping out of the way or pulling a trigger—but other times they are subtle—a shift in the eyes or a tiny frown. As an editor, you must constantly deconstruct these actions and interpret them. They are your road map to the emotional terrain of a scene. They can also be an indicator of the truth of a performance, and choosing the wrong action can quickly ruin a scene. Regardless of how the actor performed the scene on set, it is in the editing room that their performances are honed.

The action at the cut point carries the most weight because it is juxtaposed against the shot to which it refers. In this scene, there are three distinct actions. First, the agents turn their heads; second, Phil (the dark-haired agent) clenches his fist; and third, they look straight ahead, attempting to ignore Darren. (Yes, sometimes deliberately doing nothing is an action.) You could begin this shot with any of those three actions.

Like every editorial decision, there is no wrong answer, but for this lesson, you'll begin with the head turn.

17 Set an In point two or three frames before the agents turn their heads (02:48:29:02).

18 In the sequence, set an In point just as Darren looks down at his chair (01:00:49:04).

Starting here serves two purposes. Storywise, you're emphasizing Darren's apparent power over the agents by juxtaposing them looking up at him *after* he has looked away from them. Structurally, starting the shot after he looks down means you don't have to cut back to Darren. Since he's already looked away from them, you don't need his reaction to their reaction (which saves you from using any of the hammy "mocking gestures"). Finally, because looking down is the beginning of his sitting down, that tiny gesture plus the sound of the chair sell the idea that he has been seated, without having to show it on screen.

19 Set an Out point in the sequence at the existing edit point between **43Y** and **43B**. Untarget tracks A1 and A2, so Darren's chair audio doesn't get overwritten.

20 Overwrite the clip into the sequence.

21 Play the two new shots and see how they fit.

NOTE ▶ Don't worry about the small piece of audio that is left behind from the old clip. It will be cleaned up in subsequent edits.

Not bad. Now the "staring straight ahead" action accidentally serves a new purpose. It looks like the agents are reacting to the entrance of the boss. This can be enhanced further by adding a sound effect of the door opening right before they look forward.

22 In the Sound Effects bin, select **DoorOpenClose** and open it into the Viewer.

23 Play the clip and set an Out point after the door opens but before it closes.

24 In the sequence, find the frame where Phil starts to look toward the front of the room.

He does a sort of double-take, beginning to turn his head the first time around 51:17. Since you want the sound to motivate his look, it should begin shortly before that.

25 Set an In point at 51:12 and target tracks A3 and A4 in the Timeline.

26 Overwrite the door sound into the sequence.

TIP To drag an audio clip from the Viewer, click the drag-target in the upper-right corner of the window.

This sort of sound work is usually done much later in the editing process (for good reasons described in Lesson 10). However, this example shows that you can often use sound in place of (or in conjunction with) pictures in order to best tell the story.

The exchange between the agents and Darren was the first event of the scene and, although you simplified it greatly, its purpose has been served. It is your obligation not just to assemble the events, but also to interpret them and cull only the most essential beats. That finishes the Entrance section of the scene.

27 Click the disclosure triangle next to the 1 Entrance bin to collapse it.

Completing the Second Event

Next, it's time to move to the meat of the scene. Here you're going to encounter the complexities of a dialogue scene with multiple people.

Remember that it's essential to keep track of whose scene it is, since you must pay extra attention to that person (or persons). This is the agents' scene. They are the main characters in the story and, in this scene, the main action is that they are facing the consequences of their prior behavior. Don't be fooled into thinking it's Blithers' scene, just because he does all the talking.

Also, don't forget to look for the turning point of the scene. Without the context of the whole movie, it may be harder for you to spot, but there is a very definite hinge: when Phil corrects the boss's pronunciation of his name. This act of defiance is a major turning point for the character, not just in this scene, but in the film (and it supports the broader themes of the film, self-respect and self-determination).

Unlike the diner scene in "Hope," the hinge here doesn't happen right at the end of the scene, but this is a much larger, more complex scene. In some ways, that action signifies the end of one scene and the start of a new scene in the same location. (That second half has its own turning point when Blithers gives the agents a new assignment.)

Some editors prefer to begin editing a scene by cutting the turning point moment first. While this might challenge your sense of continuity, it's not a bad approach. After all, that's the most important moment, and the stylistic or pacing decisions made there should inform the way you cut the rest of the scene (and not the other way around).

To keep things simple, in this exercise you'll continue to edit the scene in chronological order.

1   Play the sequence from the end of the last edit you made until Blithers (the big bald guy with the moustache) begins talking.

   Do you see the need for an edit?

   You should only add an edit when it's necessary because some new piece of information is missing. Are the six questions all answered, or is the audience likely to be wondering about something?

   Perhaps it occurs to you that what is missing is the reaction of our heroes, the agents. What are they doing while Blithers is getting settled? Are they nervous? Confident? Still sniping with Darren?

2   Open shot **43Mb_3 MS Agents at Table**, and type *1537.* (don't miss the period at the end) to move the playhead to 02:15:37:00.

3   Play the clip from that point.

Here's the agents' reaction to Blithers' entrance. Now, look for a section to cut away to while Blithers is getting ready in the long shot. Remember, since it's a cutaway, it can come from anywhere in the shot. As long as they're not talking, nothing will appear out of sync.

4   Set an In point at 02:15:37:20 and an Out point at 39:20.

5   In the sequence, watch the scene until you reach a point that feels like the right moment to lay in the cutaway of the agents. (In the picture below, the edit happens at 01:01:00:10.)

6   Untarget the audio tracks and overwrite the clip into the sequence.

In the master shot, there is a fairly long pause before Blithers delivers his next line, but you don't have to wait for it.

7   Open **43G_3 MCU Blithers** and set an In point right before he says, "Connolly," at approximately 21:26:41:05.

8 Set an Out point a beat after he says, "Tonto" (approximately 51:20).

9 Target the audio to tracks A1 and A2 and overwrite the clip directly after shot **43Mb_3** and play this section of the sequence.

Any ideas coming to mind? You may have thought that edit would be a lot smoother if the audio came in before the picture. Kudos to you if you did think that and, if you didn't, maybe you will the next time.

There's a way to split an edit before you even add it to the sequence.

10 Press Command-Z to undo that last edit.

11 In the Timeline, position the playhead right in the middle of shot **43Mb_3** (approximately 01:01:01:10).

12 Press Command-Option-I or choose Mark > Mark Split > Audio In to set an audio-only In point.

13 Press Down Arrow to move the playhead to the next edit.

14 Press Control-I to add a video-only In point.

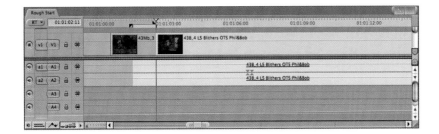

You have just defined a split In point in the sequence. Watch what happens when you edit in the shot.

15 Perform an overwrite edit.

16 View the new edit.

Voilá! Instant split edit. While this practice can be easy in some instances, many times it's just as quick to perform the edit normally and split it afterwards using the Roll and Ripple tools.

At the end of that shot, Blithers looks up and to his right offscreen, to where Kenny is sitting. Any ideas what the next shot should be?

17 Open **43E_2 MCU Kenny** into the Viewer and mark the section where he responds to the Tonto taunt (In: 01:19:36:11, Out: 38:10).

18 Overwrite it into the sequence directly after the Blithers clip.

19 Play around this latest edit.

You can hear the beginning of Kenny's laugh in the Blithers shot, and then again in the single of Kenny. This can easily be cleaned up with a little trimming, creating another split edit.

20 Press R twice to select the Ripple tool, and select the Out point of **43G**.

21 Drag the edit to the left by about 1 second to eliminate the laugh in the outgoing clip.

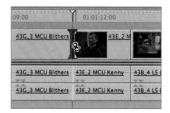

This eliminates the double laugh, but you still want to see Blithers look up to Kenny.

22 Press Command-Shift-A to deselect the edit. Press R to select the Roll tool and Option-click the video edit.

23 Drag the edit to roll it to the right, watching the Canvas until the frame where Blithers looks up at Kenny is visible.

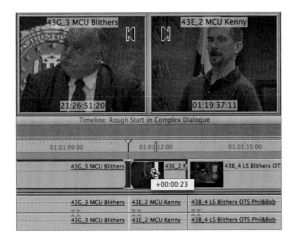

That four-step process is another common way to create a split edit. It's slower than the previous example, but it allows more precise control over the placement of the split.

Blithers' look motivates the cut to Kenny, and you might be inclined to cut back to the CU of Blithers. However, this break from the main dialogue between Blithers and the agents provides an opportunity. Stop and think about the rest of the room and who might be getting left out of the scene. Also think about who the audience is most interested in checking in with. The answer should be obvious: The agents. You could go back to the two-shot of the agents, but you've just come off the MCU of Blithers, and another MCU of Kenny. Remember the rule about matching shot sizes? Instead of returning to that two-shot, try going to one of the MCUs of the agents.

24 Open **43P_1 MCU Phil**.

There's a great expression of defeat that would fit perfectly here.

25 Set an In at 02:23:10:16 and an Out at 11:15.

26 Untarget the audio tracks and overwrite **43P** directly after the Kenny shot.

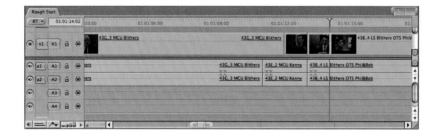

Because you've been trimming seconds from the scene as you've added each of these shots, the audio in the sequence might seem confusing, because the audio from the master shot is repeating the Lone Ranger line while Phil is fretting. However, that's easily fixed with another J-edit.

27 In the Timeline, place the playhead at the start of **43P.** Control-click the ruler and from the shortcut menu, choose Mark Split > Audio In.

28 Move the playhead to the end of **43P**, Control-click the ruler again, and from the shortcut menu, choose Mark Split > Video In.

29 Use the Recent Clips menu in the Viewer to access **43G_3 MCU Blithers**.

30 Set In and Out points around the line, "You two ever hear of protocol?" (In: 21:26:56:02, Out: 58:00).

31 Check that the audio tracks are targeted and perform an overwrite edit, automatically splitting the edit.

Before you proceed, note that the master clips that were supposed to form the foundation of the scene are getting pretty far out of sync with the edits you've made. If you were close to the end of the scene, you might disregard this, but in this instance, there's quite a bit more to go.

32 In the Timeline, set an In point at the end of the last instance of **43G_3**.

33 Set an Out point after Blithers says, "You two ever hear of protocol?" in the master shot (approximately 01:01:22:15).

34 Press Command-Shift-A to deselect all, then press Shift-Delete to ripple delete the marked region.

Now the remainder of the scene will remain approximately in sync with the clips you've already edited in. You may have to repeat this occasionally in a scene where you are cutting lines or spaces while laying in the coverage.

Keeping Track of People

The next event in the scene is Bob's rebuttal to Blithers' accusation. You could cut directly to Bob as he begins his line, or you can look for a *bridge*. In this scene, we haven't yet seen a close-up of Wright (the philosopher from the doorway). It would be helpful to incorporate him into the scene, and this moment presents the perfect opportunity.

In the story, Wright is Phil and Bob's direct superior, working between them and Blithers. In this scene, he is (not accidentally) physically sitting between them. Here's an opportunity to reinforce that relationship editorially.

1 Open **43H_1 MS Wright** into the Viewer.

2 Mark the section where Wright wryly looks from Blithers to the agents (In: 01:33:49:20, Out: 51:00).

This shot is perfect because Wright's head turn motivates the next cut. It begs the question: what's he looking at? You can answer that question with the next shot. Head turns are especially useful in complex dialogue scenes because they help clarify the physical relationships between people.

One minor problem, however, is that the audio is not good on this shot. (Bob is talking but isn't on mic.) The problem can be solved with another split edit, but this time you'll create it in a new way.

3 Open **43Q_2 MCU Bob** and mark the section where he delivers his line, "Sir, we did present the intel to."

On this particular take, Blithers' dialogue nearly overlaps Bob's. Since you don't want to have any double words (or breaths), before editing this shot, you may need to adjust the In and Out points by a frame or two.

4 In the Viewer, press Shift-\ to play In to Out.

If you hear any of Blithers' dialogue on either side, move the In or Out point until Bob's audio is totally clean. The correct In and Out should be In: 02:34:48:00, Out: 50:12.

5 Make sure the audio tracks are targeted and overwrite **43Q** into the sequence directly after **43G**.

6 Use the Recent Clips menu to reopen **43H_1 MS Wright**.

The In and Out points you previously set will still be active.

7 Untarget the audio tracks, position the playhead at the *beginning* of **43Q**, and overwrite the clip into the sequence.

8 Play back this section of the sequence and check that all the edits are working properly.

Before jumping back to Blithers, it might be nice to see what Phil's been doing during all of this.

9 Open **43P_1 MCU Phil**.

If you watch, while Bob is trying to explain, Phil provides one of those invaluable head turns, which will easily motivate (and therefore hide) your cut back to Blithers.

10 Mark the head turn (In: 02:23:24:08, Out: 25:15).

Now you must decide where to put it in the scene. This beat is a mite tricky, since Bob cuts himself off. If you put a video cut at the same moment when Bob stops talking, it will look and sound like a mistake.

That means that **43P** must begin before Bob stops talking, or after it's clear that Blithers has cut him off. Either could work, but momentum and brevity favor starting the shot earlier.

11 Position the sequence playhead right after Bob says the word "intel" (01:01:17:00).

12 Make sure the audio tracks aren't targeted (we don't want to hear the audio from the Phil shot) and overwrite **43P** into the show.

The edit still feels weird, and it's because Blithers' line is starting late. It should begin before Bob stops talking to motivate his silence. If the actors had overlapped their lines on set, you would have a very hard time controlling the edit to make the lines overlap correctly. Fortunately, there are clean versions of their lines that allow you to set the overlap to your liking.

13 Press A to select the Selection tool and, in the sequence, Option-click the audio tracks for **43Q** (Bob), then Shift-drag them to tracks 3 and 4.

14 Option-drag the left edge of the **43B** (master) audio to the left about 18 frames.

NOTE ▶ You may need to turn off snapping and/or press Command (to gear down the drag) to perform this step.

It now makes sense that Bob shuts up (Blithers cuts him off), while the cut to Phil is still sufficiently hidden.

Keeping Track of Location

You've just used a series of six close-ups in a row, featuring five different people. Where are all these people? Are you having trouble keeping track of the geography of the room? If so, the audience is probably having trouble, too.

Fortunately, in this example, the close-ups aren't that close, and you've had three different head turns to reinforce the physical relationships between people in the room. But if you were cutting a scene where the shots were tighter, and you didn't have those head-turn cues, it's very likely that your audience would begin to lose track of the physical space in the room.

Cutting back to the master at this point isn't a terrible choice. It reinforces the geography and could be justified by the natural pause in the conversation following Blithers' action of shutting Bob down. That pause provides an editorial opportunity to reset the stage, so to speak, which is exactly what a cut to the master does.

But this particular master is too wide. While it does have both agents' shoulders, they're really not part of the shot. What this moment really calls for is a shot that you don't have: a slightly tighter master that shows both the agents and Blithers in the same angle.

Since the production is long wrapped, it's not likely anyone's going to go back and pick that shot up for you, so you need to press on without it. And, in this case, the simplest answer is to go back to Blithers' MCU and hope for the best.

1   Use the Recent Clips menu to open **43G_3 MCU Blithers** into the Viewer.

2   Set an In point right before the word "stand" (as in "stand down") and set an Out point after "superiors" (In: 21:27:01:04, Out 14:15).

3   In the sequence, position the playhead at the end of Phil's CU (**43P**).

4   Make sure the audio tracks are targeted to A1 and A2, and overwrite the clip into the sequence.

There is one minor problem with this shot. A distracting camera move in the middle of this take would be best hidden. Remember that your job is about controlling the viewer's focus. That camera move pulls attention away from the content of the scene and puts the attention on the camera instead.

5   Play the sequence until just before the camera move as Blithers says, "Answer." Set an In point there (01:01:21:07).

Do you have any idea of what to use to cover it up? One idea would be to put a shot of Darren here. It's been an awfully long time since you've shown him, and it would be nice to be reminded that he's in the room. Or, you could show Bob and Phil's reaction to Blithers' attack.

Both of those are valid solutions, but here's one more. Always pay attention to both sides of an edit. Think about when you're going to come back to Blithers. If you play forward a few seconds, Blithers is looking up at Kenny.

6   Set an Out point there in the sequence, right around 01:01:22:20, just before Blithers says, "As to why my top field agents."

7   Open **43E_2 MCU Kenny** and scan through it to find an appropriate reaction.

Remember that Kenny is being reprimanded here, so you should be looking for an expression of guilt. The closest shot is right after his "Tonto" line. He has a sort of embarrassed expression.

Since the Out point is what's going to match Blithers' withering glare, you should focus more on finding the right Out point in the Kenny clip.

8   Set an Out point in the Viewer at 01:19:39:20. Press Option-I to clear the In point.

9   Make sure the audio is untargeted and perform an overwrite edit.

10   Play around the edit to see how well the cutaway works.

Build Up to the Climax

Throughout this scene, you have pretty aggressively cut out pauses and even whole lines of dialogue. Part of the reason is to make the scene shorter, but it's not quite that simple. First and foremost, your purpose is to pay attention to performance and eliminate any expendable beats where you feel the performance isn't working.

Second, you must be watching for redundancy. Scripts are often full of redundancy. It's redundant when Blithers says, "Now I have to explain to the brass…" and then a moment later says, "How do I look to my superiors…" Both lines serve the same purpose, in terms of explaining the story and explaining the character's motivations. Are both needed? No, not unless some other new information is being conveyed.

Third, you adjust the timing of a sequence as a way to control its pacing. That means that you not only tighten bits of a scene, you might also deliberately pad a moment to allow suspense to build or to draw attention to the action that follows.

At this point in the scene, Phil is finally going to own up to having hatched the whole scheme and at the same time, he is going to stand up for himself against Blithers. It's the turning point, so it deserves a little special attention. You already know how to take extra seconds out of a scene; now you'll learn how to put some back.

1   Position the sequence playhead at the end of **43G_3** and set an In point.

2   Open **43P_1 MCU Phil**.

   Rather than going straight to his line, look at the section in Phil's close-up where Blithers is saying, "How do you think that makes me look?" Phil has a great expression of total despair. The audience doesn't yet know what he's going to do, and that's exactly what you want. You want to hold that suspense as long as possible.

3   Set an In point at 02:23:36:00 and an Out point 2 seconds later at 38:00. Be sure not to include any frames at the end of the shot where he begins to look back up, as that begins his next action.

4   Make sure the audio is untargeted, and perform an insert edit.

   NOTE ▸ You can safely ignore the warning that some clips will be moved out of sync.

This creates a gap in the audio track, but don't worry. You can easily fill that gap later with room tone and other ambient elements. For now, just get the timing of the moment right.

5   Open **43Q_2 MCU Bob** and find the same section, where Blithers is blathering about his superiors.

Although these two looks happened at the same time in the scene, there's no reason you can't stack them one after the other to stretch out the moment.

6   Set an In point at 02:35:02:00 and an Out point at 03:10.

Be sure not to include any of Bob nodding as he does at the end of this bit. The idea is that they are both defeated and the physical gesture of looking down conveys a different meaning than the nodding.

This is an example where you are completely changing the actor's performance, transforming "complicity" to "despair." Don't worry, he won't mind as long as it makes the film better (and as long as you give him all the credit).

7   Insert this clip into the sequence directly after **43P**. (Again, click Yes to dismiss the Out of Sync warning.)

But that's not enough! It's not just Phil and Bob who are disappointed here. Their mentor, Wright, is also distraught.

8 Open **43H_1 MS Wright** and find the same moment in the scene.

9 Set an In point at 01:34:10:20 and an Out point at 13:13.

This shot ends with Wright looking down to Phil, presumably motivated by Phil speaking.

10 Insert this clip into the sequence following **43H**.

11 Play over the three clips you just inserted and find the frame where you should begin to hear Phil's line, so that it appears to motivate Wright's head turn (approximately 01:01:36:00).

12 Press Command-Option-I to set an audio In point.

13 Press Down Arrow to move the playhead to the end of Wright's shot and press Control-I to set the video In point.

14 Use the Recent Clips menu to open **43P_1 MCU Phil** into the Viewer.

15 Set an In point just before Phil's sigh at 02:23:40:00. Set the Out point after he says, "Angelino…Sir" at 52:05.

16 Make sure the audio tracks are targeted and overwrite the clip into the sequence.

To further heighten this moment, rather than rushing back to Blithers, you can take this opportunity to show some of the other people's reactions to Phil's confession.

17 In the sequence, set an In point after Phil says, "Responsible" around 01:01:40:20.

18 Load **43Q_2 MCU Bob** into the Viewer and find the moment where Bob turns his head to look at Phil (In: 02:35:06:00, Out: 07:00).

19 Untarget the audio tracks and overwrite the clip into the sequence.

20 In the sequence, set an In point at the end of Bob's shot and set an Out point right before Phil's brooding look, as he decides to stand up for himself (Out: 01:01:42:15).

21 Load **43G_3 MCU Blithers** into the Viewer. Find where Blithers says, "Oh really, Angelina" and set an Out just afterwards, at 21:27:19:00. Press Option-I to clear the In point.

22 Retarget the audio tracks and overwrite the clip into the sequence.

23 Play around the new edit.

The edit mostly works, but Blithers' audio has an unwanted overlap.

24 Select the audio-only edit between **43P** and **43G** (press Option to select only the audio).

25 Enter *–10* to roll the edit to the left.

26 Play the whole sequence up to this point and admire all the work you've done.

You might want to cut one more exchange between Blithers' and Phil's close-ups instead of using the master for the last part of this section, but for the sake of the lesson, you can stop here and skip to the next edit.

Mixing Doing and Talking

So far, in all of the dialogue examples, the subjects haven't been doing anything except talking. But in many instances, a scene mixes dialogue and action.

The next section of this scene, beginning with Kenny crossing behind Blithers, is a good, simple example of this.

1 In the Browser, collapse the 2 Main Scene bin and expand the Agents and Bosses bins in the "3 Ending (after Kenny crosses)" bin.

2   In the Timeline, skip to the next edit in the sequence, which begins with Kenny walking behind Blithers. Set an In point at the beginning of that shot.

3   Open **43D_4 MLS Kenny Crosses** from the Bosses bin inside the 3 Ending bin.

This is a somewhat tighter shot that has a clearer point of focus than the wider master shot.

4   Set an In point at the beginning of the shot and an Out point as Kenny reaches for the vinegar bottle (around 01:14:37:21).

5   Overwrite the clip into the sequence.

Once Kenny approaches that bottle, the viewer's attention is likely to be focused there. Because of that, the next most logical shot is the insert shot.

6   Open **43J_3 CU Vinegar Bottle.**

7   Set an In point just before Kenny begins to twirl the bottle (01:43:08:00) and set the Out point as he lifts the bottle out of the frame (13:20).

As always, use objects moving in the frame to hide the edit. In this case, the bottle exiting the frame in this shot and entering the frame in the next is one of the simplest, most traditional ways of covering this sort of action.

8   Overwrite the clip into the sequence directly after **43D.**

9   Open **43F_2a MCU Kenny & Vinegar.**

10   Set an In point as the bottle enters the frame (01:20:48:07) and set the Out point after Kenny says, "Now we know their M.O." (approximately 21:00:00).

11   Overwrite the clip into the sequence directly after **43J.**

12   Play this section of the sequence.

A little cleanup is required to eliminate the double audio between the second two clips. This is a procedure you should be very familiar with by now.

13   Select the audio edit between **43J** and **43F** (press Option to override linking).

14 Enter *-20* to roll the edit to the left.

Despite all this interesting action, never forget who the scene is really about. Kenny gets the limelight for a moment, but you quickly need to bring back the agents.

15 Use the Recent Clips menu to open **43P_1 MCU Phil** into the Viewer.

16 Mark the area where Phil is watching the vinegar gag.

Try to find a moment that includes a specific physical action, such as the way he sits back in his chair between 02:24:23:20 and 26:10.

17 In the sequence, set an In point just as Kenny says, "immersion oil," around 01:02:20:05.

18 Untarget the audio tracks and overwrite the clip into the sequence.

Although the front of this edit works, coming back to Kenny feels a little awkward because it cuts back to him after just one action (his amazement at the trick) but a beat before his next action (commending the agents).

This insert of Phil might work a little better if it was shifted to the right a few frames.

19 Position the playhead just before Kenny says, "Thanks to you two guys" at 01:02:23:08.

20 Press S twice or from the Tool palette select the Slide tool.

21 Click the **43P** clip and drag it to the right until it snaps to the playhead. (Press N to turn snapping on if it is currently turned off.)

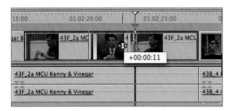

Sliding a clip moves it within the clips around it by rolling the edits on either side of the clip simultaneously. The contents of the clip don't change, but the clip's position in the sequence does.

22 In the sequence, set an In point just after Kenny puts the bottle down and right before he says, "Now we know their M.O." (approximately 01:02:25:10).

23 Use the Recent Clips menu to open **43Q_2 MCU Bob** into the Viewer.

24 Mark Bob's great reaction beginning at 02:35:41:15 and ending at 44:10.

25 Overwrite the clip into the sequence.

26 Open **43H_1 MS Wright** and mark just before and after he says, "Not bad" (In: 01:35:02:00 Out: 03:10).

27 Retarget the audio tracks and edit the clip into the sequence directly after **43Q**.

Naturally, by now you know that you are practically obligated to show the agents' reaction to Wright's compliment, but in the vein of laying down the foundation first, it may be helpful to first drop in Blithers' next line, then go back and cover up part of it with Bob and Phil's reactions.

28 Open **43G_3 MCU Blithers** and set an In point right before Blithers says, "So congratulations," and an Out after he says, "Get back to work" (In: 21:28:18:22, Out: 23:10).

29 Edit the clip into the sequence directly after **43H**.

Now you're ready to go back and drop in the agents' reactions.

30 In the sequence, position the playhead at the beginning of **43G** and untarget the audio tracks.

31 Use the Recent Clips menu to open **43Q_2 MCU Bob** into the Viewer.

32 Set a new In point at the previous Out point (before Bob turns smiling to Phil at 02:35:44:10) and set a new Out point after Bob completes his turn at 45:20.

33 Edit the clip into the sequence so it overwrites the first frames of **43G**.

34 Use the Recent Clips menu to open **43P_1 MCU Phil** into the Viewer.

35 Find the moment when Phil is looking over at Bob and turns back to look at Blithers. Set the In point just before he turns (02:24:28:16), and the Out point right after he completes his turn at 29:13.

36 Edit the clip into the sequence directly after **43Q**.

37 Play back this part of the sequence to see the results of your handiwork.

This is a perfect set of shots, as once again, the head turns serve perfectly to motivate (and therefore hide) the cuts. It's as if they hand off the focus from one to another, from Wright to Bob, from Bob to Phil, and from Phil to Blithers. Of course that's not at all what happened in the room, but through the magic of editing, you are able to integrate all of their individual actions into one seamless story.

Finish the Scene on Your Own

As you can see, despite being a relatively simple scene, all in one location with a minimum of movement or action, and with fairly limited, standard coverage, this sequence provides a wide variety of challenges and opportunities for you to experiment and hone your dialogue editing skills.

Many of the edits you made can be finessed further and enhanced using the various methods and techniques described throughout this lesson.

The project contains all of the footage you need to edit the last bit of the scene on your own, and there is a wide variety of choices available to make your version of the scene unique.

Most important, the ideas and concepts you've covered are applicable to all editing situations, whether they are dramatic, nonfiction, or experimental. All edits should be motivated, and you must consciously control the viewer's point of focus with your choices of shots, edit positions, and the specific frames you choose to edit on.

Furthermore, in all your editing projects you'll use all the techniques you used throughout this lesson such as organizing your footage before you begin, starting each sequence with a skeleton of master shots (even if you eventually replace every one of them), finding the point of no return in each scene (the hinge), breaking complex scenes into smaller sections, and so many others.

Lesson Review

1. What are three things that make dialogue scenes more complex?

2. How do you begin editing a complex dialogue scene?

3. What happens when you use too many close-ups in a complex dialogue scene?

4. What are two possible solutions to that problem?

5. What else can easily get lost in the course of editing a dialogue scene with many people?

6. How does mixing action and dialogue complicate the editing of a scene?

7. How do you create an audio-only In point?

8. How do you perform a slide edit, and what is its function?

Answers

1. More than two people, more than one position, combining action and dialogue.

2. Organize the scene into sections, create bins to group the footage accordingly, then lay down a series of master shots to see the whole scene at a glance.

3. The viewer can lose track of the geometry of the room and the actors' physical relationships to one another.

4. This can be alleviated by cutting on characters' head turns (or by following their eyeline shifts) *and* by cutting back to a wider shot that shows the characters' physical relationships.

5. Minor characters can be completely forgotten if all the emphasis is focused on the main players.

6. Controlling the focus of a scene can be tricky when there is detailed action that must be covered. Never forget the importance of characters' reactions to the action occurring.

7. Press Command-Option-I or choose Mark > Mark Split > Audio In.

8. Press S twice or from the Tool palette select the Slide tool. A slide edit moves a clip within the clips around it by rolling the edits on either side of the clip simultaneously. The clip's position in the sequence changes but the contents of the clip do not.

3

Lesson Files Lesson Files > Lesson 03 > Basic Action

Media Media > Friends Of The Family

Time This lesson takes approximately 120 minutes to complete.

Goals Learn the basics of editing action sequences

Understand how to work setups and payoffs into your scenes

Begin thinking about how footage affects style

Learn techniques to build tension in a scene

Get familiar with the Trim Edit window

Use dynamic trimming to finesse edit points

Control overall pacing and scene structure

Editing Action

Just as important as learning to cut dialogue is learning to cut basic action sequences. Action scenes come in many shapes and sizes—from something as simple as a demonstration of a coffeemaker to a full-scale laser battle in outer space. But all action scenes have some things in common, and once you learn a few concepts and rules, you'll be ready to tackle almost anything.

While all dialogue scenes are nearly identical structurally, action scenes are almost always unique. Some action scenes take place in a large physical space (for example, ballroom dancing), while others focus on tiny details in one location (such as cracking a safe). Some action scenes involve continual movement from one place to another (such as delivering milk). In any of these cases, the specific details of the action will often call for different types of coverage.

However, while actions scenes are all different, there are common editing patterns you can apply depending on the type of action scene you're cutting. If you can identify your scene as one of a certain type, that can give you clues as to the best way to approach cutting it.

Later, you'll learn to identify common action scene types such as fights, battles, chases, shootouts, and others. But don't think all fights require fisticuffs or that all shootouts require guns. These categories can be applied to all sorts of action scenes, and each has its own set of guidelines and tricks.

Telling a Story in Action

It's helpful to begin by separating simple actions from complex ones.

A *simple* action scene is one where there is one central activity, usually performed by one person (or thing). This could be as simple as someone practicing their golf swing or tying their kid's shoe, or it could be as complicated as someone taking apart a motorcycle engine or painting a house.

A *complex* scene strings together several simple actions, either sequentially (playing a whole round of golf) or simultaneously (a house-painting competition). As you might expect, complex action scenes require greater organizational forethought in order to cut them quickly and effectively.

Don't forget, however, that your basic charge is still just to tell the story. Most of the basic tenets covered in the dialogue lessons still apply to action scenes. It's usually advantageous to start wide and then move in close; most edits benefit from being split; and, of course, you should still always seek to cut on action within the frame. No matter what the content of the scene, you are still going to use pacing and shot selection to guide the audience's focus.

Most important, don't lose track of the six essential questions. Plenty of zillion-dollar action films fail to engage the audience because they get so caught up in the *what* and the *how* of the action that they don't bother to spend enough time answering the *who* or the *why*. This isn't rocket science—it's campfire storytelling.

As the editor, you are limited to the footage that the production team provides, but it is still up to you to find the best dramatic balance. You set the tempo and pacing of each scene and choose which questions get answered and which get ignored. Invariably, you will have close-ups of faces and inserts of important details. It's how and where and for how long you use them that ultimately determine the impact of the scene.

Another storytelling concept that you must incorporate into your action scenes is the fundamental idea of the beginning, middle, and end. If you ignore this essential notion, an action scene can quickly become a dense mess of disjointed details without a clear sense of progression.

There may be as many shots of the details of an action as there are pieces of a motorcycle engine. Sure, you can begin with a shot of the assembled engine, and end with a shot of the pieces spread out on the floor; but what about all those shots in between? Assuming you're not making an instructional video about motorcycle maintenance, the truth about how to take apart an engine is irrelevant. You need to determine which shots *tell the story* and arrange them in a way that conveys a sense of progress. Just like a good plot, each shot must depend on the one that precedes it, and it must compel the one that follows.

Learning Action Fundamentals

There are a few critical concepts you should learn to improve your action cutting skills. These are general principles that can be applied in almost any situation. All of these concepts are based on consciously manipulating the audience's anxiety level to induce an emotional response.

The more you understand how to control that anxiety, the more successful you will be as an editor. While this may sound clinical (or perhaps insidious), it is exactly what makes editing effective. It's no secret that certain images and certain editing techniques have a physical effect on viewers. Whether you are evoking terror or catharsis, the goal is to use that power in the service of your theme.

Creating a Setup and Payoff

Setup and payoff are broad storytelling concepts that can be applied very concretely in action scenes. Payoff is another word for satisfaction, and the only way to provide satisfaction is to set up an expectation and then deliver it. In terms of editing, this is done with specific shots. A shot of someone picking up a ripe peach is a setup that reaches payoff when she takes a big, juicy bite. Similarly, a shot of a mail truck is a setup that pays off with a shot of a letter being opened.

The peach-biting or letter-opening shots may have significance on their own, but they provide much more satisfaction for the audience when the editor builds up an expectation prior to fulfilling it.

The further you separate the setup from the payoff, the more effectively you hold hostage a part of an audience's brain. This is commonly called *suspense* because you are in effect *suspending* their attention. Providing a setup shot that establishes an expectation raises a sort of tension in the viewer. When you pay it off, you release the tension. The longer you wait to show the payoff, the more the tension builds… but only to a point. If you wait too long, you lose the audience. They either forget about the setup or, worse, they start wondering, "Gee, what was that mail truck shot about?" That means they've stepped out of the story—and the next thing you know they're checking their voicemail.

Establishing Cause and Effect

This is a subset of the setup and payoff. If you show a shot of a hand grenade, you compel a later shot of an explosion. The longer you wait to show the explosion, the more tension you create. If you never show the explosion at all, you disappoint (or confuse) the audience. If you show the explosion without the shot of the grenade, you miss an opportunity to build tension, and again you might confuse the audience. The grenade/explosion example is very clear cut, but cause and effect is often much more subtle, and you can change the meaning of a scene by rearranging the order of the shots.

For example, a thief is rummaging through a bedroom. You have three shots: an ECU of her picking up a diamond necklace; a MCU where she picks up a framed picture of a happy couple; and a CU of her face looking forlorn.

If she finds the necklace first, looks forlorn, then finds the picture, the necklace appears to *cause* the sadness, and her sadness seems to *cause* her to pick up the picture. On the other hand, if she finds the picture first, feels forlorn, and then steals the necklace anyway, you have a very different story. If you omit some of the shots altogether, you have yet another version.

Cutting an Action Scene

The scene you will cut in this lesson is of moderate complexity. It is a showdown scene that could be categorized as a unique type of action scene. The scene features multiple parties (rival gangs, in this case) preparing for a conflict. This example is very literal, but the showdown technique is applicable to any scene that leads up to a conflict: two parents on their way to a custody hearing; students preparing their projects for the science fair; or a romantic couple finally meeting for their first kiss.

The nature of a showdown is to have a gradual buildup of tension that is relieved when it explodes into a contest or is miraculously diffused at the last second. Common showdown editing techniques include crosscutting, acceleration of cuts, and copious use of reaction shots.

1   Open project Lesson 03 > **Basic Action**.

Although the scene is one continuous event, the project has been organized into two primary bins, 1 Walking and 2 Confrontation, as well as a third bin called Masters.

2   Double-click **WS Overhead_06** from the Masters bin and play it from the beginning.

This master shows the main action in the scene: two rival gangs approach each other and, rather than pulling weapons, the leaders pull out baby bottles and they all leave together to tend to their kids.

NOTE ▶ This scene is from a fundraising video for Friends of the Family, a charity that has a program specifically designed to help at-risk teen fathers get out of trouble and responsibly raise their children.

3 Click the disclosure triangle for the 1 Walking bin.

The clips in this bin have been further organized into two sub-bins: Group 1 and Group 2. These will prove to be especially helpful, since many of the shots from the two groups look very similar.

You should notice that the shots for the two groups parallel each other; both groups have "CU_Feet" and "CU_Hands" shots, and both have "ELS through bars" shots. In fact, every single shot is half of a pair—one for each gang.

This may look familiar, because it's the same thing you encountered (and took advantage of) when cutting the basic dialogue scene. These pairs of shots let you *match angles,* one of the hallmarks of effective, invisible editing.

4 Scroll the browser toward the right until the Log Note field is revealed.

The log notes can provide valuable information about which shots you'll want to use. One repeated word you may notice is "swishy." What does this mean? If you're not sure, you'd best take a look.

5   Double-click **G1_CU_swishy_01** and play it in the Viewer.

The camera continually swish pans between the gang members. While you might be inclined to cut around these messy moves, once you recognize that the footage is full of such movements, an idea should spark in your mind. Rather than avoiding that element, you would be better off to embrace it. In fact, that visual motif provides insight as to how the footage is asking to be cut.

It is always your job as editor to adapt your style to the needs of the footage at hand. Forcing a preconceived editorial style onto footage will just ruin the show. A good editor is one who can be sentimental or gritty, rigid and mathematical, or loose and organic. In this sequence, the director has provided unambiguous cues about how he wanted the scene to look and feel. You'd better respond to it or you'll risk not only the quality of the show, but the opportunity to work with that director again!

6   Double-click the *Showdown* sequence to open it in the Canvas and Timeline.

Once you've gotten familiar with the footage and its tone and style, it's time to figure out where to start editing. The shots in the Masters bin all begin in the middle of the scene, right before the confrontation, so you need to look for a master-type shot among the walking footage.

7   Open **G1 ELS through bars_02** and play it in the Viewer.

This seems like a great place to start, because it tells you *where* (a playground) and *what* (a gang is on the march). Furthermore, the compositional element of bars in the foreground evokes a prison, helping to emphasize the tone of the scene. Also, the rack focus is a great way to introduce the scene, and it will work nicely with the swish-pan style you'll incorporate later.

8   Mark an In point just before the first movement is visible from behind the bar (approximately 02:10:09:07) and mark an Out point a few steps after the shot comes into focus (around 14:20).

9   Edit the clip into the sequence.

10   Open **G2 ELS through Bars_02**.

This is the matching angle and, at least for starters, is the obvious shot to follow. Rather than starting on an empty frame like the first shot did, however, you can start these guys a little later in the shot.

11 Set the In point after the second guy becomes visible (around 02:07:10:20) and set an Out point a few steps after the focus has locked (at 15:07).

12 Overwrite the clip directly following the first clip.

Immediately, you've set up the scene. It's clear that there are two groups and, because they're moving toward each other, it's also obvious that they're in conflict. Pretty good work with just two shots.

Building Tension

Since you've so quickly established that there is a conflict brewing, you have an opportunity to heighten the stakes by immediately ratcheting up audience tension.

One effective way to build tension is with the use of close-ups, especially close-ups of details that the audience can't quite put in context. This is pretty easy to understand. Whenever a viewer is watching a movie, he is unconsciously making sense of the shots and trying to understand the story. He is assembling the pieces of the puzzle just as fast as you give them out. When you deliberately withhold information, you make his brain work harder, creating tension.

For example, if you begin a scene with close-ups and withhold the long shot to answer the *where* or *when* questions, the viewer remains in a somewhat unsettled state and doesn't quite know his whereabouts.

Similarly, in this scene, the opening shots set up a conflict. They answer the *what* and *where*, but they don't reveal the *who*. Naturally a viewer is going to crave a close-up or at least a medium shot so he can identify who the participants are. Who is the "good guy" and who is the "bad guy?" By withholding that information, you increase that tension. Of course, you can only stretch tension so far before the viewer loses interest, but you've hooked him with the instant conflict. Let's try to leverage that a bit.

1   Open **G2_CU Feet_01**.

This is a close-up of feet. It might be even more powerful if they were all wearing army boots (or more funny if they were in flip-flops); but, alas, this is what you've got.

2   Find a frame after they begin walking when the front guy's left foot lands on the ground (02:04:36:10). Set an In point there.

3   Play the clip until the next time the front guy's left foot lands and set an Out point (37:22).

In the Canvas, the guy's feet are mostly obscured by the sand pile, so you can just approximate where his left foot would land.

4   In the Canvas, set an In point at 01:00:09:20.

You now have a subtle but nonetheless useful bit of movement to cut on within the frame. Since the ELS is so far away, and the guys are not exactly all walking in unison, you could probably have gotten away with almost any In point, but why not do everything you can to make as smooth an edit as possible?

5   Overwrite the clip into the sequence.

6   Open **G1 CU Feet_01**.

Naturally, the next shot should be the matching version of the shot from the other gang.

Even though their footsteps are not literally in sync with the guys from Group 2, you can have a bit of editorial fun by doing the same kind of matching action from one feet CU to the next.

7   Find the frame where the front guy's right foot lands and set an In point (02:02:43:00). Let him walk one full stride and mark an Out (44:08).

8   Overwrite the clip directly after **G2_CU Feet_01**.

9   Press \ (backslash) to play around the edit.

The rhythm lines up nicely but the edit isn't as powerful as it could be. The action is the foot hitting the ground but, once it lands, the action is over (and a new step begins).

The optimal edit would have the foot coming down in the first shot but not landing until after the cut. That way, the viewer's eyes follow the movement across the edit, thereby ignoring it. To make that optimal edit, you would have to guess how far off the ground the foot needs to be (accounting for momentum) in each shot. This is fairly difficult, especially in a situation like this where the two guys aren't even walking at exactly the same speed.

But there's a trick! And it's one of the most useful tricks you can learn to speed up and improve the quality of your action cuts. Make the edit at the moment when the action ends (like you did in Steps 5 through 9) and then roll the edit back slightly to move the cut midway through the action.

10   Press R to select the Roll tool, and select the edit between **G2 CU Feet_01** and **G1_CU Feet_01**.

11 Drag to the left to roll the edit, watching the Canvas until the foot is halfway to the ground on both sides of the edit (about 10 frames).

> **NOTE** ▶ You may want to turn off Snapping and/or press Command (to gear-down the drag) to trim more precisely.

It's kind of fun to watch the canvas as you roll back and forth, seeing how the two shots line up, allowing you to choose the best frame for the cut.

By the way, that trick works on any action cut where you have to guess about how the momentum of a movement will play across an edit. If you have two shots of someone slamming a door, make the cut on the frame when the door is closed in both shots, and then roll the edit back so it cuts in mid-slam.

Crosscutting

From this point in the scene, you will cut back and forth from Group 1 to Group 2 back to Group 1 with nearly every edit. This is called *crosscutting*. Although it is similar to cutting back and forth between characters during a dialogue scene, both groups in this scene are technically still in different locations. Imagine that instead of the groups marching right up to each other in the playground, they were getting ready in separate buildings.

Crosscutting is another technique that builds tension. It asks the audience to keep track of what's going on with Group 1 even as you cut away to Group 2, and vice versa. You're asking them to keep track of twice as much information. This taxes their brains and causes more anxiety. Like other tension-building techniques, you can't keep up that anxiety indefinitely. You have to relieve the stress at some point or risk losing your audience's attention.

Usually in a showdown scenario, the tension is relieved when the two parties finally arrive at the same location. You'll see the same technique employed in Lesson 4 when you cut a chase scene.

1 Open **G2_CU Hands_01**.

2 Watch the Viewer and follow the stride of Andy's left foot. Try to identify the frame where his foot hits the ground and mark an In point (02:04:59:07). Play forward another full footstep and set the Out at 05:00:10.

3 Overwrite the clip into the sequence directly after **G1 CU Feet_01**.

4 Open **G1 CU hands_01**.

It's a little harder to precisely locate the footsteps in this shot, so you'll just have to eyeball it.

5 Set an In point around 02:03:08:06 and an Out point at around 09:12.

6 Overwrite the clip directly after **G2_CU Hands_01**.

Now it's finally time to reveal the gang members' faces. You must decide if you want to show all of the guys' faces or just go straight to the leaders. Since the previous two exchanges focused mainly on the leaders, holding out even longer before showing their faces might try the audience's patience.

7 Open **G2_CU Andy_02**.

Here's your first opportunity to work in one of those swish pans.

8 Set an In just as the camera begins moving up from his feet (approximately 02:05:35:02) and set an Out point after he makes that great scowl around 39:00.

9 Overwrite the clip into the sequence directly after **G1 CU hands_01**.

10 Open the matching single from Group 1: **G1_CU Pedro_02**.

This shot is a nice matching single of Pedro (the Group 1 leader), but it lacks any of that nice swish pan stuff. Perhaps there's something better in one of the other shots.

11 Open **G1_CU_swishy_01**.

This shot contains a great lateral swish onto Pedro that matches the one that introduced Andy, making it a great choice (not to mention that Pedro's performance is better in this take than in his single).

12 Mark an In just after the camera begins its swish toward Pedro and set the Out just before it starts to swish back (In: 02:04:24:04, Out: 26:15).

13 Overwrite the clip into the sequence directly after **G2_CU Andy_02**.

This is the first instance when you are deliberately choosing not to hide the edit as completely as possible. There are several reasons for this. First of all, the swish pans and rack focus shots and handheld camera work all draw attention to the means of production, so you have more incentive to complement those techniques with some similarly self-referential editorial choices. Furthermore, in this specific case, swishing onto the leads (especially if accompanied by a cool sound effect) gives them a much more powerful introduction than a straight cut.

The only problem is that you've moved so quickly into close-ups you need a way to justify stepping back out to a wider shot to show the two gangs coming together in the next section of the scene. Fortunately, you have matching POV shots that can be cut directly from the close-ups since they presumably are what the gang leaders are seeing.

14 Open **G2 (POV Group1)_01**.

15 Mark an In point around 02:01:16:18 and an Out point around 18:17.

16 Overwrite the clip into the sequence directly after **G1_CU_swishy_01**.

17 Open **G1 (POV Group2)_02**.

18 Mark an In point around 02:02:26:02 and an Out point around 28:07.

19 Overwrite the clip into the sequence directly after **G2 (POV Group1)_01**.

Having moved out from the close-ups to these POV long shots, you've implied that the groups are now in close proximity of each other. It's time to bring the two into the same location.

20 Open **WS_Overhead_06** from the Masters bin.

21 Mark an In just as the two groups cross the frameline threshold (approximately 01:55:35:01) and set an Out just before they come to a complete stop (around 37:00).

22 Overwrite the clip into the sequence directly after **G1 (POV Group2)_02**.

23 Use the Recent Clips menu to open **G2 (POV Group1)_01**.

24 Mark the area just before and after the group comes to a stop (In; 02:01:21:17, Out: 23:06) and overwrite the clip into the sequence directly after **WS_Overhead_06**.

25 Play back the sequence up to this point.

Ignore the Audio

Now you'll move from the walking part of the scene to the confrontation. To enhance the suspense during this section, you will need to spread out the dialogue a bit. During production, the guys bantered their few lines so quickly that it sucked the tension out of the scene; if these were rival gangs squaring off, they wouldn't speak to each other quite so easily. It's up to you to create pacing that makes the moment as menacing as possible.

Ordinarily when cutting dialogue, you always get the flow of the audio worked out before you worry about the picture edit, but in this case the timing of the action is more important than the timing of the dialogue, so you will do the reverse. Don't worry about all the overlapping or repeated dialogue that happens during these next few edits. You'll go back and clean it up once the picture is in and the pacing feels right.

1 In the Browser, click the disclosure triangle next to the 1 Walking bin to collapse it and click the triangle next to the 2 Confrontation bin to expand it.

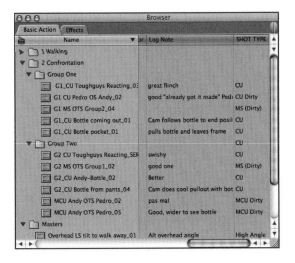

2   Open **G1 MS OTS Group2_04**. Mark the area from before Pedro says, "So what's up?" until after he clasps his hands (In: 01:57:47:04, Out: 48:15).

NOTE ▶ Although it's not ideal to back out to a wider shot here, performance trumps matching angles, and this shot had the best performance with the fewest problems.

3   Overwrite the clip into the sequence directly after **G2 (POV Group1)_01**.

4   Open **MCU Andy OTS Pedro_02**. Set an In point at 02:10:50:04 and an Out point at 51:11.

5   Overwrite the clip into the sequence directly after **G1 MS OTS Group2_04**.

6   Open **G1 CU Pedro OS Andy_02**. Set an In point at 02:17:14:16 and an Out point at 15:11.

7   Overwrite the clip into the sequence directly after **MCU Andy OTS Pedro_02**.

8   Play the sequence up to this point.

With the main shots for the dialogue section of the scene laid in with approximate timing, you can now clean up the audio.

9   Click the Auto Select control for V1 to turn it off.

10 Place the playhead at the beginning of **WS_Overhead_06** and begin to play it.

11 Mark an In point before Andy says, "What's up?" around 01:00:26:19. Mark an Out point at the end of the clip.

12 Press Command-Shift-A to deselect all and press Delete to remove that section of the audio tracks.

Because Auto Select is off for track V1, only the audio tracks are deleted.

Now, instead of Andy saying something as he approaches, you heighten the moment by having him just step up and stare. Although it's a subtle editing difference, you can see it has a dramatic effect on how the scene plays.

Also, although you are leaving a gap of total silence, this can easily be addressed later using *room tone* (an audio ambiance track recording on location) and other sound design elements.

13 Play forward past the next clip into **G1 MS OTS Group2_04**. Set an In right after Pedro says, "'S'up?" but before Andy says anything (around 1:00:30:03).

14 Press Down Arrow to move the playhead to the next edit and set an Out point there.

15 Press Delete to remove the extra dialogue.

16 Play forward and mark an In point just after Andy says, "We gonna do this?"

17 Play over Pedro's "Si mon," and into the next clip. Mark the Out just after Andy (again) says, "We gonna do this?" but before Pedro speaks.

18 Press Delete to remove the repeated lines.

19 Move the playhead back to the beginning of **WS_Overhead_06** and play the section.

Using Dynamic Trimming

The scene is looking OK, but the edits are all occurring right on each guy's lines. I'm sure you've already realized that the scene would feel a little more fluid if the edits were split. This is a great time to become familiar with dynamic trimming.

1   Turn on Auto Select for track V1.

2   Click the Linked Selection button in the button bar or press Shift-L to disable linked selection.

This step isn't necessary to make use of dynamic trimming, but in this instance, you're only going to be trimming the video, and this makes it easier to avoid accidentally selecting tracks you don't want to adjust.

3   Double-click the edit point on V1 between **G2 (POV Group1)_01** and **G1 MS OTS Group2_04**.

The edit is selected, and the Trim Edit window opens.

Trimming an edit in the Trim Edit window is identical to trimming it in the Timeline. You can roll the edit or ripple either side. The Trim Edit window just provides more detailed information, such as how many frames you have trimmed and how much media is left in each of the clips.

In order to trim effectively, you need to know which audio will be played in the Trim Edit window. This is determined in the User Preferences window.

4   Choose Final Cut Pro > User Preferences and click the Editing tab.

5   Make sure Trim with Sequence Audio is selected and Trim with Edit Selection Audio (Mute Others) is deselected.

For now, leave Dynamic Trimming deselected.

6   Click OK to close the User Preferences window.

7 Make sure the Trim Edit window is active and press the Spacebar.

The Spacebar works differently in the Trim Edit window than it does elsewhere. Here, it performs a Play Around Edit and it automatically loops. If you want to play forward (or backward) without looping, use the J, K, and L keys.

8 Press the Spacebar again to stop the loop.

Before turning on the dynamic trimming feature, you should become familiar with how the Trim Edit window works (if you aren't already). The type of edit is indicated by the green bars at the top of the window. A green bar on both sides means roll:

One bar indicates a ripple edit on the side where the bar appears:

If you're ever in doubt, you can also always check the selection in the Timeline.

You trim in the Timeline by dragging the edit point or typing in numbers, but in the Trim Edit window, you can type in numbers or you can click the trim buttons.

9 Make sure the edit is selected as a roll and click the +5 button once and then the +1 button twice.

The edit is rolled forward by seven frames.

10 Press the Spacebar to play around the edit and see how the trim improved the edit. Press the Spacebar again to stop.

This edit works, but it would have been just as easy, and taken fewer clicks, to just type +7 without ever opening the Trim Edit window.

The real reason the Trim Edit window exists is because it allows you to trim on-the-fly, also known as dynamic trimming. Dynamic trimming is very simple; when you press the J or L key the sequence plays, moving the edit point with the playhead. When you press K to stop playback, the edit is updated to the new point.

This method of trimming is far more intuitive than typing a number of frames, and it's far more useful than dragging an edit point in the Timeline.

All edit decisions should be made while playing. That's why you should always set Ins, Outs, and markers while the video is moving.

This is a very fundamental and critical point. Editing is about timing. An edit is right when it *feels* right—not when it is adjusted by a specific number of frames. And it's impossible to feel the timing of an edit while dragging an edit point in the Timeline or typing in a number of frames. But it is possible to feel the edit if you are changing it while playing. Enter dynamic trimming.

11 Click the Dynamic checkbox.

12 Press J to move the edit backward.

13 Press K to stop the edit.

14 Press L to move the edit forward.

It takes some getting used to. Don't be afraid. You can go back in the other direction if you go too far, and there's always Undo.

15 Use the J, K, and L keys to move the edit around and get familiar with how it feels.

This is a pretty short shot to practice with, but it's a real-world situation. Plenty of times you'll be trimming edits with only a couple of frames to spare.

IMPORTANT ▶ If you have pressed J or L and want to abort the trim operation, press the Spacebar or the Escape key instead of K. That will stop playback, and return the edit to its previous location.

16 Once you've got the hang of it, press L and play the edit until just after Pedro begins talking. Then press K to complete the trim.

Aim to put the edit after "So" and just as Pedro says, "What" in "What's up?" You are creating a standard J-edit, beginning Pedro's line while looking at Andy, then cutting to Pedro as if in response. This is the same type of split edit you did again and again in Lessons 1 and 2. The difference now is that you're using a new technique to do it.

17 After you think you've got the edit right, press the Spacebar to play around the edit.

Eventually this will become a habit. J... L... K... Spacebar... J... K... L... K... Spacebar. It will become second nature, and you will intuitively begin editing by feel.

18 Once you're satisfied with this edit, press Down Arrow to shift to the next edit point.

The Trim Edit window stays active, but now you're manipulating the edit point between **G1 MS OTS Group2_04** and **MCU Andy OTS Pedro_02**.

19 Again, use the J, K, and L keys to trim the edit dynamically, until you've created a J-cut, where you cut back to Andy just before he says, "Do this."

20 Press the Spacebar to play around the edit.

21 Once you're satisfied, press Down Arrow again to move to the last edit.

22 Use J, K, L, and the Spacebar to adjust this edit to your liking.

You may choose to cut to Pedro before he says, "Si mon," or just after "Si" and before "mon." There is no correct answer; just place the edit where it feels right.

As you can see, it's very easy to adjust one edit, then move on to the next and adjust that one, and so on. This is one of the reasons it makes sense to get your edits approximately right, but wait until most of the clips are in place before doing the final trimming. As you get more comfortable with dynamic trimming, you'll use it all the time.

There is a misperception that dynamic trimming is an "advanced" editing feature. It's not. It's wonderfully easy to do and, once you get the hang of it, it's fun, too! The only obstacle is that you have to know what you are trying to achieve before using it.

Stretch Out the Climax

The next event in the scene is the two leaders pull out their weapons, which turn out to be baby bottles. You could simply show this action in one shot, but to maximize the effect and enhance the surprise, you should stretch out this event as long as possible. Fortunately you have quite a bit of coverage to work with.

1 Open **MCU Andy OTS Pedro_05**. Mark the area where Andy goes for his weapon but don't include any frames where you can see what it is (In: 02:12:03:18, Out: 04:08).

This is a classic setup shot. As soon as the audience sees him going for a weapon, a host of expectations are established. The longer you can wait before paying off on the setup, the more tension you create, and the more comedy when the expectation turns out to be wrong.

2   Overwrite the clip into the sequence directly after **G1 CU Pedro OS Andy_02**.

3   Open **G1_CU Bottle pocket_01**. Set the In on the first frame where his hand moves, and set the Out just before you can identify what it is he's grabbing (In: 02:21:56:19, Out: 57:10).

4   Overwrite the clip into the sequence directly after **MCU Andy OTS Pedro_05**.

5   Open **G2_CU Bottle from pants_04** and mark the In point as he's reaching for the bottle and set the Out point once the bottle is out and held still (In: 03:03:49:00, Out: 50:00).

This is an instance when you can overlap the action slightly to stretch out the moment. This is commonly called *double-cutting*, and you see it done all the time with explosions. In reality, it probably only takes Andy four to five frames to whip out that bottle, but here you've managed to stretch it out to almost 2 seconds!

6   Overwrite the clip into the sequence directly after **G1_CU Bottle pocket_01**.

7   Press \ to play around the last few edits.

Not bad, but you can do better. Sure, you've stretched out the moment when the bottles come out, but you can stretch it even further and make it more suspenseful and funnier.

Bring in the Witness

The idea of a witness is an essential element of successful action scenes. Adding shots of someone in the room watching events unfold provides several benefits. First, it provides an emotional point of view for the viewers to identify with. Typically with most action scenes, the people performing the action are so busy doing that they don't have much time to be feeling or reacting. A witness (especially if it's a character that the audience already knows and relates to) is a perfect solution to this. It's scary to see the hero strapped to a log-cutting machine, moving inch-by-inch toward the spinning blade. But it's twice as moving if you can show that the woman who he was supposed to save tied to a chair nearby watching helplessly. Similarly, even the most mind-numbing corporate speech is made more engaging by cutting to a shot of an audience member in rapt attention.

Furthermore, the witness has another, more technical benefit. It provides a guaranteed cutaway. In the midst of a scene, there may be many reasons why you need to cut away from the action at hand. You might need to change angles or cut around a moment when the make-up artist needed to apply some fake blood. Action scenes are complicated to shoot, and they frequently are broken up into many shots. Sometimes you need to divert the audience's attention just for a moment, so you can cut around a hole in the action, or make the scene seem more seamless.

Finally, cutting away to a witness gives you the opportunity to stretch out a moment far longer than it might have been in reality. And this is exactly what you will do at this point in the scene.

8   Open **G1_CU Toughguys Reacting_03**.

A section of the shot is already marked.

9   Move the sequence playhead back to the second-to-last edit.

10 Insert the clip into the sequence.

11 Play this section of the scene.

Seeing the guy's reaction definitely improves the scene and further suspends the payoff. But there's no reason to stop there!

12 Open **G2 CU Toughguys Reacting_SERIES**.

A section of this clip has also been marked.

13 Move the sequence playhead back until it is in between **MCU Andy OTS Pedro_05** and **G1_CU Bottle pocket_01**.

14 Insert the cutaway between those two clips.

15 Play back this section of the scene.

Amazingly you have stretched this tiny moment to almost 4 seconds—and you're not done yet! You've probably stretched the buildup as much as possible, but the event itself, the revealing of the bottles, can be extended a bit as well.

16 Put the sequence playhead midway through the last clip, while Andy's arm is still moving (at about 01:00:36:10).

17 Open **Overhead LS tilt to walk away_02** from the Masters bin.

A section of the clip has already been marked.

18 Overwrite that clip into the sequence.

Because there is a camera move in both shots and because Andy's arm movement begins in shot 1 and finishes in shot 2, this makes for an exciting (maybe even dizzying) edit. Yes, the action is doubled slightly, but this is exactly the place to do it, as it draws added attention to this pivotal moment. How exciting!

However, while all of those elements would likely be the same whether they were pulling out switchblades or bananas, in fact they are pulling out baby bottles. This is an unexpected surprise and will almost certainly elicit a laugh from the audience. You can milk that laugh (sorry for the pun) by adding another shot or two of the bottles. That gives the audience a chance to laugh, plus it emphasizes the silliness of the event.

19 Open **G1_CU Bottle coming out_01**.

An area of the clip has already been marked.

20 Overwrite the clip into the sequence directly after **Overhead LS tilt to walk away_02**.

It would be nice to complement this CU with a matching CU of Andy's bottle, but another option is to go back to the MS of Andy holding the bottle.

21 Open **G2_CU Bottle from pants_04**.

While this breaks the matching angles rule, another CU of a baby bottle would potentially wear out the joke. It's not like there's any new information learned by seeing a close-up of Andy's bottle. Instead, this angle gives you the added humor of seeing the tough guys lined up behind this absurd display (not to mention Andy's delightfully serious expression).

22 Mark an In point at 03:03:51:00 and an Out point at 52:19, and overwrite the clip into the sequence directly after **G1_CU Bottle coming out_01**.

Before you dismiss this climax, one other element you set up earlier has yet to pay off. Any guess what that is? Well, remember the frightened looks on the part of the witnesses just as the boys were whipping out their weapons? What happened when they found out it was only milk?

23 Open **G1_CU Toughguys Reacting_04**.

24 Play forward past the witness's frightened reaction to see his smile of relief when he sees the bottles. Mark an In at 02:20:20:23 and an Out at 22:17.

25 Overwrite the clip into the sequence directly after **G2_CU Bottle from pants_04**.

That resolves his story, but what about the other guy?

26 Open **G2 CU Toughguys Reacting_SERIES**. Shuttle through it looking for anything that might work.

Unfortunately, this guy is so stoic that he really has no reaction to the bottle at all. However, there is still hope: At the very end of the shot, unable to keep playing the role, he breaks character and smiles. Guess what? That will work perfectly!

27 Mark an In at 02:13:05:23 and an Out at 07:02 and overwrite the clip onto the end of the sequence.

Finishing the Scene

Just like a dialogue scene, once the turning point has been reached, the right thing to do is get out quickly. This scene has a couple more lines of dialogue and then a final payoff, showing the picnic where the boys' families are all waiting.

1 Open **G2 MS OTS Group1_02**. Mark the area where Andy says, "Hey man, I'm out of formula" (In: 01:58:55:03, Out: 56:07).

2 Overwrite it onto the end of the sequence.

3 Open the reverse, **G1 CU Pedro OS Andy_02**. Mark the area where Pedro says, "I already got it made" (In: 02:17:17:22, Out: 19:06).

4 Overwrite the clip into the sequence.

5 Open **Overhead LS tilt to walk away_01**. A section of the clip has already been marked. Overwrite it onto the end of the sequence.

6 Make sure the Timeline window is active and press Shift-Z to zoom the whole sequence to fit.

You can see that the overall pacing of the show illustrates a natural progression. The early cuts are mostly of a similar length; the cuts then speed up dramatically as you reach the climax, and they slow back down in a denouement. While not all scenes are the same, looking at the big picture like this can give you clues about the pacing. Are your shot lengths generally consistent? Do they vary randomly, or is there a visible arc that matches the storyline?

7 Play the whole show and admire your work.

Of course, your work with this scene isn't done. There's loads of audio work to do to make the scene really come alive. In addition to adding room tone and environmental sounds to fill in the empty gaps you left when you cut the dialogue, you could also add military type marching for the footsteps as the gangs come together, a gasp or two as the bottles come out, and maybe a corresponding sigh of relief once the truth is revealed. Top it all with an urban-flavored rap song that comes to a suspenseful climax at just the right moment and you've got yourself a pretty amazing scene!

Lesson Review

1. What is an action scene?
2. What is a complex action scene?
3. What are setup and payoff shots?
4. What is the advantage of working in the Trim Edit window?
5. What are three common ways to increase tension?

6. What is a quick and effective trick to easily account for momentum when cutting on an action?

7. What is crosscutting?

8. What does the Spacebar do in the Trim Edit window?

9. How can you use dynamic trimming?

Answers

1. Any scene where the focus of the scene is an activity.

2. A scene where multiple activities happen, either in sequence or simultaneously.

3. A setup is a shot that elicits an expectation from the viewer. A payoff is a shot that resolves such an expectation.

4. The Trim Edit window provides detailed information, such as how many frames are trimmed and how much media is left in each clip.

5. Using close-ups without context, crosscutting, and speeding up the edits.

6. By first making the edit on the end of the action, then rolling the edit back to just before it happens.

7. Cutting back and forth between two locations, usually for action that is occurring simultaneously.

8. Play Around Edit Loop. It also aborts a dynamic trim operation.

9. Activate dynamic trimming in User Preferences by using the Trim Edit window to perform roll or ripple edits while the sequence plays. This enables you to make timing decisions in the ideal context of the flow and pacing of the video.

4

Chases and Fights

Now that you've got the hang of how to approach a general action scene, it's time to explore some of the more specialized varieties. It's true that all action scenes are unique, but some types have enough consistency that you can employ patterns and techniques that are effective regardless of the specific content.

For example, nearly all chase scenes have a similar structure. Whether the chase takes place on foot or in spaceships, in a few minutes or over decades, there are two parties; the follower and the followed, and inevitably the follower gains on the followed, suffers a setback, gains again, and ultimately either catches the followed, or does not. For the editor, a chase is an exercise in controlling tension. You can dial up the tension by showing the follower gaining, dial it down a little with a setback, and then ratchet it way up as you race to the final release.

Similarly, fight scenes have patterns that you can manipulate and techniques that you can consistently employ to control the audience's tension level and engage them in the scene.

By recognizing these common structures you can leverage viewers' expectations when you follow the structures, and create audience surprise or humor when you deviate from them.

The beauty of chases and fights is their primal simplicity: A chase is a hunt. The viewer might relate to the hunter or the hunted, but either way it stimulates his caveman-mind, stirring deep unconscious emotions. A fight is nothing short of a battle for survival—you don't get any more primal than that.

Crafting Chilling Chases

Chases are deceptively simple, and depending on the location where it takes place, the coverage is likely to be equally simple. For an editor, chases are a great exercise in skill because they render literal many of the tension-building techniques that you metaphorically explore in almost any type of scene. They reduce all dramatic tension to a single vector: the proximity of pursuer to pursued. By experimenting with that variable, you can learn what works and what doesn't work in terms of guiding your viewer's tension levels.

Keep in mind that not all chase scenes are so easily recognized. Perhaps someone is pursuing a thing instead of another person, or the object of pursuit may not even be known. Often, such scenes are not high-speed adrenaline fests; but even in a slow-burn cat and mouse game, as long as there is pursuer and pursued, the tension is building—or ought to be— and it is up to you as editor to exploit that tension.

1   Open **Chases&fights**.

The *Slapdash Chase* sequence should already be open in the Canvas and Timeline.

2   Play the scene to get familiar with it.

This scene is very straightforward, and as it is currently cut, it's not very dynamic. Sure, one guy is getting chased and the ending has a little bit of surprise, but the pacing of the scene doesn't vary at all, and the follower never really gains or falls behind the followed.

Determining Distance

An editor controls the flow of tension and improves the chase scene by varying the distance between the parties.

In the current scene, the second shot shows the guys as they get onto the train. First, Mosley (in the blue shirt) gets on in a matching-action cut from the outside of the train, and then, a moment later, Martin (in the white shirt) arrives and begins running after him.

There's no reason you have to stick with the actual timing that occurred during production. Right off the bat, you could increase or decrease the amount of time it takes for Martin to follow Mosley. However, to do so, you need a shot of Mosley running through the train that you can cut to before Martin gets on board.

1   Open **091_D2** from the Chase Clips bin.

2   Set an In point on the first frame where you begin to see Mosley (00:24:25:15).

   The length of time you allow this shot to play will determine how much of a lead Mosley has on Martin. In this case, you will start by giving Mosley a fairly long lead time.

3   Play the clip until Mosley is almost entirely down the length of the train car and set an Out point around 29:24.

4   In the sequence, find the frame in the second shot in which Mosley is halfway out of the frame (around 01:00:10:15) and set an In point.

   This will create a smooth match cut with the In point you set in **091_D2**.

5   Insert **091_D2** into the sequence.

Before you can check the edit, you need to clean up the second half of clip **091_D1** in the sequence.

6   In the sequence, mark an In point on the first frame of the second half of **091_D1**. (Step 5 should have left your playhead parked on that frame.)

7   Play forward until you see Martin get onto the train, then back up to the frame just before he enters (around 15:19) and set an Out point.

8   Press Shift-Command-A to deselect all (as a safety precaution), then press Shift-Delete to ripple delete that section of the clip.

9   Play these first few clips in the sequence.

You have given Mosley a bit of a lead on Martin, but how much lead? Figure it out exactly.

10 Set an In on the frame in which Mosley first steps onto the train (around 01:00:07:20) and set an Out on the frame in which Martin first steps aboard (around 15:00).

11 Look at the Duration field in the Canvas.

Duration field

This shows you exactly how far ahead Mosley is: about 7 and a half seconds.

12 Press Option-X to clear the In and Out frames.

13 Play ahead to the next clip (**091_D2A**).

14 Set an In point as Mosley exits the frame around 01:00:20:20 and set an Out point when Martin exits, around 25:12.

15 Look at the duration field again.

Now they're less than 5 seconds apart. Already Martin is gaining on Mosley. Is this desirable? It's up to you. Your audience won't be counting seconds, but they will have an implicit sense of timing and will feel that the pursuer is gaining ground.

If you're careless about these measurements, you might have Martin bounce around, being 7 seconds behind in one shot, then 4 seconds behind in another, then 8 seconds behind a moment later. Your audience won't be taking out their stopwatches, but they will very likely sense that the continuity of the scene is off. That might get them looking at their wristwatches, which is a very bad sign.

If you want to hold Martin off a little, you can do so by adding another shot into the scene.

16 Shot **091_D2** should still be loaded in the Viewer; set an In on the first frame where Martin enters the shot (around 00:24:31:20).

Since you know you want to keep Martin about 7 seconds behind, you know exactly how long you want this shot to be—about 2 to 3 seconds.

17 Press Tab to access the Duration field. Type *2.15* and press Enter.

An Out point is automatically set to ensure this duration.

18 Make the Timeline or Canvas window active and press Option-X to clear the In and Out points you set earlier.

19 Move the playhead to the edit between the second instance of **091_D1** and **091_D2A** and insert **091_D2** into the sequence.

20 Play around the section.

By creating consistent timing across two shot sequences, you reinforce a sense of the reality of the scene. Now, when you show Martin gaining on Mosley in the next section, there will be a concrete sense of tension.

Using Subjective Shots

Another way to get your audience engaged in the chase is to use shots that put the viewer in the shoes of the characters. The *lockdown* shots you used in the first section are essential for conveying the relative distance between the parties (just the way a 2-shot provides a sense of relationship in a dialogue scene); but once that pacing is established, you can heighten tension by using tracking shots.

1   From the Chase Clips bin, open and play **091_D4**.

   This is a tracking shot, showing Mosley's face as he runs. Even though a chase scene sustains your audience's attention by raising their adrenaline, to keep them fully engaged, you must answer all of the story questions. This shot adds a little *who* to the *what* and *where* you've already provided.

   Because this shot doesn't give you a natural entrance and exit (like the lockdown shots did), you must find another element within the scene that can serve as a beginning and an ending.

2   Set an In point as Mosley crosses the first threshold into the train car (at 00:26:02:17) and set an Out as he enters the next threshold (at 00:26:06:06).

3   Overwrite this clip into the sequence directly after **091_D2A** (at around 28:02).

4   Open and play **091_B5**.

   This is a similar shot, but featuring Martin. Just as in other scenes, matching angles (MCU tracking shots, in this case) is a good way to hide edits and keep your audience focused on the story instead of the construction.

5   Set an In point just as Martin crosses into the car at 00:15:14:08.

   Here, you can further use the train car thresholds to provide a sense of continuity, even though you are actually shifting from one character to another.

This is just like syncing up the footfalls between Andy and Pedro in Lesson 3. Even though neither example is actually a *continuity cut* (where an onscreen action carries you across the edit), you are using the similar composition and movement in each frame to hide the edit.

6　In the sequence, set an In point on the first frame following **091_D4**, and play forward until Martin enters the frame in **091_D9** (around 01:00:33:18) and set an Out point here.

7　Overwrite **091_B5** into the sequence.

Cutting back to the static shot here reminds the audience of the context, and gives you another chance to check in on the distance between the two participants.

8　Play across the next few shots.

9　Set an In just as Mosley gets to the middle of the round bar (around 01:00:38:21).

10 Set an Out when Martin reaches the same point in the car (around 43:25).

11 Look at the Duration field.

Now they are only 5 seconds apart. This is perfect, as it shows Martin gaining on Mosley and thus ratchets up the tension level. Now it's time to give Martin a little setback.

12 Press Option-X to clear the In and Out points.

Creating a Setback

The specifics and the severity of the setback are determined by the events in the script and the way the scene was shot, but it's up to you to determine where and how to use them. In this scene, there really isn't a setback to work with, at least not an intentional one, so you have to be extra creative to construct one out of the footage you have.

Why is it important to include this moment? To maximize tension and make the most of the scene, you need to create punctuation. You must take a single minute-long event with a constant level of tension, and turn it into a series of moments in which the tension ebbs and flows. This is how you keep your viewers on the edges of their seats.

1 Open **091_C4** and press Shift-\ (backslash) to play from In to Out.

This clip shows Martin struggling to get around a doorway. It's not much, but it's all you have, and you can employ it to signify the moment when Mosley begins to gets ahead of him.

The trick is figuring out how to work it into the sequence. It's obviously a different part of the train, so you need something that will get you from this well-lit area into the darker part of the train where Martin hits his obstacle.

2 Open **091_D4**.

You've already used part of this clip, but there is a section near the end that could help you transition into **C4**.

3 Play the section of the clip past the section you previously marked.

At around 00:26:11:00, Mosley enters another threshold, and this one seems very dark. Even though this isn't actually the part of the train where Martin's obstacle is located, no one will ever know the difference.

4   Set an Out point at the darkest point in the frame, before the camera pans away from Mosley (around 11:23). Moving backwards, set an In point just as he recovers from his near-stumble, around 09:20.

5   In the sequence, position the playhead at the edit between **D10** and **D8** (around 45:12).

6   Insert **091_D4** into the sequence.

7   Open **091_E3** and play from In to Out (Shift-\).

This is the section of the train beyond Martin's obstacle. By showing Mosley getting here in a hurry, it will accentuate the delay when Martin gets stuck. In reality, Mosley had to go around the same bulkhead, but you don't have to show it!

8   Insert **091_E3** directly after **D4**.

Now you're ready to put in Martin's setback.

9   From the Recent Clips pop-up menu in the lower-right corner of the Viewer, choose **091_C4**.

The section of the clip is already marked.

10   Insert the clip directly after **E3** and play around this whole part of the sequence.

Doesn't seem like a setback yet, does it? That's because **E3** is just the setup. You still have to show the payoff that results.

11   In the sequence, play across clip **D8** and stop after Mosley clears the frame, but before you can see Martin appearing in the distance (around 55:20). Set an In point here.

12   Press Down Arrow to move the playhead to the next edit, and set an Out point there.

13 Press Shift-Command-A to deselect all, and press Shift-Delete to ripple delete this part of the shot.

By cutting here, and showing the empty hallway behind Mosley, you sell the idea that Mosley has gained some distance from Martin. This is the payoff to the setup in **E3**. Until you show another shot in which you can see both guys in the same frame (or show both of them pass a recognizable landmark in close succession), the audience will assume that Mosley has a substantial lead on Martin.

This is perfect, because in this particular scene, the surprise ending is the thug waiting in the last car. The more we think Mosley is getting away, the bigger the surprise when the "thug" appears.

In another chase, you might use this technique to show the hunted party appearing to get away; but then something else happens that sets *him* back, and brings the hunter back into the game.

14 Open **091_B12** and play from In to Out (Shift-\).

Here is a tight CU on Martin. Cutting to this close-up after the setback appears to raise the stakes. The audience has seen that he's losing the race, and now they want to see how he feels about that. Showing the close-up here and now gives them a glimpse of that feeling, *even though the shot was not intended for that purpose!* The meaning of this shot is derived from the shots around it.

15 Insert **091_B12** into the sequence, directly after **D8**.

16 Press Shift-Z to fit the entire sequence into view.

Notice anything about the pattern of shots? They get shorter toward the end of the sequence, right up until the denouement at the very end. This is virtually the same pattern as the Friends of the Family scene, and that's not a coincidence. This is another classic technique for building tension. Speeding up the edits as the scene progresses will add intensity. This is especially applicable to cross-cutting scenes (which chases almost always are) because there is a natural climax when the two parties come together in the end.

To appreciate the scene in its final form, you can add some music.

17 Drag **Bodo.aiff** directly from the Browser into the Timeline, onto tracks A5 and A6.

18 Play the whole scene.

This is fairly standard chase music, but it still undeniably adds to the scene.

Creating Compelling Combat

To an editor, a fight scene is really nothing more than a dialogue scene in which the parties exchange physical actions instead of exchanging words. To this end, you can expect good fight coverage to parallel standard dialogue coverage with establishing masters, OTS singles, CU singles, inserts, cutaways, and so on.

In contrast to dialogue scenes, fights will likely have more wide shots so the physical action is visible in the frame, and you will have more opportunities to cut back out to them. You will also likely have more inserts or specials that cover details of the action. Perhaps the most significant difference from a dialogue scene is that fight coverage is most often broken up into many more individual shots. Fighters frequently move during the course of the fight. Each time they move from one part of a room to another, a new angle must be shot. Also, fights often incorporate special effects or make-up changes that require frequently stopping and starting the action on set. The result of this is that you have far more shots to manage in your bins, but the resulting editing pattern remains very similar to that of a dialogue scene.

Fights are not always fisticuffs or swordplay. Often the "blows" in a fight are more symbolic or subtle. In fact, many times the line between fight and dialogue becomes blurred. Picture a courtroom scene in which a lawyer grills a defendant on the stand, or a verbal fight between separating spouses. And even in physical fights the combatants might alternate their corporal blows with verbal ones. In essence, a fight is any action in which two parties are in opposition.

1 Double-click the *Broken Fists* sequence.

2 In the Browser, click the disclosure triangles to collapse the Chase Clips bin and expand the Broken Fists Clips bin.

This bin contains the first few shots of a martial arts fight from the film "Broken Fists."

3   Open and play **A-16_A-4 Master.**

This shot will serve as your master shot. In addition to the opening camera move that sets up the scene and introduces the character, it contains the whole first episode in a long shot.

4   Set an In just before the camera starts moving and an Out when the actors stumble forward and stop (In: 07:06:37:00, Out: 57:00).

5   Edit the clip into the sequence.

Cutting fights requires being able to break them down, blow-by-blow (literally). You must identify each individual action, so you can identify the best cut points and avoid skipping or overlapping the action of the scene.

This scene is especially challenging because there are nine actions in about 7 seconds. Here is a rundown: Hope (the woman in black) begins with three quick kicks to the left, and then does a roundhouse kick to the right. That is followed by a lateral move with her left arm, then an overhand move with her right. Then Ruby (in blue) grabs Hope's right arm and twists it around. Next, both women block each other with their forearms, and, finally, Hope connects with an elbow to the face. This fight (like all fights) was carefully choreographed, and it's part of your job to deconstruct the choreography to bring it to life editorially.

You need to understand how each blow affects the story. As in the chase scene, you want to manipulate the audience's anxiety level by deliberately increasing and decreasing the tension. Each time one of the fighters gains or loses advantage, the stakes change and the tension is impacted. You can emphasize certain moments with close-ups, or tone down other moments by covering them long, or even cutting them out altogether.

6 Open and play **A_16_FB-1 MS Favor Hope.**

This is a reverse, covering the exact same action, but from the other side, and a bit tighter. Because the fight is so active, you could almost cut on any of the nine actions. How do you choose?

Remember the ideas put forth in Lesson 1? You should only cut when there is new information to show, and you should cut to the shot that shows that new information. In this clip, you can see that on Hope's third kick to the left, Ruby blocks with her arm. That information was completely absent in the master shot, so it provides a good reason and opportunity to cut.

7 In the Viewer, set an In on the frame when Hope's foot hits Ruby's arm (at 07:11:50:13) and let it play all the way until they exit the frame (around 57:20) and set an Out point there.

8 Find the frame in the sequence when Hope's foot reaches its full extension (on her third kick) at 01:00:13:00.

9   Overwrite the clip into the sequence.

10   Play around the edit.

By cutting directly on the action of the foot block, you actually miss seeing it happen.

11   Make sure Linked Selection is turned on, then press R to select the Roll tool and roll the edit to the left about 6 frames.

NOTE ▶ You may need to zoom in and/or turn off snapping (press N) in order to perform step 11.

Now the edit happens as her leg is going up, and that movement hides the cut. You slip into the closer shot without drawing attention to it, and show that the kick was blocked. Perfect! But you may be wondering why you didn't cut on this frame in the first place?

It's much easier to match the action across edits by finding the end of the action in both clips. If you guessed, and made the edit "about halfway" through the movement, you would have to judge the momentum in both shots, which may be difficult. This is especially true when working with differing angles and different takes in which the action may have occurred at different speeds. By first making the edit on the clear ending of the action in both shots, you can then confidently roll the edit freely in either direction and maintain sync.

12 Press A to deselect the Roll tool, and play the sequence.

The problem with that medium shot is that you can "feel" the choreography; the actors pause slightly after each exchange, almost like they are counting time (which is frequently how fights are staged). But you don't want the audience to see those pauses, so you need to find a way to cut around them.

The first egregious pause comes right before Hope's overhand right blow (at around 15:00). It looks like this is your next place to cut.

13 Open and play **A_16_FA-2 MS Favor Ruby.**

This is a matching reverse of **FB-1**—a medium favoring Ruby.

14 Set an In just before Hope grabs Ruby's arm at 07:10:50:00 and set the Out after they run offscreen, around 56:00.

15 In the sequence, look for the action that matches the In point you just set, and set an In there, at 15:05.

16 Overwrite the clip into the sequence.

Hopefully, you can see the parallels to a dialogue scene: Begin on a wide master, and cut back and forth between matching OTS shots for the bulk of the scene. The last step is to move into close-up for the climax.

17 Open and play **B_16_A-2 MCU Favor Ruby.**

Toward the end of the shot, it becomes a tighter angle on Ruby, which will be perfect for the elbow to the face.

Another thing you need to keep in mind when cutting fights, especially hand-to-hand combat, is that you have to choose the angles that look like actual contact was made.

18 In the Viewer, step through the shot, especially in the section where Hope makes her final blow (01:14:28:14).

Because the camera is directly on axis with the action it's fairly difficult to tell whether or not she actually made contact. (Actually, in this take, Ruby reacts a frame late, but that tiny difference will easily be overlooked when played at full speed.)

19 Open **B_16_FB-1 Profile MCU**.

This shot is already parked on the frame of "impact," and it's very clear that Hope's elbow never touches Ruby. This profile shot may be perfectly useful for other parts of the scene, but to convey the illusion of a solid blow, it's a terrible choice.

20 Reopen **B_16_A-2 MCU Favor Ruby**.

21 Set an In point on the previous action, where both women use both arms to block each other (around 01:14:28:00).

22 Find the matching frame in the sequence (01:00:17:14).

23 Overwrite the clip.

For the sake of the exercise, don't worry about the Out point or the end of the sequence.

24 Press R to select the Roll tool, and roll the edit to the left about 10 frames.

25 Press A to deselect the Roll tool, press Home to return to the head of the sequence, and play through the whole sequence.

This is a very simple sequence but it works. You could choose to make a cut for every one of the nine actions. That might seem more exciting, although it would primarily serve to severely disorient your audience (which may or may not be desirable).

In general, you should avoid overcutting. Let the action unfold without interfering any more than is required. Like dance or comedy (see Lesson 5), fights are choreographed to have a specific style and character. If you cut too aggressively, you risk losing that delicate artistry that was chosen for deliberate reasons.

Of course, if the choreography isn't working to tell the story, then by all means do what you can to save it. Your primary obligation is to your audience, and if they are confused or bored or distracted, you've failed at your job as storyteller.

Using Sound Effects

There is one more tiny thing you can do to bring the scene (or at least that final blow) to life. It's difficult to feel the impact of the scene without hearing the sound effects of the various hits and blows. You would never expect any audience to buy the scene without the sound in place, and while the show will certainly go through an extensive sound design once you're finished cutting, it can't hurt to drop in a sound effect when it's really essential.

1   In the sequence, position your playhead on the precise frame where Hope's elbow is supposed to connect with Ruby's face (at 01:00:18:05).

2   Drag **Body Hit 11.aiff** directly from the Browser into the Timeline onto track A2 and A3, lining it up to begin at the playhead and overwrite it into the sequence.

3   Play around that section of the scene.

It's amazing what a difference that sound makes! You don't want to spend much time with sound effects this early in the process, but every so often a little cue like that can have a significant impact on the way the scene plays.

Fights with Weapons

Your editing style must take into account the type of weapons your combatants wield. In a gunfight, the parties will be physically separated. This means that, in many ways, tying the two parties together is an exercise in cross-cutting between separate locations, and you will have to pay special attention to clarifying the geography of the scene. Also, the pacing of a scene is directly affected by the means of battle.

1   Open and play the *Hope Fight* sequence.

This is another scene from "Hope," in which Anne, the angel, fights the arch devil Temeluchus. Notice that this scene, too, has elements of the traditional dialogue structure, using masters, over-the-shoulders, and close-ups.

The two combatants fight with large weapons, giving the scene a very different feel than the hand-to-hand combat of the scene from "Broken Fists." For one thing, swinging a broad sword takes a few seconds, while throwing a punch takes only a few frames. This significantly slows the pacing of the scene.

You have other similar issues, however, and even though the overall scene is slower, the pacing still needs to be consistent within its own rhythm.

2 Play the sequence from about 15 seconds in.

There is an unnatural pause that occurs before Ann thrusts away Temeluchus' spear. The director presumably wanted this moment to play as a moment of struggle, but in this wide shot, it just looks like a mistake.

3 Collapse the Broken Fists Clips bin and expand the Hope Fight Clips bin.

4 Open and play **15AV-2z**.

This CU of the same action provides you an opportunity to tighten the timing of the scene, while adding emphasis to the struggle of that moment.

5 Set an In point just before Anne pushes his spear away (around 06:11:01:00).

6 Set an Out point just as she escapes him and spins out of the way (around 02:15).

7 In the sequence, set an In where you want to insert the close-up. You could put it imme-diately after Temeluchus lands his spear, or you could wait a bit to add to the sense of struggle. In the image, the In point is set at 01:00:18:00:

8 Overwrite the clip into the sequence.

9 Play around the edit.

The timing feels great for the beginning of her action, but now Anne does the whole pushing-away action twice.

10   In the sequence, set an In point on the frame after **15AV-2z** ends, and set an Out after the second pushing away. Attempt to match Anne's position from the end of **15AV-2z**. In both shots, she should just be crossing the second post behind her (around 01:00:20:02).

11   Press Shift-Delete to ripple delete the duplicated action.

12   Play around the new edit.

Incorporate a Witness

One of the editor's secret weapons for improving a fight scene is the *witness*. Cutting away to a third party who is observing the fight serves multiple significant purposes. Story-wise, it gives perspective and point of view. It gives the audience an ally, someone within the story to watch the fight with. Typically it's someone who is invested in the story: the boxer's trainer, the victim who is being saved, the child whose custody is being fought over. This witness illuminates the stakes of the fight. Even the most elaborately choreographed and spectacularly violent fights can still seem impotent without this crucial element.

The other reason for the witness is more technical. Filming a fight requires stopping and starting between almost every exchange. To give the editor a consistent and convincing series of cutaways, you need more than a shot of a clock on the wall. You need a separate but connected action.

1   In the sequence, press Down Arrow once or twice until your playhead is at the edit point between **15AW-3** and **15AP-3**.

2   From the Hope Fight Clips bin, open **15AF-4**.

3   Press Shift-\ to play from In to Out.

Earlier in this scene, before he began the fight with Anne, Temeluchus knocked out Asteroth. Although you're watching this fight out of context, the audience won't be. And they're sure to be wondering what happened to Asteroth. Now is your opportunity to answer that question, along with using him as the witness for all the great reasons just described.

4   Insert **15AF-4** into the sequence directly before **15AP-3**.

To make this shot feel like it's a part of the scene, you need to hear the fight going on in the background. Due to the production track having the fight choreographer counting throughout, there is no useful track for you to use at this point. You'll just have to use your imagination until the final sound mix.

5 In the sequence, play across the edit between **15AX-2** and **15BA-2**.

This is a sort of jump cut. The two are still battling, but apparently some time has passed because they are in a new part of the room. This is a spot where adding another bit of Asteroth would link the two sections of the scene.

6 In the Viewer, play the rest of the scene after the marked Out point.

7 Set an In point just as Asteroth begins to get up (around 05:05:01:05) and set an Out after the door opens (around 16:12).

8 In the sequence, position the playhead between **15AX-2** and **15BA-2**.

9 Insert the shot into the sequence.

10 Play the whole sequence back.

Intercutting Asteroth's story with the fight scene adds a significant level of complexity and excitement. Now, in addition to the tension created by the fight itself, the audience is following Asteroth's story at the same time. This scene actually continues, with Asteroth bringing the little girl out of the cell, just as the fight comes to a draw.

The footage for this whole scene is in the Hope Raw Clips bin. Experiment with cutting the scene your own way, with and without the witness and using different choices of shots.

Lesson Review

1. What is the main vector of tension in a chase scene?
2. How can you measure the time/distance between characters?
3. How does a close-up inform a chase scene?
4. How do you use an action within the frame to make a good edit?
5. What kind of shots are best for hiding stage fighting?
6. How do the weapons used in a fight impact the editing style?
7. What does a "witness" provide in a fight scene?

Answers

1. The distance between hunter and hunted.

2. Set an In point when the first character passes the edge of frame, set an Out point when the second character passes the same spot, and observe the Duration field in the Canvas.

3. The close-up reminds the viewer of the feelings of the characters involved in the chase.

4. Make the edit on the hard ending of the action, then roll the edit point forward or back slightly.

5. Shots that are on-axis with the action best disguise stage fighting.

6. The larger the weapons, the slower the pacing of the scene.

7. A witness provides a point of view as well as a consistent and compelling cutaway.

5

Lesson Files   Lesson Files > Lesson 05 > Comedy

Media   Media > FBI Guys Pencil Scene

   Media > FBI Guys Pepper Spray

Time   This lesson takes approximately 90 minutes to complete.

Goals   Construct the funniest scene from the available footage

   Find and exploit expectations to maximize surprise

   Increase humor with repetition

   Use reactions to make the audience laugh

   Understand comic timing versus action timing

   Use the axis to control the seriousness of a scene

   Use wide shots instead of close-ups to keep it light

Editing Comedy

Comedy is serious business, especially for an editor. Nothing stings more than comedy that isn't funny. You already know how critical it is for an editor to be a good storyteller. If you want to cut comic sequences, you must also learn to tell jokes well.

It's very difficult to describe what makes something funny, and humor is notoriously subjective and fleeting. But the structure of comedy can be learned, and techniques can be applied to maximize the potential humor in a scene.

Finding the Laughs

It's unlikely that an editor can successfully wring laughs from bland writing or from performances that aren't funny, but it's easy to squander hilarious material by treating a comedy scene as if it were drama. Similarly, great comic performances can be ruined by a zealous editor working too hard to make it funny.

What makes something funny? Almost always, it can be traced to one of two parallel categories: Someone reacts to a situation in an inappropriate or unusual way, or someone does something predictable and the result is unexpected or unsuitable. The more out-of-place the reaction is, or the more outrageous the result is, the funnier the gag is. Both of these concepts rely on a very simple and familiar concept that is particularly useful to the editor.

Surprise.

Surprise is the lifeblood of comedy. At its simplest, surprise is the result of contradiction. The more surprised a viewer is by the unexpected elements of a scene, the more the potential there is for humor. This theory can be translated to editing in a very tangible way. You already know how to recognize "setup" and "payoff" shots. The editor can control how funny something is by choosing the right setup and payoff shots, and through the precise placement of those shots.

Cutting Comic Dialogue

For the most part, dialogue is dialogue, whether it's intended to be funny or tragic or somewhere in the middle. However, there are decisions you can make that will tilt a scene toward the dramatic or toward the comic.

1   Open project **Comedy**.

2   Double-click **Scene 29 Edit** to open it into the Canvas and Timeline.

3   Play the sequence to get familiar with it.

   This is a scene from "FBI Guys," in which the two desk agents are going through "cold" files looking for a case that they might be able to revive. The humor comes primarily from a gag in which Bob throws a pencil into the wall behind Phil every time a case is no good.

   There are several elements that can be highlighted to enhance the humor. The first is repetition. This can be funny because the audience expects that something different should happen but, instead, the same thing happens again and again.

In this case, two elements are repeated. The first gag is that all of the cases relate to Teamsters. The second is the pencil. Each time a case turns out to be related to the Teamsters and Bob throws the pencil, the scene gets funnier.

One way to enhance the humor is to see if you can squeeze any more repetition out of the scene, perhaps by using different takes of the same action.

4   From the Scene 29 Clips bin, open **A19-29A_1**.

5   Set an In point just before Bob picks up the pencil (19:23:39:09) and set an Out point before he grimaces (41:00).

6   Place the sequence playhead at the fifth edit, between **29B** and **29C**.

7   Insert the new clip into the sequence.

This shot resolves the exchange that previously ended in the shot on V2. This provides the room to add a new back and forth. Now you can insert another shot of Phil.

8   Open **A19-29C_3** and set an In just as Phil says, "Teamsters" (03:22:30:00) and an Out as Bob raises his arm (31:13).

9   Insert this clip after **29A**.

10   Use the Recent Clips menu to reopen **A19-29A_1**.

11 Set an In just as Bob throws the pencil (19:23:43:02) and an Out just before he grabs for the next one (43:18).

12 Insert this clip immediately after **29C_3**.

This adds one complete exchange: Phil says "Teamsters" and Bob throws a pencil. However, you can't cut from Phil saying "Teamsters" right to Phil saying "wait a minute" without creating a sort of jump cut. So you need to add one more "Teamsters," this time from Bob.

13 Open **A19-29C_1** and set an In before the pencil strikes the wall (19:19:58:10) and an Out as Bob picks up the next pencil (20:01:10).

14 Insert this clip right after **29A**.

15 Open **A19-29A_1** again and set an In point before Bob closes his folder (19:23:41:10) and the Out point before he reaches for the pencil again (43:12).

16 Insert this clip right after **29C**.

To end this exchange, rather than adding another clip, you can extend **29C**. Because the clip on V2 will move along as you ripple **29C**, it will remain a good edit and lead right into the remainder of **29C**.

17 Choose the Ripple tool from the Tool palette or press R twice and click the right side of the edit you just made, between **29A_1** and **29C_3**.

18 Drag the edit to the left to extend **29C_3** about 3 seconds until just before the pencil hits, at 03:22:41:20. (Watch the display in the Canvas.)

19 Play the sequence from the beginning to this point.

You may need to finesse some of the edit points, but you have successfully added another round of Teamster reports and two more pencil throws—all fabricated entirely from the existing footage. Each time Bob throws the pencil, it's likely to get at least a giggle from the audience, and the more it happens without Phil doing anything, the funnier it gets.

Using Replace Edit

There is one problem with the edits you just made. You actually used the same portion of **29A_1** twice. It's not obvious, but it might appear strange to see Bob furrow his brow twice in exactly the same way. This can be easily remedied; plus, it gives you an opportunity to use the replace edit feature.

Most edits are performed by lining up an In or an Out point (or both), but replace is a way of performing an edit by choosing a frame within the body of the clip.

1   Press A to choose the Selection tool.

2   In the sequence, position the playhead in **A19_29A_1** just where the pencil leaves Bob's hand (at approximately 01:00:27:20).

3   Open **A19_29A_2** and find the frame where the pencil leaves Bob's hand (at 19:12:58:20).

You do not need to set any In or Out points. The points would be ignored in the Viewer, and they would limit the effect of the replace edit in the sequence.

4   Untarget audio tracks A1 and A2. Drag the clip from the Viewer onto the Canvas and pause until the Edit Overlay appears, then drop the clip on the Replace edit target.

Take 2 replaces take 1, giving a slightly different performance; but because you precisely lined up the action with the replace edit, the timing should match perfectly.

5   Play the sequence to check your work.

Using Reaction Shots

Comedy is all about surprise and upsetting expectations, but something can be very funny even if it's not a surprise to the audience—as long as it's a surprise to someone. Think of the classic banana peel. There is a setup shot, warning the audience that danger lies in the path ahead. When the hapless victim inevitably slips, it can still be funny, as long as the actor appears convincingly surprised. You can enhance the humor of a scene by showing how the participant's expectations are confounded.

This theory can be applied to this scene at the point when Phil finally catches the pencil. The audience is surprised and it's a little funny, but what about Bob? Bob is surprised too, and it's his reaction that makes the unexpected action not just surprising, but funny.

1   Find the moment in the sequence when Phil catches the pencil and holds it up beside his head. Set an In point at 01:00:52:23.

2   Open **A19-29Ap_SER** and find the moment when Bob reacts to Phil catching the pencil in the last take in the series. Set an In at approximately 20:16:13:15 and an Out at approximately 14:20.

3   Overwrite the clip into the sequence.

4 Play that part of the sequence back.

You'll probably agree that the scene is funnier when Bob's reaction is included.

Choosing the Right Performance

In any scene, it's important to find the best performance for each line; but "best" is subjective, and what's best for drama or suspense might not be best for comedy. Also, every time you make an adjustment to a scene, you may change the impact of the other shots in the scene.

In this scene, adding Bob's reaction shot improved the scene, but now his performance in the following line assumes a shift in tone. When Phil catches the pencil, the new reaction shot indicates that it briefly befuddles Bob, but he gets over it less than 2 seconds later in the next shot.

This can be remedied by finding another version of Bob's "force equals mass times acceleration" line in which he still appears somewhat shaken. This not only makes the performance seem more consistent but also makes the scene funnier, since Bob's reaction is unexpected.

1 In the Timeline, position the playhead anywhere over **A19-29Ap_SER** and press X to mark the clip.

2 Press F to load the master clip **A19-29Ap_SER** into the Viewer.

3 Play through the first take in the series. Set an In point at 20:14:59:06 and an Out point at 15:08:07.

4   In the Timeline, press Command-Shift-A to deselect all, and press Shift-Delete to ripple delete the marked clip.

5   Re-target A1 and A2 then insert the clip in the Viewer into the sequence.

6   Play the entire sequence to check your work.

The old performance is replaced with the new one. The new performance is more consistent with the earlier shots, and his embarrassment is funnier to boot.

Cutting Comic Action

Great physical comedy is an art in itself. In many situations, it should be photographed and edited more like dance than like dramatic action. In general, you should let the action unfold without editorial interference, as the essence of comedy is often dependent on the subtle timing and physical actions of the performers. The magic of a performance can evaporate when those precisely executed actions are used to carry edits or are broken across multiple shots.

Unfortunately, there is no simple formula for achieving great comic timing, or for acquiring the equally important ability to recognize when the timing is hurting the comedy.

Often, a sequence waits too long to reveal the payoff, allowing the tension of the setup to dissipate. Other times, the pacing is too fast and doesn't give the viewer enough time to enjoy the joke.

This next scene from "FBI Guys" is excerpted from a later scene when Bob and Phil bumble their way into the villain's lair and engage in a fight with her lieutenants and henchmen. Just as in scene 29, this situation has solid comic moments, but the editing is not realizing its full comic impact.

1   Double-click **Scene 41 Edit** to open it into the Canvas and Timeline.

2   Play the first 10 or 15 seconds of the sequence.

Bob screams, "Freeze!" (a classic "setup" shot). Then the henchmen react (functioning in the witness role), then Bob pulls out his pepper spray, which turns out not to work (the payoff). If you analyze the shots, everything seems right, but it's just not as funny as it could be.

In this edit, the joke happens when the pepper spray doesn't work so well, but there's a joke that has been skipped right over: the fact that he's using pepper spray instead of a gun.

This situation contains the short-term humor of undercutting the audience expectation that he's got a firearm. It also serves the story at large by reminding the audience that these desk-bound agents are trying to solve a real-world case. It adds to the humor to show that they don't even have real weapons.

This scene can be much funnier if you split this gag into two separate jokes: first, the reveal of the pepper spray and, second, its ineffectiveness.

First, use dynamic trimming to expand the "Freeze" beat in an organic way.

3   Press R twice to select the Ripple tool, and double-click the right edge of **B10_41X_2**.

The Trim Edit window opens with the left window selected (ripple outgoing).

4   Make sure Dynamic Trimming is enabled.

5   Press J to back up the edit to before Bob says, "Freeze," and press the Spacebar to stop playback.

NOTE ▶ If you stop playback by pressing K instead of the Spacebar, you may get a warning that you can't set an Out point earlier than a disabled In point. If this happens, no harm is caused; just click OK and proceed with the following steps.

6   Press L to play the clip. After Bob says, "Freeze!" wait a short beat, and press K to set a
new Out point (approximately 20 frames later).

Indicates how
many frames
have been
trimmed

7   Press the Spacebar to play around the edit.

If you aren't happy with the timing, repeat steps 5 through 7 until you are satisfied.

8 Press Down Arrow to move the selection to the next edit without closing the Trim Edit window.

The edit will still be selected as an outgoing ripple. This will allow you to add frames to the end of the henchmen shot.

9 Press J to back up the edit to before Bob says, "Freeze," and press the Spacebar to stop playback without trimming.

10 Press L to play the clip. When the guys begin laughing, press K to set a new Out point (approximately 2 seconds).

11 Press the Spacebar to play around the edit.

Next, you will split the edit so the video leads the audio.

12 Press U twice to switch the edit selection to an incoming ripple edit.

13 Drag the jog wheel to the right until Bob is midway through his movement of revealing the spray.

14 Press I to set a new In point.

15 Turn off Linked Selection (Shift-L), and then in the Timeline, Command-click each of the selected audio edits to deselect them.

16 Click the title bar of the Trim Edit window to make that window active again.

17 Press U twice to change the edit selection to a roll.

18 Press J to roll the edit to the left until just before Bob begins his movement (about 13 frames) and press K to stop and perform the edit.

19 Press the Spacebar to play around the edit.

Hopefully, you feel that the scene is improved. If you don't, continue trimming the edits until you find the humor is most apparent.

Using the Axis

One key to enhancing humor is to stay away from techniques that emphasize drama. For example, it's a fact that the closer an actor's eyelines are located to the axis of the camera, the more likely the viewer is to be engaged emotionally. This is why OTS shots are so popular in dialogue scenes.

Therefore, the further off-axis a shot, the more objective is the audience's reaction. This is helpful for comedy. You don't want your audience emotionally involved with your characters, especially when they're supposed to be laughing at them.

You can apply this technique here by adding an objective shot of Bob spraying the pepper.

1   In the sequence, set an In point before the camera begins tilting up from the spray on the floor (around 01:00:11:20) and an Out point after the camera move is complete, but before the henchmen look at each other (around 14:00).

2   From the Scene 41 Clips bin, open **A11_41X_4**.

3   Set an Out point after Bob looks up at the henchmen (around 11:51:50:10).

4   Untarget tracks A1 and A2 and overwrite the clip into the sequence.

5   Press \ (backslash) to play around the edit.

You could also choose to replace the first shot of the pepper spray with this profile angle, but in some ways the performance is preferable in the existing shot. However, using this shot at this point provides an additional opportunity to laugh at poor Bob and does so in the less personal off-axis shot.

Additionally, this shot has the benefit of providing an angle on Phil, showing his reaction to Bob's failure. This serves the traditional witness purpose (giving the audience someone onscreen to relate to), and it serves as a subtle setup for Phil's next action when he pulls out his gun.

Using Wider Shots

You can also maximize comic potential by choosing wider shots instead of close-ups. This is one of the most useful general rules for comedy scenes, though like all of these techniques, its impact is subtle.

Close-ups tend to bring the audience into a more intimate, subjective relationship with the actors, similar to the effect of on-axis shots. This effect is magical in drama but it can be deadly in comedy. Additionally, comedy is often physical and, just like dance, cutting in too close can suck some of the energy out of the scene.

You can see this in most cinema or television. Dramas tend to use tighter close-ups than comedies. A tight close-up puts the viewer inside the character's head and, most of the time, that just isn't very funny. There are exceptions, but this is another of those subtle visual cues that audiences have been conditioned to perceive.

In this scene, there is a sudden close-up on Phil when he pulls his gun (around 01:00:24:00).

This works wonderfully, because it's not supposed to be comic (except that he calls the villains "cheese sticks"). It's a surprise, but not a funny one.

However, what follows is a series of three MCUs during the exchange between Bob and Phil. This moment is supposed to be funny, and it *is*. Both actors' performances are terrific; but, the moment still feels too much like drama because the camera is in close and the editing falls into the traditional matching MCU angles. The scene can be funnier by stepping out to a wider shot instead.

6   Place the sequence playhead just after Phil's CU around 01:00:25:00.

7   Open **B10_41V_4**.

A section of the clip has already been marked.

Interestingly, this angle, which was too on-axis for the exchange between Bob and the henchmen, is actually perfectly off-axis for the exchange between Bob and Phil. Unlike the close-ups, this shot is ideally suited for maximum comic effect.

8   Retarget tracks A1 and A2 and overwrite the clip into the sequence.

9   Play the whole sequence.

The comedy editor faces a unique dilemma in that it's very difficult to laugh at footage that you've watched hundreds of times and deconstructed and reconstructed in multiple ways. It's not uncommon for an editor to lose track of how humorous a scene will appear to a fresh audience and, in the worst case, reedit the "funny" right out of it.

Always bring in a fresh eye, a second person, to provide objective feedback. This is advisable for all projects, but especially for comedy. It's also important for your test viewer to be similar to the target audience. Don't expect your teenage son to be an adequate surrogate for a target audience of retired military brass. He might just talk you into cutting a scene inappropriate for the latter's awards dinner.

Now that's a funny scene.

Lesson Review

1. What is the nature of humor?
2. What are the two most common comic structures?
3. When does repetition make something funnier?
4. What tool can be used to adjust the start and end points of clips?
5. How do you perform a replace edit?
6. How do close-ups affect humor?

Answers

1. Humor arises from the contradiction of expectations.
2. A person reacting in an inappropriate or unexpected way or a predictable action resulting in unexpected outcome.
3. Repetition is funny when it is unexpected. The more times something repeats when the audience expects a change, the funnier it will be.
4. The Ripple tool.
5. Drop a clip on Replace edit in the Edit Overlay window.
6. Close-up shots tend to illicit a more intimate connection with a character, which are usually less comic.

Cutting Nonfiction
Material

6

Editing Documentaries: Cutting Interviews

Documentary film includes everything from educational nature shows and concert films to scientific polemics and political tirades. There are as many interpretations of the documentary form as there are variants of dramatic film.

From reality television to concert films, there are endless shapes and sizes that fit in the documentary category, and innovative filmmakers are continually blurring the lines between traditionally discrete genres. Like all art forms, the documentary is continually evolving, but no matter what technique is in use, your goal as an editor remains the same: Control the viewer's point of focus through shot choice and pacing in order to convey information in the form of a story.

Defining Documentary

In general, documentary film is synonymous with nonfiction film, though that connection is by no means required. The "truth" of the subject is less relevant than the technique used to convey it. Whereas dramatic films tend to bury their themes in the intricacies of relationships and plot, documentaries wear their themes more blatantly on their sleeve. Instead of featuring characters who speak dialogue, documentaries are more often populated with interviews or scripted narration. Still, both categories always have an underlying theme or purpose, and fiction or not, both categories are still storytelling.

While it may be easy to identify the story underlying most dramatic footage, the elements of story in documentary footage may be more subtle. The beginning, middle, and end may not be inherent in the material, but don't be fooled into thinking they aren't essential. You must find a way to create such a structure. You must also answer those who, what, where, when, why, and how questions and weave them into a logical, engaging story.

Cutting Interviews

One of the most common and basic components of documentary footage is the interview. Just as dialogue is the heart of most dramatic material, interviews are the heart of most documentaries. Even though both are essentially shots of people talking, they require decidedly different editing skills and techniques.

The purpose of interviews generally is to provide supporting evidence for a hypothesis. Sometimes the hypothesis is stated explicitly by one speaker and corroborated by others. Other times the theory emerges from what is said by a combination of speakers. A film occasionally might focus entirely on a single interviewee (such as director Errol Morris's fascinating Robert McNamara documentary, "The Fog of War"). More often, though, several interview subjects are used. This serves an obvious purpose; the more voices that support a theory, the more credibility the documentary has.

Unfortunately, nothing is more mind-numbing than watching a series of talking heads—no matter what they are saying. So, documentary editors must come up with ways of making the content engaging. You can flesh out the story using B-roll footage or graphics or other supplemental materials, but the interviews are the show's spine. Unless they construct a lean, coherent (and entertaining) story, no amount of flash techniques will keep the audience from changing the channel.

Too often, documentaries get bogged down by long-winded or convoluted interviews. Beginning documentary editors are often timid about cutting aggressively, concerned that cutting will compromise the integrity of the interview. Such fear is folly. If you can't make a documentary engaging, no one will see it anyway.

Once you get over this concern, you'll find there are limitless possibilities for manipulating footage to make a point in a clear, concise, and engaging manner. This often means combining phrases from different speakers to make a single point. Sometimes you must rearrange a speaker's phrases, or even take phrases or words out of context.

While there is always a danger in rearranging footage to the point of contradicting the intended meaning of what was said, you generally can leave moral questions to the director or producer. They are not likely to allow you to defeat the purpose of the interview, and they're the ones who will have to answer to the interviewee's objections. Your job is to illustrate the script points in the best way the footage permits.

1   Open **Interviews**.

This project contains select footage from a "Making of" featurette from the DVD of the film "Artistic License."

2   Click the disclosure triangle to open the Interviews bin.

Like in any project, you must begin by becoming familiar with the footage.

3   Open and play each of the interviews.

Regardless of what other materials you will incorporate into the sequence, the first step is to pull together the interviews into a rough assembly that makes sense and has a good rhythm.

Conceiving the Script

Many documentary directors will provide a script that will identify the intended structure of the show. Just as often, that structure will be determined in the editing room, based on the interview content. In the latter case, you must seek out themes and consistent elements in the interviews that you can combine to create the show. If the interviewer was good, some of those sections will be obvious. She may have asked the same question of every subject or elicited answers that are narrow enough to group easily.

At first glance, you may feel that there is no useful footage. The interviews all stink; no one spoke in clear, simple sound bites; and the purpose of the documentary seems utterly absent from the hours of talking heads. Relax. That feeling is entirely normal.

In fact, if you don't feel that way, you should worry. If the speakers simply parrot what the director wanted them to say, it will seem inauthentic or staged. The nature of good interviews is that they are subtle. Just as in a dramatic piece the theme is best conveyed in the subtext of dialogue and action, the essence of a documentary is best conveyed through the *combinations* of what people say. The theses and ideas should be inferred by the audience. Your job is to craft the show in such a way that the viewer feels as if he came up with the ideas on his own. And if your show requires that specific words be spoken, you can script a narration.

Sometimes the interviews don't support the hypothesis. In that case, you need to rethink what the movie is about or scrap the footage and start over again. Otherwise, you must find a way to tell the best story you can with the footage you have available.

In the footage used in this lesson, one of the consistent themes is the good vibe on the set and how much everyone liked working together. Other elements that are mentioned in more than one interview are discussions of the cast and descriptions of the story.

By identifying these three elements, you have the beginning of a framework to build around. In some cases, you can literally break up the interviews into segments with title cards (for example, The Crew, The Cast, The Story), or you can subtly weave the sections together by finding transition points in the interviews.

Pulling Selects

Once you've sketched out the overall structure, you begin the editing process by identifying sections of the interviews you are likely to use. Remember, when cutting interviews, you must ruthlessly search for the essence of what is being said. Look for redundancy. People love to repeat themselves when they speak, clarifying their point or trying out different phrasings; but in the final piece there isn't time to hear that repetition. You must find the simplest, shortest segment possible and discard the rest.

Typically, this honing process requires several passes. At each stage you'll shave a word or two off the beginning or end of a sound bite, or even eliminate a whole sentence until you've whittled the material down to its most indispensable elements.

4 Open **Michael Interview**. Set an In point just before the first words he speaks, "The cast and crew…," at 00:54:38:03, and set an Out just after he says, "I feel completely blessed," around 42:13.

5 Press Shift-\ (backslash) to play from In to Out.

You may hear a little bit of his next line at the end of the clip.

6 Make sure your playhead is at the Out point, and press Left Arrow once, then press O to set a new Out point.

7 Press Shift-\ again.

Can you still hear any of his next line? If so, repeat steps 6 and 7 until you just have the clean line.

8 Choose Modify > Make Subclip or press Command-U.

A subclip is created in the Interviews bin.

9   Name the subclip with the text of what it contains. Type *MW: The cast and crew are amazing...*

10   In the Viewer, skip ahead to where Michael says, "Carlos, the A.D.," around 00:55:09:08. Set an In point there, being careful not to include any of the preceding word.

11   Play forward until after he talks about Seamus the D.P. and set an Out point after he says, "This has been a great experience so far," (approximately 29:05).

12   Press Shift-\ to play In to Out.

Make sure you don't hear any extraneous words at the head or the tail of the clip. If you do, adjust the In or Out point until the section you want is clearly marked.

13   Press Command-U to make a subclip and in the Browser, name the new subclip *MW: Carlos and Seamus...*

14   In the Viewer, play forward to where Michael says, "And Divi and Nate producing this thing," (around 36:18).

Notice that he says, "And, uh… And Divi and Nate…"

There's no reason for you to include that first false start. Interviews are full of these extraneous "uhs" and "ums" and flubbed words and other minor mistakes. You must make it a habit to mark exactly the words you need and nothing else. You may think it's impossible to cut around some of these—perhaps two words are slurred together into one sound—but you almost always can. Final Cut Pro can make audio edits down to 1/100th of a frame. There's no excuse for leaving in extra words or sounds. Great interview editing is all about making tiny subtle edits. Just start moving frame by frame, setting a new In or Out point and playing from the In to the Out (Shift-\) until you get it right. For those rare cases when you can't make a successful edit, just get it close, and later you can add subframe-level keyframes in the Timeline.

Unlike editing dramatic dialogue in which you generally avoid manipulating the nuances and pacing of speech, good interview editing requires precisely this ability.

15 Find the frame right before the second "And" (37:04).

This time, instead of making a subclip by setting an In and Out, you will use an extended marker.

16 Press ~ (tilde) to set a marker on that frame.

17 Play forward until just after he says, "Blown away," at 42:08.

18 Press Option-~ (tilde) to extend the marker.

The marker now lasts the duration of that section of the interview. You will see that the clip in the Browser also now has a disclosure triangle next to it.

▼ Michael Interview	00:00:20;00	00:55:09;08	00:55:29;07
Marker 1	00:00:05;04	00:55:37;04	00:55:42;07
Murphy Interview	00:00:23;29	Not Set	Not Set
Murphy Interview 2	00:00:19;06	Not Set	Not Set
MW: Carlos and Seamus	00:00:20;00	Not Set	Not Set
MW: The cast and crew are amaz	00:00:04;09	Not Set	Not Set

19 Click the disclosure triangle.

20 Name the marker *MW: Divi and Nate...*

▼ Michael Interview	00:00:20;00	00:55:09;08	00:55:29;07
MW: Divi and Nate...	00:00:05;04	00:55:37;04	00:55:42;07
Murphy Interview	00:00:23;29	Not Set	Not Set
Murphy Interview 2	00:00:19;06	Not Set	Not Set
MW: Carlos and Seamus	00:00:20;00	Not Set	Not Set
MW: The cast and crew are amaz	00:00:04;09	Not Set	Not Set

You can use extended markers and subclips interchangeably in Final Cut Pro.

There is just one more section to mark in this clip.

21 Find the section in which Michael says, "And the actors," and set a marker that begins on frame 00:56:04:09.

22 Play until just after he says, "It's been really good," at 18:25 and press Option-~ (tilde) to extend the marker.

23 In the Browser, name the marker *MW: The Actors...*

▼ 🎬 Michael Interview	00:00:14;17	00:56:04;09	00:56:18;25
🔖 MW: Divi and Nate...	00:00:05;04	00:55:37;04	00:55:42;07
🔖 MW: The Actors...	00:00:14;16	00:56:04;09	00:56:18;24
🎬 Murphy Interview	00:00:23;29	Not Set	Not Set
🎬 Murphy Interview 2	00:00:19;06	Not Set	Not Set
🎞 MW: Carlos and Seamus	00:00:20;00	Not Set	Not Set
🎞 MW: The cast and crew are amaz	00:00:04;09	Not Set	Not Set

24 In the Browser, Command-click the two markers and the two subclips and drag all four items into the Interview Snippits bin.

25 Click the disclosure triangle next to the Interview Snippits bin to expand it.

Name ▼	Duration	In	Out
Finished Interviews	00:02:14;18	Not Set	Not Set
Interview Sequence	00:00:00;00	Not Set	Not Set
▼ Interview Snippits			
AK Working with MW	00:00:04;11	Not Set	Not Set
DC: Origin of the Idea	00:00:22;23	Not Set	Not Set
DC: Wanted a comedy	00:00:18;26	Not Set	Not Set
JE: An awesome project...	00:00:23;03	Not Set	Not Set
JE: Brianca is a very controlling...	00:00:10;02	Not Set	Not Set
ML: It's been a great set	00:00:06;27	Not Set	Not Set
ML: It's been fantastic to work wit	00:00:03;10	Not Set	Not Set
ML: Very professional	00:00:02;23	Not Set	Not Set
MW: Carlos and Seamus	00:00:15;14	Not Set	Not Set
MW: Divi and Nate... from 'Michae	00:00:08;29	Not Set	Not Set
MW: The Actors... from 'Michael Ir	00:00:13;22	Not Set	Not Set
MW: The cast and crew are amazi	00:00:04;14	Not Set	Not Set
▼ Interviews			
Aaron Interview	00:00:42;24	Not Set	Not Set
David Interview	00:01:21;01	Not Set	Not Set
Divi Interview	00:01:48;23	Not Set	Not Set
Jennifer Interview1	00:00:18;05	Not Set	Not Set

Notice that the two markers you just dragged now appear as ordinary subclips. Most of the other sound bites have been selected already and are collected in this bin.

Pulling Selects in the Timeline

The process just described is efficient and allows you to go through all of your interviews and identify which sections you will be using. You can further categorize them in the Browser, assigning labels or grouping them in different bins according to where they're likely to fit in the show.

However, sometimes it can be easier to do some selecting in the Timeline. This can be especially useful if you think you may want to rearrange the order of some of the clips.

1   Double-click *Interview Sequence* to open it into the Canvas and Timeline.

2   Drag the **David Interview** clip from the Browser into the Canvas.

3   Play the whole clip to hear what you have to work with.

The entire clip will be edited into the sequence. Obviously you won't be using the entire thing, so the first thing to do is eliminate the sections of the clip you know you don't want.

4   Play the sequence until just after David says, "He's extremely passionate," and set an In point there (around 01:00:13:00).

This mark indicates the beginning of the section you will be deleting.

5   Play forward until just before David says, "His obstacle is," (at around 28:00) and set an Out point there.

6   Press Shift-Delete to ripple delete the unwanted section.

7   Play forward and stop just after he says, "Brianca," at 17:24. Set an In point there.

8   Set the Out point just before David says, "He's kinda eccentric," at 35:06.

9   Press Shift-Delete to ripple delete this section.

10   Set a new In just after he says, "In his head," at 28:16.

Since you'll be deleting the remainder of the clip, no Out point is necessary.

11 Press Delete to eliminate the marked area.

You have whittled the clip down to three sections that you may want to use. However, the clips can be rearranged so they make better sense. In the first and third clips, David is talking about his character, but in the second clip, he's talking about his boss, Brianca. It is a bit more logical to move the third clip before the second one.

12 Select the third clip and drag it to a position between the first two clips. Make sure snapping is on (by pressing N), then press Option to perform a swap edit.

The swap edit (indicated by a curved arrow) rearranges the clips in the Timeline without leaving any gaps.

NOTE ▶ Don't press the Option key before you begin dragging or you will copy the clip instead of moving it. Also be sure to release the mouse button before releasing the Option key, or else you will just move the clip.

13 Play the whole sequence.

The edit between the first two clips is a little rough, mainly because of the extra "He's" at the beginning of the second clip.

14 Play the sequence and park the playhead just before he says, "Kinda eccentric," (at 14:05).

15 Press R twice to select the Ripple tool and drag the right edge of the edit until it snaps to the playhead position.

> **TIP** ▶ This technique of positioning the playhead at the desired place and then drag-trimming to that point is a great way to trim in the Timeline without the guesswork that dragging usually entails.

16 Press A to release the Ripple tool.

17 Press \ to play around the new edit.

Don't worry about the obvious visual jump cut. In fact, while putting together the framework of interviews, you generally should ignore the picture entirely. In many cases, you're better off just closing your eyes and listening to the audio. You can always fix jump cuts later using B-roll (discussed in Lesson 7) or, in the worst case, using *soft cuts* (short-duration cross-dissolves).

Assembling the Clips

Once you've collected your sound bites, you're ready to assemble them. Because there's no inherent order to the clips and because it's easy to rearrange things in the Timeline, one way to start is to drag several clips into the Timeline at once, rearrange them, and trim them there. You probably wouldn't want to do this with an hour's worth of interviews, but for shorter sequences it's sort of fun.

1 Drag the Interview Snippits bin from the Browser directly into the Timeline, performing an insert edit at the head of the sequence.

Be sure not to release the mouse until you see the insert arrow, and the clips appearing as outlines and not solid blocks.

2 Press Shift-Z to zoom the Timeline to fit all the clips.

All of the clips are now in one place, but they are in random order. If you think back to the organizational plan you made earlier, there were three main sections: the crew, the cast, and the story. So, continue by grouping the clips into those categories.

The first clip features Aaron talking about working with the director. That clip would fall into the crew section, so leave it where it is for now. The second and third clips show Divi talking about the origin of the story and wanting to make a comedy. These probably fit in the story section, which is going to go to the end of the sequence.

3 Drag **DC: Origin of the idea** and **DC: Wanted a comedy** to the end of the sequence.

There's no harm in leaving a little gap between these two clips and the clips of David.

4 Press Shift-Z to zoom the Timeline to fit.

5 Select the gap left by the two missing clips and press Delete.

The next clip shows Jennifer talking about how great the crew is, so it stays at the front. The clip after that, **JE: Brianca is a very controlling**, is clearly about her character, which is part of the cast section.

6 Drag **JE: Brianca is a very controlling** to just after David's last clip. Be sure to line up the front of the clip with the end of the David clip, then press Option and release the mouse to perform a swap edit.

The next clips feature Michael talking about the crew, so you can leave them alone; but **MW: The Actors** needs to be moved to the cast section. Since this is a great introduction to that section, it's only logical to place it at the head of that section.

7   Drag **MW: The Actors** to just before David's first clip. Be sure to line up the beginning of the MW clip with the beginning of the **David Interview** clip, then press Option and release the mouse to perform a swap edit.

The remaining three clips all feature Murphy and are about the crew. Since these three clips are fairly redundant, it's very likely that at least one of them will get cut before the sequence is finalized. For now, there's no harm in leaving them there.

To clarify the three sections, you can create a gap between the crew and the cast sections.

8   Deselect **MW: The Actors**. From the Tool palette, select the Track Forward Select tool (or press T) and click the **MW: The Actors** clip.

All the clips are selected from that point forward in time.

9   Drag the clips to the right about 3 seconds.

You may want to turn off snapping (by pressing N) to make dragging easier.

Next, you will arrange the clips in the first section.

10   Drag a marquee around the first section and press Option-Shift-Z to zoom into the selection.

11 Press Command-Shift-A to deselect all.

You need to identify a good clip to begin the sequence. Fortunately, this footage provides a pretty obvious choice: **MW: The cast and crew.**

12 Drag **MW: The cast and crew** to the head of the sequence, and perform a swap edit.

While the Aaron clip is not a bad choice to follow, it talks about the specific role (director), and there are some general crew comments that fit best at this point.

13 Drag **JE: An awesome project...** to the left until it lines up with the edit between **MW: The cast and crew** (clip 1) and **AK: Working with MW** (clip 2). Press Option to perform a swap edit.

If you previously turned off snapping, you should turn it back on to make sure this edit lines up precisely.

Beginning the Edit

Now that the clips are organized into rough categories, you need to think about the specific order of individual clips. Creating a flow across the edits requires continuity to hide the edits, just the way physical gestures provide continuity to hide edits in an action sequence. With talking heads, there aren't many physical gestures to work with, so you must find continuity in the thoughts conveyed.

1 Play the first two clips.

While their contents are similar, it's a pretty awkward edit. Part of the problem is that Michael begins a thought and then Jennifer expresses the same thought all over again. You have to trim down the Jennifer quote to its essence, trusting that the setup from the first shot will provide the necessary context.

When you play her clip, you may recognize the heart of what she's saying. Don't get stuck looking for phrases that start at the beginning of sentences. In the middle of one sentence she says, "All these people come together and donate their time, their talent, their craft." This is a perfect quote. It continues naturally from the first clip, adds several new pieces of information without being redundant, and even has a nice, natural rhythm. The whole quote felt a bit long-winded and rambling, but by reducing it to that 5-second sound bite, she sounds succinct and focused.

2 Set an In point at the beginning of the Jennifer clip and set an Out point just before she says, "All these people," at 01:00:07:18.

3 Press Command-Shift-A to deselect all, then press Shift-Delete to ripple delete that section of the clip.

4 Play forward and set a new In point just after Jennifer says, "Their craft," at 9:24.

5 Press Down Arrow to move the playhead to the next edit, set an Out point there, and ripple delete that section as well.

Great job! Are there any other clips that would naturally follow? Perhaps there is something to finish the thought begun by Michael and elaborated by Jennifer. Aaron's quote starts a new thought, so that won't work, though it would be nice to bring in a new face. How about Murphy?

6   Play the three Murphy quotes.

Voilá! His third quote is a perfect follow-up to those opening shots.

7   Drag **ML: Very professional** to the end of **JE: An awesome project**, carefully lining up the edit. Press Option to perform a swap edit.

Next, you'll introduce some of the individual crew members. This will be great fodder for a B-roll later on, as it will be very easy to show a shot of Carlos or Seamus as they're being described.

8   Drag **MW: Carlos and Seamus** to the spot after **ML: Very professional** and press Option to perform a swap edit.

This is the perfect place for Aaron's quote about Michael's directing. You are building a very natural structure, talking about the whole crew at the beginning, and then moving into the specifics and talking about individuals. This is akin to starting a dramatic scene on a wide shot and moving into the close-ups. Coincidence? Not really. It's the same basic storytelling technique. First you tell the *what* and *where*, and just as the audience begins to wonder about the *who*, you provide that information, too.

9   Back up and play through **MW: Carlos and Seamus**. Stop the playhead just after he finishes talking about Carlos and before he mentions Seamus (around 01:00:20:20).

This is a long section and seems like it could be broken up right here. Are there any other clips that might fit? Perhaps something that relates to Carlos or Seamus? There's not a lot left to choose from, but there is one perfect choice.

10 Drag **ML: It's been a great set** to that spot in the middle of the **MW** clip and press Option to perform a swap edit.

TIP ▶ As this edit illustrates, you can perform a swap edit anywhere, not just at the head or tail of a clip.

To finish this section you need to think about how this section is going to bridge into the next one, which is about the actors. This might be a good time to step back and take a look at the big picture.

11 Press Shift-Z to zoom the Timeline out to show the whole sequence.

It would be nice to fit in one of those Divi quotes a little earlier. Since Michael mentions her in the second-to-last clip in the first section, that might be a nice transitional element. Try it out.

12 Drag the **DC: Wanted a comedy** clip to the end of section 1 and press Option to perform a swap edit.

13 Play the whole sequence.

Transitioning Between Sections

It's mostly working very well. The only awkward transition seems to be between Murphy's last line, "It's been fantastic," and Michael's introduction of Divi and Nate. If only there was a clip that could bridge that gap; something that was one of the cast or crew following up Murphy's sentiment, but also introducing that next section (about Divi and Nate).

Well, there was a part of Jennifer's quote that you deleted earlier in which she said how great it was to work with Michael and Divi and Nate. That might just do the trick. This reinforces how important it is to familiarize yourself with all of your raw footage.

1 Place the playhead anywhere over the second clip (**JE: An awesome project**) and press F to perform a match frame.

The source clip is opened into the Viewer.

2 In the Viewer, play the Jennifer quote to see if there's a section that might work here.

3   Set an In just before, "I've enjoyed working," at 00:45:32:05 and an Out just after, "Nate," (but before her next word) at 35:23.

4   In the sequence, place the playhead right before **MW: Divi and Nate** (around 47:00) and perform an insert edit.

This works wonderfully well. It's a slightly overused but nonetheless effective interview editing technique to repeat exact words across an edit to add emphasis. This is similar to the action scene technique of *double-cutting* a dramatic action for emphasis (described in Lesson 3).

Now, when the audience hears, "Divi and Nate," twice, they're going to be anticipating some information about Divi and Nate. Unfortunately, you don't have any Nate clips to work with, but you do have a clip of Divi, and it's one that explains why everyone's talking about her. She's the producer, and the film was her idea.

Now you have to get from her clip into the next section about the actors.

5   Select the gap between **DC: Wanted a comedy** and **MW: The Actors** and press Delete.

6   Play around that edit.

The edit doesn't work as it is. This is another case in which the second clip introduces a new thought rather than continuing a thought that would carry the viewer across the edit. However, if you trim the first few words of that clip, it suddenly appears that Michael is following up on her thought about the development of the project.

7   Set an In at the beginning of **MW: The Actors** and set an Out just before he says, "We spent a long time casting," around 01:01:16:10.

8   Ripple delete that section and play around the edit.

Much better! Now it makes an organic segue.

This is an important lesson. Pay great attention to the intonations and phrasing of your interviewees. Often, the key to a good edit lies in linking the beginning of a sentence in one clip to the middle of a sentence in another, and the ending of a sentence in a third.

Butchering an Interview

There's no way around it; sometimes you simply have to roll up your sleeves and chop up an interview to make it work. In fact, the more interviews you cut, the more you'll realize it's not a rare occurrence at all. Even brilliant speakers often pause, go off on tangents, hem and haw, or repeat themselves—basically doing everything possible to make it impossible to cull a great sound bite. But if you're good, you can squeeze blood from those stones. And the more comfortable you get slicing and dicing, moving words and even syllables, the easier it gets. That's good because you can salvage a great piece of interview that says something critical to your story but in an awkward or convoluted way.

1 Zoom in on the last clip, **DC: Origin of the Idea**.

2 Play across the clip.

The sentiment of the clip is wonderful, but there are several problems. The first sentence about "sitting outside smoking and talking" paints a nice picture, but it doesn't make any sense out of context. We don't know who she's talking about or how it relates to the rest of the story.

One great test to see if you can cut a word or phrase from an interview is this: Listen to the quote without it. Does it still make sense? Is some essential piece of information missing? If the answers are yes and no, respectively, there's only one thing to do: Cut it.

3 Position the playhead just after she says, "You know," and before she says, "What would be a really funny concept" (around 01:02:15:00).

4 Make sure you have the Selection tool selected and drag the clip's left edge to the right until it snaps to the playhead.

Next, you need to tackle the tangent about whether the person in her story is a "kid" or a "guy." This one is tricky. Obviously, it was important enough to her to stop and correct herself. You don't want to ignore that and disrespect your interview subject. But the way she interrupts herself really ruins the flow of the quote. How can you trim this section to eliminate this unwanted sentence?

5   First, play across the clip and try to set an In just before she says, "a kid."

This is a very difficult edit, because the words "about a" are basically one indivisible sound.

6   Instead, try to set the In after the word "a" but before "kid."

This is a little easier, at around 01:02:18:10.

NOTE ▶ The timecode numbers in this section might not match yours exactly because earlier when you moved this clip to the end of the sequence, you were not instructed to place it at a precise location. Try to perform the edits based on the nuances of the audio rather than the timecode numbers.

7   Set an Out point just after the "a" and before the "guy" in her phrase, "A guy who works at the DMV," (at around 22:28).

8   Ripple delete the marked section and play across the edit.

Even if you got the timing just right, her intonation of the word "guy" doesn't match the phrase leading up to it.

9 Press Command-Option-W to display audio waveforms, and click the Track Height control to increase the tracks to the second-largest preset.

It's pretty obvious from the waveforms that the word "guy" is much too loud. Fortunately, you happen to have another instance of that word from a few seconds earlier in the clip.

10 Press F to perform a match frame, and load the source clip in the Viewer.

11 Switch to the Audio tab and find the section where she says, "Or a guy, I shouldn't even say kid," (around 00:19:38:03).

12 Zoom in, if necessary, and set an In and Out around the word "guy" in the Viewer.

13   In the sequence, untarget track V1, place the playhead one frame before the edit point, and overwrite the new "guy" into the sequence.

14   Play across the new edit.

Depending on exactly how you made your edits, you will probably need to further finesse this edit to make it work naturally.

15   Select the Ripple tool. Position the tool over the right edge of the edit between "Guy" and "who works," and drag the edit two or three frames to the left.

Getting this right may be very difficult, but it is possible. Just be patient and add frames one at a time. Be sure to listen to the edit with your eyes closed. Seeing the jump cut will always distract you.

With that edit fixed you can still improve one more piece of this quote. A few seconds later, Divi says, "And he wants to take a picture… every picture that he wants to take." In natural speech most people would understand what she is trying to say, but for the sake of getting things perfect, why not eliminate that double phrasing?

Again, this is not a simple fix because, for the phrasing to sound natural, she should say, "*And* every picture," but the "and" must come from the first phrase and the "every" from the second.

16 Set an In point just after she says "and" but before "he wants" (around 22:01) and set an Out *about four frames before* she says "every picture."

17 Ripple delete the marked area and play back over the edit.

Those few frames of space are critical to getting a natural-sounding edit. If you don't like the sound of your edit, use the Ripple tool to adjust each side of the edit until it sounds natural.

Editing Subframe Audio

Often, to make each edit sound right, you will want to perform little fade-ins or fade-outs at each edit point. Professional audio editors never let any piece of audio begin or end "hard." Such hard Ins and Outs can generate pops or subtle but abrupt changes in sound quality.

Final Cut Pro allows you to create as many as 100 audio keyframes within the duration of a single video frame. So in this case you can create a tiny subframe fade to smooth the edit.

1 Zoom in the Timeline all the way, centered on the edit point between "And" and "Every."

The dark gray area in the ruler indicates the duration of one video frame.

2   Press Option-W to turn on keyframe overlays.

3   Option-click the audio level envelope for the outgoing clip to add a keyframe about half a frame before the edit point.

4   Add a second keyframe very close to the edit point and drag it down to the bottom of the clip to create a fade-out effect.

That tiny, half-frame fade-out will be barely audible, but it will help to hide the edit ever so subtly.

Finishing the Sequence

When you've completed the surgery on this clip, you still need to choose its place in the project. There is one obvious natural place for it to go, and that's mixed with David's description of his character.

1   Press Shift-Z to zoom the Timeline to fit all the clips.

2   Find the place in the sequence when David says, "He's the photographer that takes the pictures at the DMV," (around 01:01:37:20). Park the playhead there.

3   Select the whole group of clips that comprise the last Divi quote and drag them until they line up with the playhead. Press Option to perform an insert edit and release the mouse.

Before

After

4   Play the entire sequence.

The only remaining problem is that there is no ending beat. The sequence just ends with Jennifer's last line. One easy solution is to split in half Michael's last comment about the actors.

This is another common tactic: taking one sound bite and breaking it in half to book-end a section.

5   Play through the **MW: The Actors** clip and park the playhead right after he says, "Bring something to this," (around 23:05).

6   Select all the clips to the right of that clip, beginning with the first **David Interview** clip.

7   Drag left the group of clips until the group snaps to the playhead position. Press Option to perform an insert edit and release the mouse.

8   Play the entire sequence again.

That bookending helped, but it didn't give the ending punch that the sequence ought to have. Perhaps there's something else in the raw clips that can serve as a final shot.

9   Go back to the Interviews bin and open **Jennifer Interview2**.

10   Set an In point just before she says, "And everyone's been really sweet," (00:46:07:22) and an Out point just after she says, "Because we love to work," (22:22).

11   Make sure track V1 is targeted and overwrite this clip onto the very end of the sequence.

Awesome! A great last sentiment, but there's one last nagging thing. At the end of her line, she flubs the word "love" making it sound like "larve." Is this fixable? Is it worth fixing? You've come so far; why not try?

12 Go back to the Viewer and play past the Out point.

In the very next sentence, she says the word "love" clearly.

13 Set an In and Out around that word in the Viewer (In: 00:46:24:10, Out: 00:46:24:15).

14 Press Shift-\ to play In to Out a few times to make sure you cleanly marked only that word (without any of the previous or next words included) and adjust the edit one frame at a time if necessary.

15 In the sequence, zoom in on that last section of the Timeline and set an In point just before the word "love" (around 01:02:29:28).

16 Untarget track V1 and overwrite the "love" into the sequence.

17 Play the whole sequence once again.

There are probably some edits that still need trimming. Tiny fade-ins and fade-outs may improve or smooth out some of the edits, and as with dialogue scenes, splitting the picture and audio edits often helps to improve the overall flow.

You might get ambitious and further tighten things by removing more pauses or "um's." However, your goal should be to create a sequence that sounds like a natural flow of conversation. Remember, it's very important that you close your eyes or get used to listening for the rhythm without being distracted by untidy picture edits. Those jump cuts can be fixed once you begin the second phase: adding B-roll.

Lesson Review

1. What purpose do interviews serve in a documentary?
2. Should you edit interviews based on picture or sound?
3. How do you create a subclip?
4. What is the functional difference between a subclip and an extended marker?
5. How do you create an extended marker?
6. Describe the function of a swap edit.
7. How do you perform a swap edit?
8. True or false? Swap edits can be performed only on existing clip boundaries.
9. How many audio keyframes can be added on one video frame?
10. What does the Show Match Frame command do?

Answers

1. Interviews present and provide evidence to support a hypothesis or theme.

2. Sound

3. Set In and Out points in the Viewer and choose Modify > Create Subclip or press Command-U.

4. There is no functional difference.

5. Press M or ~ (tilde) to set the starting frame of the marker, then press Option-~ (tilde) to set the ending frame.

6. A swap edit rearranges clips within the Timeline without leaving any gaps.

7. Drag a clip to a new position on the same track in the Timeline, then press Option.

8. False

9. 100

10. Show Match Frame opens the source clip into the Viewer parked on the same frame currently visible in the Canvas.

7

Editing Documentaries: Adding B-Roll

By the time you finish editing your interviews, you should have a tight, coherent sequence that smoothly moves from one subject to the next and tells some kind of a story. But the interviews are just the skeleton. Next you must flesh out the sequence by adding shots to illustrate or expand upon what is being said. Talking heads are notoriously boring to watch, but supplemented with the right B-roll footage you can create a captivating and engaging scene.

B-roll is an old television news term that originated when editing was performed on reels of film. While the primary "A" roll contained the interviews, whenever an edit was necessary, the editor would cut to the secondary "B" footage. Although today nearly all editing is done digitally, that cutaway and supplemental footage is still referred to as B-roll.

In some cases, the B-roll isn't shot until after the interviews have been edited. This ensures that you have cutaways that correspond precisely to what is being said. This usually is the case for shows based on written narration instead of unscripted interviews.

However, documentary editors more often are handed a huge pile of footage that may or may not relate specifically to the contents of the interviews. The editor must wade through all of this B-roll looking for images that will match what is being said.

Organizing B-roll

In many ways, choosing and placing these shots is where great documentary editors show their prowess. The best editors look past the obvious contents of the footage and find the symbolic or inferred meaning that will illustrate the interview and expand upon it. This requires looking at the footage with a very open mind and thinking about how it might be used beyond its most obvious purpose.

1   Open **B-roll**.

2   Double-click the b-roll bin to open it in its own window.

Name	Duration	In	Out	Cast or Crew	Description
Aaron & David Lo <	00:00:24;06	Not Set	Not Set	Cast	Window scene
Carlito & michael	00:00:06;22	Not Set	Not Set	crew	
Carlos "That's a wrap"	00:00:07;25	Not Set	Not Set	crew	
David hugs mpw & divi	00:00:23;00	Not Set	Not Set	Cast	"Cut! Loved it!"
David turns to Jenn	00:00:06;12	Not Set	Not Set	Cast	David and Jenn
director & producer	00:00:07;22	Not Set	Not Set	crew	
Divi watching monitor (CU)	00:00:03;27	Not Set	Not Set	crew	
Divi with David laughing	00:00:05;24	Not Set	Not Set	crew + cast	David
Giggling Gaffer	00:00:05;17	Not Set	Not Set	crew	
Grip with reflector	00:00:04;09	Not Set	Not Set	crew	
Jenn "look vidal sassoon"	00:00:11;01	Not Set	Not Set	Cast	David and Jenn
Jenn Bunny-rip	00:00:05;09	Not Set	Not Set	Cast	Jenn High angle
Jenn destroys photo booth	00:00:21;22	Not Set	Not Set	Cast	
Jenn torturing BTS camera	00:00:15;18	Not Set	Not Set	Cast	Jenn
lunchroom rehearsal	00:00:07;04	Not Set	Not Set	Cast	rehearsal
▶ Movie Excerpts					
mpw & jennifer	00:00:07;19	Not Set	Not Set	crew + cast	Jenn
mpw & scripty	00:00:08;22	Not Set	Not Set	crew	
mpw & seamus planning	00:00:11;01	Not Set	Not Set	crew	
mpw blocking actors	00:00:22;25	Not Set	Not Set	crew + cast	David and Aaron
Nate blowing balloon	00:00:09;09	Not Set	Not Set	crew	
NateDancing	00:00:07;08	Not Set	Not Set	crew	
Post-shot meeting	00:00:05;20	Not Set	Not Set	crew + cast	
Seamus at eyepiece	00:00:02;07	00:12:39;05	00:12:41;11	crew	
Seamus hand signals	00:00:02;10	00:19:21;21	00:19:24;00	crew	
Seamus handheld	00:00:00;21	00:25:46;23	00:25:47;13	crew	
Seamus on dolly	00:00:05;00	Not Set	Not Set	crew	
The Kiss	00:00:01;11	00:54:30;15	00:54:31;25	Cast	David and Jenn
The sixth hug	00:00:07;14	Not Set	Not Set	Cast	David and Aaron
Tilt from roof to ground	00:00:09;03	Not Set	Not Set	crew	

As in all projects, the first step is to get very familiar with your footage. These clips have been culled from several hours of behind-the-scenes footage from the "Artistic License" shoot.

3   Watch all the clips.

The behind-the-scenes videographer had no idea what would be said in the interviews, so he just gathered random bits of activity over the course of two days. Matching that footage to the interviews is typical of the challenge you will face in many documentary situations.

The more thoroughly you organize your B-roll shots, the easier it will be to find what you're looking for. You can do this organization in any of the common ways, such as creating a hierarchy of bins and sub-bins, using labels, or typing descriptive comments in the various comment fields. Entering specific and descriptive information helps you search for the shots you need by using Final Cut Pro's Find feature.

At the very least, you can group these clips into a couple of sub-bins.

4   If necessary, scroll the Browser until you can see the column labeled Cast or Crew.

5   Click that column header to sort the bin by that data.

6   Press Command-B twice to create two new bins.

7   Label one of the bins *Cast* and the other *Crew*.

8   Select all of the clips marked Cast (in the Cast or Crew column) and drag them into the Cast bin, and drag all off the Crew clips into the Crew bin.

Since the other four clips have both cast and crew in them, they are labeled as *crew + cast*. Rather than choosing which bin to put them in, there's no reason not to put them in both.

9   Select the remaining clips that are labeled *crew + cast* and Option-drag them into the Cast bin.

This puts a copy of each of those clips in the Cast bin but leaves a copy loose in the b-roll bin.

10 Select the clips again and drag them into the Crew bin.

11 Close the b-roll bin.

Spotting the Sequence

Once you are familiar with the B-roll available to you, you should begin thinking about how and where you can use it in your sequence. *Spotting* is the term for watching a program and marking all of the "spots" where something must be done. You might spot a show for moments that need sound effects or for edits that need finessing. In this case, you will look for spots where you think B-roll should be used. This includes long sections of one person talking, jump cuts that require covering, or content that seems to beg for a cutaway to the subject.

Your project contains a version of the interview sequence that has been finessed and is ready for this next step.

1 Double-click the *Finished Interviews* sequence and play through it, specifically thinking about B-roll.

Remember, your goal in editing is to construct a story that illustrates a theme by juxtaposing shots. In this case, the B-roll serves to corroborate what's being said. Sure, these people say it was a great shoot, but why should you believe them? By cutting away to B-roll shots that effectively support their points, the theme is communicated clearly.

You can use markers to identify the spots you want to address.

2 Press M to add a marker where you want to add your first cutaway.

It's not important that the marker go on a specific frame, but it will be helpful if you label the marker something useful.

3 While the playhead is parked on the marked frame, press M again to open the Edit Marker window.

4 In the marker Name field, type *Production Crew* and click OK.

5 Play the sequence until Michael says, "Carlos, the A.D.," and add another marker there.

6 Press M to open the Edit Marker window and name this one *Carlos*. Click OK to close the window.

7 Play forward until the next shot of Murphy.

As he says, "There's a whole lot of production going on," he's looking offscreen, which is very distracting. This is a perfect example of a section that ought to be covered by B-roll. But what should the content of the B-roll be? He's talking about, "a whole lot of production going on," which could be almost anything. It might be nice to see a shot of him on set, or it might be okay to use generic shots of the crew working. Since his first sentence is about how relaxed the set is, perhaps you can show a shot of people having fun and then follow it up with people working hard. Either way, another marker should go here.

8 Press M to add another marker, and press M again to open the Edit Marker window. Name this one *Relaxed -> Working hard.*

Because it's important here that the B-roll cover the entire section when Murphy is looking offscreen, you can indicate that by extending the marker to the end of his shot.

9 Play forward to the end of the shot and press Option-~ (tilde) to extend the marker.

10 Play forward into the next quote.

At this point where Michael is talking about Seamus the D.P. a gap was removed, resulting in a jump cut. This is another place where a shot of B-roll is all but required to hide the jump cut and illustrate what's so "stellar and crazy" about Seamus. Perhaps you've got something in the B-roll to communicate that idea.

And so on. Rather than spotting the whole show step by step yourself, the project supplies a sequence that has already been spotted.

Adding the B-Roll

As you add the B-roll shots to the interviews, you need to consider what kind of overall balance you want between the two components (talking heads and B-roll). Depending on the nature of the film and the intended audience, you may favor one or the other. This also may be influenced by how compelling the interviews are on their own, as well as how exciting or engaging the B-roll shots are.

Serious subjects tend to favor more heads and fewer cutaways. Likewise, if the interviews are particularly emotional, cutting away may seem to cheapen or undermine the intensity of what is being said. For lighter material, such as the behind-the-scenes sequence at hand, the more B-roll, the better. Similarly, if you were cutting a piece about athletes or musicians performing amazing feats, you would want to show as little interview as possible to maximize exposure of the (presumably) illustrative B-roll footage.

However, you rarely want to completely omit the talking heads. Seeing the face of a speaker provides context and a grounding that gives the piece its structure. When you have several people speaking, as in this sample project, it's important to show their faces, at least the first time they speak. Like all rules, this one can be broken, often to dramatic effect, by withholding the face of a well-known interview subject until after you've heard her speak. By delaying the reveal, you can increase the surprise and enhance the significance of her testimony.

1   Open the **Spotted Sequence**.

This version of the sequence has already been filled with markers. Each one indicates a place or a section where B-roll ought to go, and each is labeled with a suggestion of the type of footage that might fit.

2   In the Canvas, Control-click the Current Timecode field.

The shortcut menu that appears contains a list of all the markers in the sequence. (This list can also be found by Control-clicking anywhere on the Timeline ruler.) Selecting one of the names automatically jumps the playhead to that marker.

3   Choose Seamus from the shortcut menu.

The playhead moves to Michael's quote about Seamus the cinematographer.

4   Click the Browser window to give it focus, and press Command-F to open the Find window.

5   Type *Seamus* in the search field and click Find All.

The Find Results bin appears, containing several shots featuring Seamus. The green ones are B-roll, and the remaining clip contains the interview.

You must first determine how much time you need to cover in the sequence.

6   In the Timeline, press Up Arrow to move the playhead to the beginning of the clip, and set an In point.

7   Press Down Arrow twice (first to go to the jump cut, then to go to the end of the second half of the quote) and set an Out point.

The Canvas Duration field shows you how long this quote is: 5:16. You don't need to cover that entire quote, although you can if you want to, since you've already seen Michael's face in the opening quote.

8 Go back to the Find Results bin and play the first clip: **mpw & seamus planning**.

This clip shows Michael doing all the talking, and Seamus is just listening. It's a nice shot to show their relationship, but it doesn't exactly complement the quote.

9 Audition the rest of the clips in the Find Results bin.

Unfortunately, none of them show Seamus doing anything particularly "stellar" or "crazy." The closest is the hand signals shot, where at least he's doing something physical.

10 Open **Seamus hand signals**. Set an In point just as the camera pans over to him (00:19:21:20) and set an Out after his hand signals end and he looks down to the camera (24:00).

11 Press Shift-\ (backslash) to play In to Out.

This is a nice active shot, but it's only 2 seconds long. You can keep hunting for a longer shot that will fill the space in the sequence, or you can use more than one B-roll shot. In this instance, try the latter approach.

12 Make the Timeline active and press Option-O to clear the Out point.

13 Target the audio to tracks A3 and A4 and perform an overwrite edit.

14   Press \ (backslash) to play around the edit.

Not too bad; it covers the jump cut but, predictably, it feels a little brief. This might be improved by adding a second shot, but which one should you use? Ideally, you should pick something that builds on the content of the first shot. This could be a shot with a matching camera move (the hand signals shot featured an aggressive pan), or it could be a shot featuring a similar or complementary angle. Or perhaps there is something else that can speak to the idea of the quote.

15   Open **Seamus handheld**.

Near the end, he does some weird gesture with his fingers. This could be exactly what you're looking for! The two hand gestures are unrelated, and neither one is all that "crazy" by itself; but combining the two just might elicit the right feeling.

16   Set an In point just before the "finger-talking" at 00:25:46:23 and an Out point when he finishes at 47:13.

17   Overwrite this clip directly after **Seamus hand signals** and play the section.

Is it working? Well, you are probably distracted by the audio from the B-roll. While it's unlikely you'll want to hear much of that background noise over the interview, you may later want to include some portion of the B-roll audio in the mix. For that reason, it's good to include it in the sequence, but there's no reason you need to listen to it while you edit.

18   Disable the audio for tracks A3 and A4.

19   Play this section of the sequence again.

The two shots are improving the portrait, but so quickly that they're a little confusing. Adding a third shot might do the trick. Identify where you'd like it to go in the sequence. Think about where you'd like to come back to the interview. One good idea is to return just for Michael's last phrase, "And I love that."

20 Set an Out point just before that line (around 31:20) and, moving backward, set the In point at the edit point with **Seamus handheld**.

21 Open **Seamus at eyepiece**. Set an In just before he leans toward the camera (around 00:12:39:05). The Out will be calculated automatically.

22 Overwrite the clip into the sequence.

23 Close the Find Results bin window.

24 Play around the entire area.

Now that's starting to feel much better. If you had a single shot of him dancing or swinging from the rafters, that might have worked, too. But this is a great example of making do with what you've got. Rather than a single piece of B-roll, you're using three snippets to convey much more information. Seeing Seamus in three different settings, always with the camera and always moving, does give a sense that this is an energetic person, and lends credence to the point about him that you're trying to support.

Splitting the Edit

As it stands, cutting to the shots of Seamus at the exact moment that Michael starts talking about him feels a little stiff. Just like edits in dramatic sequences, this edit can benefit from splitting the audio and video so they happen at separate times. However, this is not a typical edit in which the audio and video are from the same clip, and the video isn't even a single shot, but a mini-montage of three shots. Regardless, the edit will be improved if you create an L-cut, so you see the shots of Seamus a moment before you hear about him.

The Slide tool moves a clip earlier or later in the sequence by changing the durations of the clips on either side without modifying the length of the clip itself.

Before

After

Slide is not very widely used in dramatic editing, but it can be invaluable in cases like this where you want to move around a piece of B-roll. There's only one catch: Final Cut Pro can slide only one clip at a time. In this case, you would need to slide each of the three clips individually. This is tedious, and you could accidentally change their individual durations unless you were careful and slid them all the exact same number of frames, which defeats the purpose of using this handy tool.

However, there is a workaround. You can slide multiple clips at once if you do it numerically. Slide works just like Ripple, Roll, and Slip: If you have the tool selected, typing a number automatically performs that type of edit on the Timeline selection.

1   Select the three clips you want to slide.

2   Choose the Slide tool from the Tool palette or press S twice.

3   Type *-10* and press Enter.

The three clips are slid together.

4   Press A to release the Slide tool.

5   Play around the edit.

Now, the clips of Seamus lead the interview audio, creating a sort of split edit. This eases the viewer into the subject change, creating a more sophisticated, organic editorial sensibility. Naturally, this is a stylistic choice and might not be appropriate in every instance.

Integrating B-Roll Audio

Frequently, you will want to mix the audio from the B-roll with the main interview audio. While the content of the interview is obviously paramount, adding a little bit of the sound from the B-roll shot can greatly enhance the overall mix, bringing both components to life in a unique way.

1   Control-click the Timeline ruler and choose the David's Character marker.

The playhead is moved to the section where David and Divi are describing the main character in the movie: a photographer who takes outrageous driver's license photos.

This section of the sequence contains quite a few jump cuts and will need an extended section of B-roll to cover the whole section.

2   Set an In point before the first jump cut (right after David says, "David is the photographer," at 01:01:19:00). Play through the entire Divi interview and set an Out point after the last jump cut (just after David says, "Kinda eccentric," at 34:00).

3   Locate the Movie Excerpts bin inside the b-roll bin and open **PhotoMontage**.

This is a montage of the wacky license photos David takes during the film. Since you'll use this clip from the first frame, you don't need to set In or Out points.

4   Overwrite the clip into the sequence.

5   Enable the A3 and A4 audio tracks.

6   Play across this section of the sequence.

This clip has music and the sound of the camera flashes. At full volume it competes too much with the interviews.

7 Press Option-W to turn on clip overlays.

8 Drag the level envelope for the **PhotoMontage** audio to –15dB.

9 Option-click the level envelope near the beginning of the clip to add two keyframes and create a fade-in effect.

NOTE ▶ You may need to zoom in on this section of the Timeline to effectively build the fade-in effect.

10 Option-drag the right edge of the **PhotoMontage** audio clip to extend it as far as it will go.

11 Option-click the level envelope to add a keyframe just before the end of the video of the **PhotoMontage** clip.

12 Option-click to add another keyframe at the far right edge of the clip.

13 Drag down that keyframe to create a slow fade-out effect, as illustrated below.

14 Play across this entire section of the sequence.

The music and sound effects from the movie clip nicely complement the interviews. While this is a fairly easy example, using some of the ambient sounds or practical sound effects from any typical B-roll clip can enhance the integration between interviews and B-roll in an organic and subtle way.

Inserting Clips

Sometimes a piece of B-roll requires the audiences' full attention. You want them to listen to the full-volume audio and watch the clip by itself without any interview over it. This technique has many merits. It changes the pacing of the sequence, breaks up the monotony of the interviews, and can suggest an engaging call-and-response feeling.

But beware of losing track of the structure of your show. Don't forget that you are telling a story. Each section of your show must lead to the next; each event must propel the story forward. The edited interviews serve this purpose (assuming you crafted them well). B-roll elements typically illuminate the story but don't advance it.

Furthermore, these "stand-alone" B-roll pieces must be fully integrated into the shots around them. This can be accomplished by splitting the edits going in and out of them, or inter-weaving them with the interviews, where the audio goes back and forth in a seemingly seamless way.

1 Control-click the Timeline ruler and choose Brianca.

The playhead jumps to the next edit, when David introduces "his obstacle" Brianca. This time, instead of laying the B-roll over the existing interview, you will cut to a shot of her delivering a line of dialogue that illustrates their relationship.

2 In the Cast bin, open **brianca into cam**. Play the clip and set an In right before she says, "You have 75 seconds per person," at 00:49:32:15 and set an Out just after she says "Snappin'!" at 38:20.

3 Perform an insert edit.

The clip is inserted into the sequence between David's and Jennifer's interviews. This succeeds in describing what David is saying in a way that would have been nearly impossible without hearing her line.

However, the clip can be integrated into the sequence much more smoothly if you turn it into an L-edit, where the picture begins while David is talking.

4 Press R to select the Roll tool, then Option-click only the video edit at the head of that clip, where **David Interview** ends and **brianca into cam** begins.

5 Drag the edit to the left until it snaps to the previous edit point.

6   Press A to release the Roll tool.

7   Play around this part of the sequence.

The B-roll is seamlessly integrated into the sequence.

There are no rules about how to mix the audio from the B-roll and the interviews; you can completely insert it, or just fit it between the words or phrases without any inserting required.

8   In the sequence, play forward into the interview with Jennifer. Set an In point just after she says "Controlling" (01:01:55:05) and an Out before she says "Manager" (56:08).

9   Open **Jenn Bunny rip** from the Cast bin. Set an In point just before she rips the head off the stuffed bunny (00:26:45:15).

10   Overwrite the clip into the sequence.

11   Press R to select the Roll tool, and Option-click the video edit at the head of the **Jenn Bunny rip** clip.

12   Roll the edit to the left about 10 frames to create a slight L-edit.

13 Press \ to play around the edit.

To perfect the edit, you might want to add a quick fade-in and fade-out on the B-roll audio.

The goal is to marry the B-roll and the interviews together so they feel intimately linked. Indeed, regardless of whether the production team intended for certain images to go with certain lines spoken in the interviews, your job is to make the viewer feel that they were conceived and created for no other purpose.

Having Fun with B-Roll

In addition to supplementing the narration created by the interviews, your B-roll also provides material that can be used to create montages. Such montages can serve as an interstitial or transitional element connecting multiple interview-structured scenes, or it could serve as an introductory or concluding element.

1 Open Media > **Art_Lic_BTS.mov**.

2 Study the opening and closing montages.

Building such montages is beyond the scope of this lesson, but some broad guidelines include paying special attention to juxtapositions in composition, isolating action within the frame, matching camera movement across edits, and controlling pacing. Using the shots in the B-roll bin, experiment with creating your own version of an opening montage.

Expanding the Documentary Form

Although the majority of documentary programs are structured around interviews or narration, as illustrated in this chapter, such projects frequently contain additional scenes that may take a wide variety of forms. Often a film will include dramatic scenes featuring dialogue or action elements that can be cut based on the principles described in Section 1, "Cutting Dramatic Material." Such scenes range from fully scripted reenactments featuring actors to fly-on-the-wall observations of real events as they transpire. While these scenes may not have coverage as carefully crafted as you would expect from scripted material, good directors will always provide you with some coverage to allow for editorial options.

Another common format employed by documentaries is a different type of interview, where one subject is interviewed extensively and the interviewer is part of the scene. In such a scene you would typically have shots of both interviewer and interviewee, and possibly even a master-type 2-shot. These scenes can be cut just as if they were a simple dialogue scene.

One type of scene that does have its own unique editing guidelines is a scene that documents an event such as a wedding or a spelling bee. This type of scene is described in detail in the next lesson.

Lesson Review

1. What makes for good B-roll?
2. What does "spot" mean?
3. How do you spot a sequence for B-roll?
4. How can you navigate directly to a sequence marker?
5. How can you slide multiple clips simultaneously?
6. What must each section of a documentary accomplish?
7. Can an edit be split if the audio and video come from different sources?
8. How can B-roll audio improve a scene?

Answers

1. Good B-roll not only supports or corresponds to the audio that accompanies it, but it also enhances or expands upon it.
2. To identify sections or moments of a show that may require further attention.
3. Play the sequence and add markers whenever the narration suggests a B-roll shot might be helpful. Be sure to name the markers appropriately.

4. Control-click the Current Timecode field in the Canvas, or the ruler in the Timeline.

5. Select them with the Slide tool and edit numerically.

6. It must propel the story forward.

7. Yes

8. You can use B-roll audio to split edits and to integrate the B-roll more tightly with the primary footage.

8

Lesson Files	Lesson Files > Lesson 08 > EventDoc
Media	Media > Destinations Market
Time	This lesson takes approximately 90 minutes to complete.
Goals	Structure an event into a story with a beginning, middle, and end
	Manipulate reality while retaining the truth of an event
	Organize footage in different ways
	Make narrative-like sequences using footage without coverage
	Construct montages using a variety of techniques
	Make effective jump cuts
	Use Slip and Slide tools to create precisely timed edits
	Identify an editing pattern to give your show stylistic cohesion
	Use narration to make sequences more accessible

Documenting an Event

Aside from interviews and B-roll, documenting an event is probably the most common type of nonfiction film you're likely to encounter. The event could be a wedding, a corporate press event, or a live performance. It could be a road trip to Niagara Falls or a political protest rally.

In each of these cases, you must whittle multiple hours of footage into a concise film that captures the spirit of the event, chronicles the important episodes, and engages your audience.

For starters, it's pretty obvious that you can eliminate an hour of wasted footage shot between speakers at the protest rally, or trim the 20 minutes a bride and groom waited before cutting the cake while someone retrieved Grandma from the dance floor. But once you've pulled the selects—the important moments that must be included—how do you assemble them? How do you tie the moments into a *story*?

By now, the answer should be familiar to you. Just as with narrative films, you need to identify the beginning, middle, and end; to assemble events from a series of moments, each of which depends upon the one it follows and compels the one it precedes.

Construct Your Own Reality

Don't fall into the trap of maintaining the "reality" of the event at the expense of a clear, concise story. For example, at a corporate press event, the flamboyant CEO may have spent 10 minutes demonstrating obsolete technology as a buildup to unveiling the new product. In the video version, you would have 10 minutes screen time when the story isn't progressing. Those minutes might undermine the momentum of the piece and even confuse your viewers. Cut them.

Even the actual order of events is usually not very important to documenting an event. What's far more critical is to assemble scenes so they progress in a natural flow. Of course, you don't want the groom to kiss the bride before the vows; but in your road trip movie, you can relocate the funny moment that happened on the way home right up front, especially if it ties together two other shots or moves the story forward.

Don't get caught up in objectivity when the very nature of shooting and editing an event dictates a subjectivity that you simply cannot escape. Inevitably you are abridging the story, and that requires a degree of interpretation. Don't shy away from that fact—embrace it. If you understand the underlying essence of your event, you'll stay true to your theme without becoming a slave to the chronology or other "realities" that will make a boring or confusing video.

Organize Creatively

Whenever you begin a project you examine all of the available footage. This is especially true with an event documentary in which you'll probably have a huge amount of footage covering a wide range of subjects. As always, the process of reviewing the footage is invaluable for familiarization; but, additionally, it helps you find ways to organize and categorize the footage.

For example, the wedding might be divided chronologically into the arrival, the ceremony, toasts, dancing, cutting the cake, tossing the bouquet, and receiving gifts. But you could also identify the footage using different criteria. You might group all the shots of the bride's family, shots of the groom's family, and shots of friends.

You might additionally call out shots featuring outrageous dancing, laughing, kisses, babies. or celebrating. While these shots won't make up a single scene, they could be perfect for a montage or as a thematic element. You might end each segment with a shot of someone hugging the happy couple. Finding such a motif provides a unifying framework that ties your show together.

Thinking about your program this way opens your mind to new ways of telling the story. Events are chronological, yes, but they also have thematic and content-based structure. There's no reason your video of the political rally couldn't group the three speeches about the environment, even though speeches discussing other issues were delivered between them. You could even go a step further and *intercut* the three speeches into a single segment featuring highlights from each.

Examine Your Footage

This lesson features footage from a travel show called "Destinations." While the show is very structured overall, individual sections are shot in a documentary style, and a wide range of footage is assembled into a story in the edit room. This particular section features the show's host visiting a public market on the Caribbean island of St. Lucia.

The current segment is much simpler than a typical "documenting an event" project, but it provides a sort of micro-event that allows you to explore the same techniques you would employ on a larger show.

1   Open **EventDoc**.

   The footage already has been grouped into two main bins, Inside and Outside, plus a bin labeled "Intro & transition." This organization defines the overarching structure of the piece. There is an Intro, then you'll move Inside, then there is some sort of transition and you'll move outside.

2   Click the disclosure triangle to expand the Inside bin.

▼ 🗀 Inside			
▼ 🗀 Shopping			
▦ Bag Shopping	00:00:15;27	Not Set	Not Set
▦ Big Hat	00:00:12;03	05:12:21;04	05:12:33;06
▦ Hot Sauce	00:00:11;27	05:16:39;24	05:16:51;20
▦ Hot Sauce Bottles	00:00:02;26	05:16:15;13	05:16:18;08
▦ Maracas	00:00:01;24	05:18:07;11	05:18:09;04
▦ Postcards	00:00:09;08	05:13:04;04	05:13:13;11
▶ 🗀 Spice Vendor			
▶ 🗀 Outside			

The Inside bin has been subdivided into two sections: Shopping and Spice Vendor.

3 Watch each of the clips in the Shopping bin.

These clips have no obvious or relevant chronological order. They are merely a variety of shots of two women as they wander around the market. They could just as easily be walking around a tradeshow floor in your corporate communications piece, or exploring the lookouts and other sights at Niagara Falls State Park.

4 Expand the Spice Vendor and play each of the clips.

This footage all takes place at the spice vendor's stall. There are several elements, each of which could be edited into a mini-dramatic sequence, and the whole visit to this stall could be arranged as a scene with its own beginning, middle, and end.

5 Expand the "Intro & transition" bin and open **Establishing – market**.

This is a typical establishing shot. Although the zoom into the sign is a little clumsy, the shot succeeds in identifying the location.

Just as in dramatic scenes, you answer the *where* and *what* questions by beginning with an establishing shot, thereby providing a context for the scene to follow. This is a great place to begin your sequence.

6   Set an In point before the child crosses the road (around 05:06:31:12) and set an Out after the sign has been onscreen long enough to read (around 40:00).

7   Double-click the **Castries Market** sequence to open it into the Canvas and Timeline.

8   Edit the **Establishing – market** shot into the sequence.

9   Collapse the "Intro & transition" bin.

Constructing a Montage

Next, you will assemble a montage composed of the shots from the Inside bin. Just like assembling the interview sequence, you can begin by pulling selects and throwing them all into the Timeline. At the outset, don't worry about getting everything in the right order. You can rearrange and fine-tune things as the feel of the montage emerges.

1   Open **Bag Shopping** into the Viewer.

The camera operator built some coverage of this event right into the shot. He begins on a wide shot, zooms into a CU on the bag, and then zooms back out as the women move on. You can cut out the zooms to condense the shot, speed up the scene, and better control your audience's focus.

While you could set three sets of In and Out points and perform three edits in the Viewer, it is quicker to add the whole clip and just remove the zooms in the Timeline.

2   Set an In point after the women begin walking (around 05:11:49:18) and use the end of the media as an Out.

3   Edit the clip into the sequence following **Establishing – market**.

4   In the sequence, set an In after Sandi (in the blue shirt) lifts the bag but before she moves it to the right (around 01:00:11:00).

NOTE ▶ When referring to sequence time, be sure to look at the sequence current timecode field, and not the burned-in timecode in the Canvas window.

5   Set an Out after the camera has zoomed in, just before Sandi begins twirling the bag (around 16:24).

This will make a nice edit because the beginning of her arm movement will naturally turn into the twirling motion she makes in the CU. This is the sort of serendipitous continuity you should always be on the lookout for.

6   Deselect all and press Shift-Delete to extract the zoom.

7   Play around the edit (\).

How does it look? One minor problem is a sort of audio jump cut. Sandi's line in the close-up cuts off her own line in the long shot. This can easily be remedied by rolling the audio from the CU back to cover over the line from the LS.

8 Press R to select the Roll tool, then Option-click the audio edit and drag it left about 10 frames.

9 Press A to release the Roll tool and play around the edit again.

Cutting out that first zoom succeeds in directing focus to the colorful bag and manages to squeeze out 5 seconds. Now direct your attention to the second zoom. This one happens very quickly and actually achieves exactly what you want: a smooth transition of focus from the bag back to Sandi. So there is no reason to make another edit.

The rest of the clips in the Shopping bin have already been trimmed, so you can edit them all in as a group.

10 Select the rest of the clips in the Shopping bin and drag them into the Timeline, directly following the last clip in the sequence.

11 Press Shift-Z to see the whole sequence in the Timeline.

Now, you should choose a shot that could be used first in the sequence. This is the same dilemma you face with every new scene, no matter what the content. The most traditional approach is to move gradually from wider shots to closer ones, which, in this case, would mean looking for the widest shot of the inside of the market.

If you look at the footage available to you, both the **Bag Shopping** and the **Big Hat** shots provide a wide angle that could naturally lead you into the scene, but how can you choose between them?

If you examine them further, the background of **Bag Shopping** shows the middle of the market, while the background of **Big Hat** shows what looks like the edge of the market. The second shot is much more sparse, and you can see light coming in from the outside doorway.

Bag Shopping   Big Hat

It could be argued that **Big Hat** implies that the women have just arrived in the market, while **Bag Shopping** looks like they've been shopping for a while. In reality, none of this may be true, but you must create (and stick to) a logic for the scene that will give the viewer subtle clues about the structure of events.

12 Drag **Big Hat** to line up with the edit between **Establishing – market** and **Bag Shopping**. Before letting go of the mouse, press the Option key to perform a swap edit.

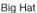

This sequence provides a great opportunity to use a dissolve effect. The dissolve will further identify this shot as the beginning of the sequence and will create an organic transition from outside the building to inside.

13 Control-click the edit point between **Establishing – market** and **Big Hat** and choose Add Transition 'Cross Dissolve'.

14 Play the sequence.

It should be obvious that the close-up of the hot sauce bottles would fit naturally as an insert in the preceding shot. Rather than spend time lining it up before editing it in, you can drop it in just about anywhere and use the Slide tool to fine-tune its placement.

15 Option-click only the video of **Hot Sauce Bottles**.

16 Release the Option key and drag the clip to the middle of the **Hot Sauce** shot.

17 Press S twice to select the Slide tool.

While you can drag the clip with the Slide tool and reposition it in the **Hot Sauce** clip, it's far more effective to play the sequence and make a decision while playing to determine where the cutaway should begin or end.

18 Play the **Hot Sauce** clip in the sequence, looking for a good place for the insert.

You don't want to begin the insert after you see Jasmin (in the black dress) reach for the bottles, because if you did, her hand logically should be visible in the insert.

This is an important concept. Even though this is a documentary, continuity errors or apparent jump cuts will still be distracting and pull viewers out of the "story." When editing this type of scene you should strive to make it feel like a dramatic scene in which all the coverage was carefully planned, and each cut was provoked and justified.

To that end, note that Sandi looks up at the sauces that Jasmin is pointing out at around 01:00:31:15. This look is a perfect cut point, making the insert serve as Sandi's POV.

19 Position the playhead at 01:00:31:15 and Option-drag **Hot Sauce Bottles** with the Slide tool until it snaps to the playhead. (If snapping isn't on, press N.)

20 Press A to release the Slide tool and press Command-Shift-A to deselect all.

Now the insert is in the right place, but the audio from that clip is still sitting there after the **Hot Sauce** clip.

21 Option-click the audio for **Hot Sauce Bottles** and press Shift-Delete to ripple delete it from the sequence.

Creating Effective Jump Cuts

The montage is beginning to take shape, but each shot of the two women appears like a jump cut as they move around the market. This style of editing is acceptable in this context, and it might play pretty well with some Caribbean music tying the scene together, but you can do better. Instead of cutting from two-shot to two-shot, you can use cutaways or different angles to smooth the edits.

Cutting montages is its own art, and often you must use the composition of shots to create effective edits. That means matching physical similarities across edits (linking two shots because they both feature strong vertical lines, for example) or deliberately juxta-posing compositional elements to emphasize the change. A jump cut is when two shots are very similar, but not exactly the same. If the shots are sufficiently different, it no longer reads as a jump cut, but as a scene change. This is why montages frequently employ techniques such as alternating close-ups and wide shots, the more extreme the better.

In this sequence, the edit from **Bag Shopping** to **Hot Sauce** is a perfect example of this problem.

This jump cut can be alleviated by inserting a different shot of the women, such as the **Maracas** shot, between the two shots.

1   Select **Maracas** and drag it to the left until it snaps to the edit between **Bag Shopping** and **Hot Sauce**. Then press Option to perform a swap edit.

2   Play across the new edit.

Technically, this is still a jump cut; it's a two-shot of the women cut against another two-shot of the women. But not only is the **Maracas** shot a little tighter, it's more on-axis, and the activity of shaking the maracas makes it very clear that this is not an accidental edit but a deliberate choice.

This edit can be greatly enhanced by using another tactic that should be old-hand by now: splitting the edit. If we begin hearing those maracas before we see them, it softens the transition and improves the edit. In fact, you can split both sides of the edit, so the sound not only leads the edit but trails into the next shot as well.

3   Press R to select the Roll tool, then Option-click the audio edit between **Bag Shopping** and **Maracas** and drag it to the left about 10 frames.

4   Option-click the audio edit between **Maracas** and **Hot Sauce** and drag right about 10 frames.

NOTE ▶ You may need to zoom in and/or turn off snapping to roll the edit effectively.

Unfortunately, the sound of those maracas is pretty loud, and the audio edits are now drawing undue attention to themselves. Both sides would benefit from audio dissolves.

5   Press A to select the Selection tool, then in the Timeline button bar, click the Link button to turn off linked selection.

6   Control-click the audio edit between **Bag Shopping** and **Maracas** and choose Add Transition 'Cross Fade (+3dB)'.

7   Control-click the audio edit between **Maracas** and **Hot Sauce** and choose Add Transition 'Cross Fade (+3dB)'.

8   Click the Link button again to turn on linked selection.

9   Press Shift-Z to zoom out the Timeline and then watch the sequence again, looking for other possible jump cuts that need addressing.

Note that the next edit between **Hot Sauce** and **Postcards** works acceptably well because the people change screen direction across the cut. Changing screen direction is another classic way to accentuate a jump cut.

Building a Scene

Within the bigger context of your event there will be many little episodes that you can edit into scenes. However, editing such material can be challenging. Typically, you will have footage from only one camera, and events aren't repeated, so there's no coverage to work with. You could let the episode play out in real time, but it's unlikely that will make for good cinema, unless the event was utterly captivating and the camera operator was extremely gifted. More likely, you'll have to find ways to abridge the scene, locating key moments and inventing a beginning, middle, and end. You will have to search for visual or content-related links to tie essential bits into a coherent whole. You may have to live with some jump cuts or awkward edits, but when done well, the content of the scene will stand out and have a flow of its own. Any subtle editorial imperfections will be overlooked.

The Spice Vendor bin contains a collection of shots from just such an episode in the Castries Market video.

1 Collapse the Shopping bin.

2 From the Spice Vendor bin, open **Spices Scene**.

   This is a long clip that shows the bulk of the scene at the spice vendor.

   The shot is very repetitive and not very entertaining. Sandi and Jasmin ask about various spices, and the vendor explains what they are. There is no beginning and no ending. How on Earth can you turn this into a scene worth watching? Well, before you panic, look at all the footage you've got to work with.

3 Play **For the Men**.

   This clip is more promising. It contains a humorous exchange about an aphrodisiac. It also starts on a nice close-up on the wood and pulls out to reveal the three women. This could prove to be a good opening for the scene.

4 Set an In point before Jasmin says, "I heard there's a myth," at 05:30:48:28 and set an Out after Sandi says, "An extra mile… Okay," around 31:09:15.

5 Overwrite this into the sequence after **Postcards**.

6 Use the Recent Clips menu to open **Spices Scene** again.

   Now that the scene has been opened, you can grab a section of this clip to fill out the middle of the scene. The opening exchange about honey is clearly not good. The beginning of the conversation is cut off, and Sandi is playing with her tongue, which is distracting.

7 Set an In point on the clean close up of Sandi around 05:26:53:20 just before she reaches forward and the camera pulls out.

Don't bother setting an Out point. You can clean up the shot in the Timeline.

8 Overwrite the clip after **For the Men**. Press Shift-Z to zoom your Timeline to fit the entire sequence.

This shot is long and repetitive, but you need to find an effective way to shorten it. The beginning is nice, and the bit about the laxative at the end is also funny, but all the spices in the middle seem virtually interchangeable.

You need to start looking for possible edit points. How can you trim a section of this clip without making a glaring jump cut? Look for physical actions within the shot that are repeated. Around 01:01:49:20 Sandi reaches offscreen for the first of several times. This reaching action could provide a cut point.

9 Set an In point at 01:01:49:20.

10 Play forward, looking for a matching action.

By 02:31:00, the camera has moved into a closer shot, and once again Sandi reaches offscreen. Because one shot is a LS and the other an MCU, and because the action is so similar, this will make a transparent edit that will succeed in eliminating a whopping 43 seconds from the scene!

11 Set an Out point at 01:02:31:00 and Shift-Delete to extract the marked section.

Naturally the audio needs to be cleaned up, but that's easy.

12 Press R to select the Roll tool, Option-click the audio edit, and drag it to the left about 2 seconds.

13 Press A to release the Roll tool, and play this whole section of the scene.

14 Open **Spices OUT**.

This is a staged shot, but it provides an ending to this scene: The women say goodbye, walk away, and even allude to the produce market outside, making for a perfect segue to the next segment.

The clip already has an In and Out point set.

15 Overwrite **Spices OUT** directly after **Spices Scene**.

16 Play around the edit (\).

Unfortunately, the edit is terrible. The new shot cuts off the action in **Spices Scene**, creating an abrupt and unpleasant transition, but it is salvageable. What you need is a cutaway to bridge the edit.

17 Open **Panning Spices**.

This is a simple cutaway shot panning across all the spices on the table. It's a perfect neutral shot that will cover up the awkward edit you just made. A section of the clip is already marked.

18 Untarget audio tracks A1 and A2, and put the sequence playhead at the beginning of the **Spices OUT** shot.

19 Overwrite **Panning Spices** into the sequence.

20 Play around the edit (\).

The cutaway helps, but something still looks awry. The screen direction of the pan contradicts the movement of Sandi's arm in the end of the spices shot. It's a subtle problem, but one that's easily fixable.

21 In the Timeline, select the **Panning Spices** shot and choose Effects > Video Filters > Perspective > Flop.

This changes the screen direction of the pan, and the cutaway is better integrated into the scene.

Defining a Pattern

While each scene you build has its own structure, you must also pay attention to its place in the framework of the whole show. It's ideal if you can find an editing pattern to repeat for each of the scenes. This gives the show an overall cohesion that makes the end product more professional and makes the story easier to follow.

For example, in this show, each section begins with a brief montage and is followed by a short dialogue scene with one of the locals. As the show progresses, viewers become increasingly familiar with the pattern, allowing them to better understand the story.

Equally important is creating a consistent technique for transitioning between sections. Such transitions can be as complex as animated title sequences or mini-montages, or they can be as simple as differently shaped wipes. The overall tone of the film is often defined by these brief interstitial moments. This is your opportunity to get really creative and incorporate multilayered motion graphics compositions or special effects.

The show in this lesson plays things safe, and the transitions between scenes are just simple cross-dissolves.

1 In the Browser, collapse the Inside bin and expand the Outside bin.

2 Open **WS Produce Market.** Set an In point after the camera begins panning at 05:34:45:00 and set an Out point as the camera stops panning around 48:00.

3   Retarget audio tracks A1 and A2, position the sequence playhead at the end of the last clip, and drag **WS Produce Market** to the Overwrite with Transition target in the Canvas Edit Overlay (or press Shift-F10).

This is a one-step method for adding a clip to the sequence and automatically adding the default transition at the head.

This clip introduces a new location: the outdoor produce market. For this sequence, the montage will be a collection of shots showing the market, followed by a short scene in which Sandi and Jasmin meet a friend who invites them to dinner. This parallels the structure of the scene inside the market, which began with the shopping montage and was followed by the short scene with the spice vendor.

4   Open **CU Tracking Produce**. Play from In to Out (Shift-\).

This is a close-up tracking shot of the local fruits. An In and Out point have already been marked.

5 Overwrite the clip into the sequence directly following **WS Produce Market**.

It's important to note that these two shots cut together well because they are both moving shots. If you let the **WS Produce Market** shot come to a standstill before cutting to **CU Tracking Produce**, you would undermine the momentum of the scene.

When a moving shot comes to a stop onscreen, it draws the viewers' focus to the stopping point. For example, if the produce shot tracked along and then came to a stop on a particular pile of bananas, the audience would assume that something important was going to happen with those bananas. If you end on the bananas, even though they hold no significance, your audience will be distracted, waiting for a "payoff" that never comes. By cutting out of these shots while they are moving, you keep the focus of the scene on the overall market rather than on one detail.

6 Open **Produce Vendor CU.** Play from In to Out (Shift-\).

The clip features a CU shot of one of the produce vendors. This is a nice transition from the broader images of the market to the specific people working there.

7 Overwrite the clip into the sequence directly following **CU Tracking Produce.**

8 Play around the edit (\).

This shot fits nicely, but that moment when someone walks past the camera can be put to much better use by moving it to the head of the clip so it helps to hide the edit. Since the clip is already in the sequence, this can be done with the Slip tool.

The Slip tool changes the In and Out points of a clip without changing the duration of that clip. So, for example, in this case it allows you to make the passerby occur earlier in the shot without disturbing the length of the shot or its position in the sequence.

9 Press S to select the Slip tool.

10 Click the **Produce Vendor CU** shot and drag it to the left. Watch the Canvas until the frame containing the passerby is just entering the left frame (about 24 frames).

NOTE ▶ You may need to zoom in on the sequence and/or disable snapping to have enough resolution to slip effectively.

Now the passerby appears right on the cut, effectively wiping the produce vendor shot onto the screen. Alternatively, you could have slipped the shot in the other direction and used the passerby to motivate the next edit.

11 Press A to release the Slip tool.

12 Open **Cutting Tuber**. Play from In to Out (Shift-\).

Again, a section of the shot has already been marked. In this case, the shot opens with the action of the vegetable being cut, then the camera tilts up to the woman doing the cutting.

13 Overwrite the clip into the sequence directly following **Produce Vendor CU.**

14 Play across this entire section.

This completes this brief montage. Remember that it may seem easy to find good shots like these, but in the real world you would likely have to scour through several hours of footage to find these 3-second nuggets—and they're easy to miss. Always be on the lookout for movement within the frame or brief moments where the camera comes upon a nice framing of the subject at hand.

Although you don't need to edit the entire next section, it will be helpful to add one more clip to introduce it.

15 Expand the Friend bin and open **Encountering Friend**. Overwrite the clip into the sequence directly following **Cutting Tuber**.

16 Press Shift-Z to view the entire sequence in the Timeline.

17 Play the entire sequence.

Incorporating Narration

You can see how the entire sequence is coming together, and it makes even more sense in the context of the rest of the show. But event documentaries like this frequently can benefit from a bit of narration to tie the story together and provide additional background or context. When a 30-hour event is compressed into a 30-minute show, it often helps to have someone explain what had to be cut out. Narration also allows you to provide a tour guide for the event being documented. The narrator gives a point of entry for the viewer: someone to trust and provide a personal perspective on the film.

Narrations don't always help a show. A narration that just says aloud what is obvious in the images only distracts the audience with unnecessary redundancy. Furthermore, a narration is a performance. A poor or inappropriate performance can hurt a documentary just as much as bad acting can ruin a drama.

Narrations are done in two ways. In one approach, the narration is written first like a script, and the show is edited to fit the words and phrases it contains. In the second, the show is cut first, and the narrator watches the final cut and provides commentary to supplement the edit. From an editor's standpoint, the former is handled much like the interviews described in Lesson 6. For the latter, it's just a matter of dropping in the narration and perhaps making minor editorial adjustments to integrate it into the edit.

1 In the Browser, expand the "Intro & transition" bin and inside that, expand the Narration bin.

2 Open and play **Jasmin's Friend VO.aif.**

3 In the Viewer, press Shift-Z to fit the entire audio clip into view.

4 Set an In right before her first word and an Out right after her last word. You can use the visual waveforms as a guide.

5 In the sequence, find the place in the last clip when Jasmin says, "Hey Allison." Set an Out point before she starts speaking (around 01:02:47:20).

6 Target the audio track to A3 and overwrite the voiceover (VO) clip into the sequence.

You certainly will want to spend more time finessing the audio levels later, and the whole sequence will likely have music mixed in. For now, you at least need to lower the level on the montage clips to hear the VO.

You can turn on clip overlays and use the rubberbands to lower the levels, but there is a quicker, more efficient way to change audio levels on multiple clips at once.

7   Select the four clips from the second montage.

8   Choose Modify > Levels or press Command-Option-L.

The Gain Adjust window opens.

9   Set the slider to *-12* and in the Make Changes pop-up menu, choose Absolute.

10   Click OK to close the window.

The selected clips all have their audio levels reduced to –12dB.

11   Play across the section to hear how well the narration complements the scene.

This gives you a sense of how narration can improve the overall feel of your sequence. There are two other VO clips in the narration folder. You can experiment with working them into the earlier part of the sequence.

Experiment with Additional Footage

There are additional clips in the "Intro & transition" bin that provide options for opening the sequence and transitioning from inside to outside. Experiment with ways you can construct this sequence and tell different versions of the same story.

More than most other types of shows, event documentaries are very flexible and can be edited in almost unlimited ways. This chapter illustrates just a few of the important characteristics that make event documentaries successful.

Lesson Review

1. What are three ways of organizing footage from an event documentary?
2. What makes a jump cut work?
3. How do you create the beginning of a scene?
4. How do you create a dissolve between clips?
5. How do inserts and cutaways figure into documentary editing?
6. What is an editorial pattern?
7. What is the advantage of the Slip tool?
8. Describe a one-step method for inserting a clip with a transition.
9. What is the purpose of interstitial elements?
10. How can you simultaneously change audio levels on multiple clips?
11. How can narration improve an event documentary?

Answers

1. Chronologically, by subject, or by theme.
2. Juxtaposing compositional elements in the frame.
3. Show people entering a location or a frame, use wide shots that introduce a setting, or use doors opening or other metaphorical images.
4. Control-click the edit point between clips and choose Add Transition 'Cross Dissolve'.
5. Inserts and cutaways are essential for covering jump cuts and making scenes feel more narrative.
6. Repeating certain structures in every segment of your show, such as montages, consistent uses of wide shots or close-ups, moving cameras, music, or recognizable pacing.
7. The Slip tool changes the In and Out points of a clip without changing the duration of that clip, which allows you to change the contents of a shot without disturbing its length or its position in the sequence.
8. Drag a clip to the Overwrite with Transition or Insert with Transition targets in the Canvas Edit Overlay.
9. The connective tissue between main segments gives you an opportunity to incorporate stylistic elements to add flavor and flair.
10. Select the clips, then choose Modify > Levels or press Command-Option-L. Gain adjustment is applied to the selected clips.
11. Narration can provide a human voice or point of view for the audience to identify with.

9

Lesson Files	Lesson Files > Lesson 09 > MusicVideo
Media	Media > SweetSound Music Video
Time	This lesson takes approximately 60 minutes to complete.
Goals	Understand the difference between editing music videos and editing other formats
	Sync lip-synced video clips to prerecorded audio
	Use Gang Sync to ease editing of time-locked material
	Use the Roll tool to adjust positions of clips in a sequence
	Incorporate B-roll into a music video context
	Line up edits with musical beats using dynamic trimming

Lesson 9
Music Videos

The music video format is one of the most flexible and exciting types of shows that an editor gets the opportunity to cut. All the rules described in earlier lessons are "up for grabs" because the goal of cutting a music video is fundamentally different from most other projects. In a music video, the picture is there to serve and supplement the sound, and this means that the usual rules related to continuity, coherence, and plot are supplanted by an emphasis on mood and tone.

This lesson covers some of the techniques frequently employed in music video editing, specifically focusing on the common scenarios of performers appearing in multiple locations and incorporating seemingly unrelated elements that nonetheless help to emphasize the tone of the song.

Understanding Technique and Approach

While the freeform creativity of editing a music video means there are fewer ways to make traditional "mistakes," it also means you have less structure to guide you in your editing decisions. We've all seen music videos that work; they are fun to watch, they complement the song, and generate enthusiasm and support for the artist. Most importantly, they are memorable and engaging. You've also probably seen music videos that don't work. They feel gimmicky and trite. Sometimes they halfheartedly try to tell a story, or sometimes they are so promotional that they look and feel like an advertisement.

Like other shows, the problems with a bad music video often aren't the editor's fault, but it's still the editor's job to make the best finished piece she can with what she's given. And the unstructured nature of music videos makes it possible to completely reconceive them in the edit room.

Emphasize Tone

Perhaps the single most important rule to keep in mind is that the key to a successful music video lies in identifying and incorporating the tone and mood of the song and reflecting that in the images and editing style you impart. Bouncy, upbeat songs lend themselves to brighter imagery, rhythmic pacing, and jump cuts. Somber, slower songs typically call for slower cutting, moving camera work, and longer shots. Of course, these are just suggestions. The specific song (and corresponding footage) will determine how you should approach your project.

Serve the Audio

One of the things that makes music video cutting deceptively easy is that there is basically no audio editing to worry about. The soundtrack is prerecorded and not malleable. You can literally lock the music track and focus entirely on picture. Of course, the downside to this is that manipulating your soundtrack is one of the most powerful secret weapons in the editor's arsenal. In a music video, you have to work with (or work around) the existing audio. Remember, the picture is merely a way to enhance and complement the track.

1   Open **MusicVideo**.

This is the project for a music video called *Sweet Sound*. In this lesson, you will focus on only one portion of the song at a time.

2 Double-click the *First Verse* sequence to open it into the Canvas and Timeline.

This sequence already contains a short portion of the song.

3 Click the Lock Track control for audio tracks 1 and 2.

It is pretty much a given that you can begin any music video sequence by laying in the music track and locking the tracks.

Examine the Footage

Like any other project, effective music video editing is predicated on a thorough and comprehensive understanding of the source footage. With music videos, you may have the opportunity to juxtapose footage from completely different scenes and even use bits of footage from the heads and tails of shots or "bad" takes that ordinarily would be considered useless footage due to camera errors or light flashes. This makes it all the more essential to meticulously review all of your source footage.

The first thing to check out is the song that you'll be cutting to.

1 Press the Spacebar to play the song.

What do you think? Whether or not it's your musical cup of tea is not relevant. What's important is identifying the feeling the song evokes and how you can enhance that feeling editorially.

Of course, there's no right or wrong answer. You might latch on to one particular aspect of the song—the vaguely Latin beat, for instance, or the eerie guitar synth sounds that undermine an otherwise upbeat melody. Or, you might pay special attention to the lyrics.

Now, while retaining those thoughts and impressions in your head, it's time to check out the video files. This project has two bins of footage. One bin is labeled B-Roll and the other is labeled Lip-sync.

2 Double-click the Lip-sync bin to open it in its own window.

The production crew recorded the vocalist in a variety of locations. By stitching these locations together, you will create the backbone of the video.

3 Open and shuttle through a couple of the clips to get a sense of the footage you will be working with.

4 Close the Lip-sync bin and double-click the B-Roll bin to open it in its own window.

5   Open and shuttle through a couple of these clips to get a sense of them.

You can see that the overall tone of the footage is rural and rustic. Although the footage maintains a consistent tone and style, there aren't many narrative or continuity-based elements. The painter shots offer an opportunity for a little bit of storytelling, but only in an abstract manner.

6   Close the B-Roll bin.

Syncing the Video

As with most music videos, no audio exists on these video clips. During production, the song was played back on a timecode-capable DAT deck and the camera photographed a smart-slate at the head of each shot. That way it's very easy to precisely sync the clips to the music.

1   In the Lip-sync bin, double-click **MCU Static woods** to open it into the Viewer.

The slate shows the timecode from the audio playback device, but the timecode in the Current Timecode field has a completely different number. That number is the actual timecode on the videotape from which the clip was captured.

To take advantage of the timecode information that the slate provides, you need to view it in the Current Timecode field.

2 Choose Modify > Timecode.

The Modify Timecode window appears. The Source TC fields show the original timecode. It's very important not to alter that; otherwise you may never be able to recapture the clip properly.

To add the slate's timecode to the clip, you must add an auxiliary timecode track. This way you can use two different timecode values for the clip.

3   Select the checkbox next to Aux TC 1.

4   Make sure that the Frame To Set pop-up menu at the top of the window is set to Current.

This indicates that you are establishing the new timecode value based on the current frame position, rather than the first frame of the clip.

5   Enter *Music TC* in the Reel/Roll field and, in the Timecode field, enter the timecode visible on the slate. In this case, enter *00010215*.

NOTE ▶ You may need to move the Modify Timecode window out of the way to see the image in the Viewer.

6   In the Format pop-up menu, choose Non-Drop Frame, and in the Rate pop-up menu, choose 30.

7   Click OK to close the window.

The clip now stores the music timecode in the Aux 1 track, but the Viewer is still showing the Source timecode in the Current Timecode field.

8   Control-click the Current Timecode field and from the shortcut menu choose Aux TC 1.

Now you can view the music timecode for any frame in the clip, which will make it easy to sync it to the music track.

Preparing to Edit

Once you have made sure that all of your clips are prepared and properly synced to the music track, getting started is simple. For this lesson, the first verse of the song has been isolated in the *First Verse* sequence.

Although the music clip has the same timecode as your clips, the sequence begins at 01:00:00:00. Editing in the video clips is a lot easier when the sequence timecode matches the music timecode.

If your music timecode begins at or around the sequence timecode, you can simply line it up with the matching number, but in this case it doesn't.

One trick to working around this timecode discrepancy is to temporarily set the sequence timecode to match the music timecode. To do that, you need to identify the timecode of the first frame of music used in this sequence.

1   Press the Up Arrow to move the playhead to the first frame of the clip.

2   Choose View > Match Frame > Master Clip, or press the F key.

The master clip is loaded into the Viewer at the current frame. The number in the Current Timecode field is the number you are looking for (00:01:11:15).

3   Select the Current Timecode field and choose Edit > Copy (Command-C).

4   Click the Canvas or Timeline to give the sequence focus.

5   Choose Sequence > Settings and click the Timeline Options tab.

Sequence Settings

Name: First Verse

General \ Video Processing \ Timeline Options \ Render Control \ Audio Outputs

Starting Timecode: `01:00:00:00` ☑ Drop Frame

Track Size: Custom ▾

Thumbnail Display: Name Plus Thumbnail ▾

Audio Track Labels: Sequential (A1, A2, A3, A4) ▾

Track Display
- ☐ Show Keyframe Overlays
- ☐ Show Audio Waveforms
- ☑ Show Through Edits
- ☐ Show Duplicate Frames
- ☐ Show Audio Controls

☐ Clip Keyframes

Video:
- ☑ Motion Bar
- ☑ Filters Bar
- ☑ Keyframe Editor
- ☑ Speed Indicators

Audio:
- ☑ Filters Bar
- ☑ Keyframe Editor
- ☑ Speed Indicators

Load Sequence Preset...   Cancel   OK

6   Press Command-V to paste the timecode value into the Starting Timecode field.

General \ Video Processing \ Timeline Options \ Render Control \ Audio Outputs

Starting Timecode: `00:01:11:15` ☐ Drop Frame

Track Size: Custom ▾

7   Click the Drop Frame checkbox to deselect it and click OK to close the window.

Now the music timecode is represented in the Timeline ruler and in the Current Timecode indicators in the Timeline and Canvas.

TIP   Remember that if you plan to output this sequence to tape, you may want to reset the sequence timecode when you're done editing.

Beginning to Edit

The sequence timecode now matches the music timecode, and it's time to lay in some video clips. In many cases, you'll have storyboards or other guidance from the director;

but, in this case, the director has left the creative decisions up to you. With all that freedom, where do you start?

1   In the Lip-sync bin, double-click the **MCU Guitar** clip to open it into the Viewer.

You'll use this clip as your "base" track. You could have chosen one of the other shots, but this one seems to capture the essence of the song better than the others.

2   Click the Canvas window to make it active, and then press Home to ensure that the playhead is on the first frame of the sequence.

3   Option-drag the timecode from the Canvas Current Timecode field to the Current Timecode field in the Viewer.

This is a quick trick to automatically move a timecode value from one field to another. It works in any timecode field in Final Cut Pro. In this case, it causes the Viewer play-head to move to the frame that matches the audio in the first frame of the sequence.

4   In the Viewer, press the I key to set an In point at the playhead position.

5   Enter *2916* in the Viewer Duration field to set an Out point.

6 Drag the clip from Viewer to Canvas to perform a basic overwrite edit.

7 Play the sequence to verify that the video and audio are in sync.

8 In the Lip-sync bin, double-click **MCU Static woods** to open it into the Viewer.

Since you've already added matching timecode to this clip, you can edit it into the sequence virtually anywhere and remain in sync, as long as you begin the edit on a matching frame.

9 In the Current Timecode field in the Viewer, enter *1.22.00* (with no trailing period).

10 Set an In point on that frame.

11 Option-drag the timecode from the Current Timecode field in the Viewer to the Current Timecode field in the Canvas.

12 Set an In point on that frame in the sequence.

NOTE ▶ You may have to click the Canvas or Timeline windows to make them active before you can set a sequence In point.

13 Play the sequence forward about five seconds until just after the vocalist sings the lyrics "learn to unwind" and set an Out point there.

14 Press F10 or drag the Source clip onto the Overwrite target in the Canvas Edit Overlay.

15 Play the sequence to see how your new clip fits.

Using Gang Sync to Simplify Edits

One of the delightful things about cutting material in which the action matches perfectly in every shot is that there are so many shortcuts and tools to aid in editing. One of those tools is the Gang Sync feature, which locks the Viewer and Canvas playheads together so if you move one, the other follows along.

1 Place your sequence playhead anywhere over the **MCU Static woods** clip.

2   Press the F key to perform a match frame, thereby opening the master **Static Woods** clip into the Viewer, with the playhead parked on that frame.

3   In either the Viewer or Canvas, click the Playhead Sync menu button and choose Gang.

With the Viewer and Canvas ganged together, the two windows move in tandem. This makes it easy to edit another section of this clip into the sequence, while ensuring that the new section will automatically be in sync.

4   Play the sequence forward until about 00:01:31:00 (after the vocalist sings the lyric "feeling better than good") and set an In point.

The Viewer is automatically cued to the matching frame.

5   Set an In point in the Viewer.

6   In the Canvas, play forward until the vocalist sings the lyric "enough to go there" (at approximately 00:01:36:00) and set an Out point.

7   Overwrite the clip into the sequence.

8   Play the sequence to see how your edits look.

Next, you'll add one more sync clip to the sequence. This one has been pre-marked to speed up this lesson.

9 Open **MCU in front of painter** into the Viewer.

This clip already has an In and Out point selected. But before you can edit it into the sequence, you need to make sure that the clip timecode matches the sequence.

10 Play the clip from In to Out (Shift -\).

11 Option-drag the Current Timecode timecode from the Viewer to the Canvas.

The timecode represents the Out point in the Viewer, so in order to make the edit line up properly, set an Out point on that frame in the Canvas.

12 Overwrite the clip into the sequence and play it back to ensure that everything is correctly in sync.

Using Roll Edit to Finesse Edits

Another advantage to knowing that all of your clips will always be in sync, no matter where you put them, is that you can easily roll any edit point without causing problems. In this way, you can even move clips to an entirely new position by rolling the edits on both sides of the clip.

1 From the toolbar, choose the Roll tool, or press the R key.

2 Roll the end of the **MCU in front of painter** clip to the right about two seconds.

You may agree that the edit is stronger when it occurs mid-phrase, rather than neatly between words or phrases. This is just like splitting edits in dialogue scenes. Moving the picture edits off the natural sound edits (in this case, the phrases of the lyrics) helps to both hide the edit and to make the juxtaposition more striking.

Another way to roll an edit is to use the Extend Edit command.

3 Select the next edit between **MCU Guitar** and **MCU Static woods** midway through the sequence.

4 Play the sequence forward, stopping right in the middle of the word "breath" (at approximately 00:01:22:23).

5   Press the E key to perform an extend edit.

This automatically rolls the edit to the current playhead position.

You can extend an edit forward or backward. So, if you don't like the resulting edit, just move the playhead to a new position and press E again.

Best of all, extend edit can be used *while the playhead is moving*, allowing you to perform one type of dynamic trimming without even opening the Trim Edit window.

6   Experiment with rolling the other edit points in the sequence.

There is no right or wrong edit and, as you'll see, the vocalist is always in perfect sync.

Adding B-roll Elements

Now it's time to add some of the supplemental, textural elements to enhance the video. Remember that the purpose of a music video is to entrance the viewer by reflecting the mood and tone of the song. This affords you tremendous flexibility. Simply put, you can drop these B-roll elements in nearly anywhere and they'll probably work.

In addition, this is one of the rare cases that I would recommend using a second video track.

1   In the Timeline, Control-click the track header area above track V1 and choose Add Track.

2 Drag the Source target to V2.

The next clips you edit into the sequence will go onto that new track.

3 From the B-Roll bin, open the **Painter Misc** clip B-roll and press Shift-\ to play from In to Out.

This clip contains a variety of angles of the painter. For this exercise, In and Out points have already been chosen, but feel free to ignore them and choose your own.

Although you can probably drop this clip anywhere into the sequence without ruining the video, it might be more effective in one place than another. Because the painter is introduced in shot two, it makes sense to add this clip somewhere after that point. In this case, you'll add it midway through that shot.

4 Drag the clip from the Viewer directly to the Timeline, dropping it onto track V2, above the second half of the **MCU in front of painter** shot, aligning its Out point with the existing Out in the sequence.

NOTE ▶ You may need to enable snapping (N) to align the clip precisely.

5   Play around the new clip in the sequence.

6   Now open **MS Woodswalk** from the B-Roll bin.

7   Press Shift-\ to play In to Out.

Notice that the marked area features the woman coming into focus. In other types of shows, this section might be discarded as junk; but here, that shift from out of focus to in focus articulates the sultry tone of the music and is a perfect part of the shot to use.

Again, choosing where to add this shot to the show is fairly loose, but it seems safe (or at least consistent) to show it after the forest has been introduced in the singing shot.

8   Set an In point in the sequence midway through the first **MCU Static woods** shot (at approximately 00:01:25:00).

9   Drag the source clip to the Canvas to overwrite it into the sequence.

10 In the Viewer, play the clip forward until the section where the vocalist is obscured by a tree due to the camera move.

Entrances and exits always make for good edit points, and this sort of in-camera "exit" is no exception.

11 Set an In and Out point around that section, beginning at approximately 00:02:15:00 and ending about three seconds later.

12 Edit this clip into the sequence about midway through the second **MCU Guitar** shot (around 00:01:29:00).

13 Play your sequence.

It's coming along. You can see that as the B-roll is added, the show becomes more interesting, and the mood and tone emerge as the threads that tie the pieces together.

Fixing (Human) Errors

You'll add one more piece of B-roll, only this time it will be for a practical reason. When editing music videos, you often can bend the usually inflexible rules of continuity and storytelling, but you can't easily ignore sync errors.

Although the timecode guarantees that the shots should all be in sync, that doesn't take into account the possibility of human error. The vocalist has to lip-sync the song again and again, and occasionally she might flub a line or maybe even sing it in a slightly different way that doesn't look quite right.

That kind of event occurs at the beginning of the second shot where the vocalist sings the lyric "you'll come around." It's not exactly out of sync, but it just doesn't look right. Using a piece of B-roll, you can cover that up, as well as open the section with a shot to emphasize a certain mood, thereby improving the video overall.

1   From the B-Roll bin, open the **Swinging Park** B-roll.

This shot shows yet another location, but it also introduces a bit of playfulness that helps to brighten the overall tone of the video from its somewhat somber palette. In this case, the shot will help you control the tone of the piece, not just reflect it.

2   Drop the **Swinging Park** shot onto track V2, beginning right at the head of the sequence.

3   Play the entire sequence.

Finding the Beat

This sequence is by no means finished. You could easily add several more B-roll shots and continue to tweak the edits points. However, one easy way to make the video feel just a bit more professional is to adjust each edit point to ensure that it lands precisely on the musical beats.

To do this, you must, of course, find the beats. While some music software can automatically detect beats, when using Final Cut Pro, you must do this manually.

1   Unlock the music tracks.

2   Select the audio clip in the Timeline and press the Home key to move the playhead to the beginning of the sequence.

3 Play the sequence and, as you hear each beat, tap the M key to add a marker on that frame.

 This often works best if you close your eyes while listening.

4 After you've completed the sequence, listen to it again, and watch to see if the markers look like they're positioned accurately at each musical beat. You can also visually note if they appear evenly spaced in the track.

If you want to try again, just press Control-~ (tilde) to delete all markers and start over. It might take you a few tries to feel confident, but once you get the rhythmic hang of it, it's pretty easy to mark the beats accurately (or close enough).

When the beats are marked, you're ready to adjust the edits so they land directly on those beats.

5 Zoom in to the first edit point.

Make sure snapping is turned on.

6   Drag the edge of the **Swinging Park** clip until it snaps to the nearest marker.

7   Press the Down Arrow to jump to the next edit.

8   Drag the edge of the **Painter Misc** clip to line up with the nearest marker.

9   Press the Down Arrow again, and adjust the Out point of the **Painter Misc** clip.

10 Press the Down Arrow again and use the Roll tool to adjust the next edit so that it snaps to the nearest marker.

11 Press the Down Arrow again and repeat the same steps for each edit.

In some cases, you may have clips on V2 that are obscuring edit points on V1. If so, be sure to align the clip on V2 with the marker. The edit on V1 is irrelevant.

12 When you're done, go back and watch the whole show.

Pretty cool, huh? It's fun to have the video move along with the music so tightly. You can amplify this effect by making all of the shots the same length (for example, exactly one measure, or half a measure).

While editing directly on the beat gives your show a satisfyingly uniform rhythm, remember that it's not a requirement. Some music videos beg for more rhythmic cutting, and some work better when cut irregularly. You might cut a song's chorus on the beat and the verses off the beat. Or cut on the beat again and again, and then finally break the pattern to add extra emphasis to one shot. You might consistently cut on the upbeat instead of the downbeat.

Using Effects

Music videos are continually evolving. New ideas and techniques are being introduced all the time. Frequently, a variety of special effects find their way into music videos. Just like editing, these effects should be motivated by the style, tone, and mood of the song. You'll commonly find effects such as step-editing (removing frames), ramp speed effects, and complex color correction effects that can all be accomplished right in your Final Cut Pro sequence.

Lesson Review

1. What is the overriding guiding principle for editing music videos?
2. How do you assign new timecode to a clip to match an onscreen slate?
3. How do you set sequence timecode to match a clip's timecode?
4. When are roll edits useful with dealing with music video footage?
5. How can you quickly move a timecode value from one field to another?
6. What would you use to lock the Viewer and sequence playheads together, and when would you do this?
7. Describe a method for marking musical beats in Final Cut Pro.

Answers

1. Cut for tone and feeling instead of story and continuity.

2. Choose Modify > Timecode, create an auxiliary timecode track, and enter the data from the slate.

3. In Sequence Settings, copy the timecode from the clip's first used frame into the Starting Timecode field.

4. Because the footage has identical timing on both sides of the edit, you can roll with impunity.

5. Option-drag it.

6. Use Gang Sync. When the timing of the clip in the Viewer matches that of the sequence and the two are ganged together, you can line up new edits automatically.

7. While playing a clip (preferably with your eyes closed to improve concentration), press M as you hear each beat to place a marker at that point in the sequence.

Working with Audio

10

Lesson 10
Sound Design

If seeing is believing, then perhaps hearing is feeling. While the visual component of your show contains the information and hard details of the story, it is the subtle combination of voices, sound effects, and music that are woven together to create a tapestry of emotion and tone.

A film's soundtrack is often the indicator of its level of professionalism and quality. Amateur filmmakers finish cutting their picture and call it done. For professionals, *locking* picture is only the beginning of a new phase of postproduction.

On professional shows, every line of dialogue is organized, balanced, equalized, and filtered; ambiances are constructed for each scene, usually composed of many different sources; sound effects are inserted for every justifiable onscreen activity that might make a sound; and, finally, music is mixed to complement and supplement the other components.

Waiting Until the Picture Is Locked

While you typically do a fair amount of sound editing during the picture editing process, it's wise to save the bulk of the sound editing for the last step. For example, take a simple case in which a shot has audio that fades in at the beginning and fades out at the end.

If later in the editing process you wind up tweaking that edit and shortening the clip by five frames, you will have to completely rebuild your fade-out.

If it only happens occasionally, this isn't a big deal, but it can amount to a significant amount of duplicated effort over the course of an entire show. This is especially true because by the time your show is complete, every single audio clip in your sequence should have a tiny fade at the beginning and end.

Furthermore, during the sound editing process you will add hundreds of tiny sound effects files. Keeping track of these and making sure they remain in sync with every edit is a headache you can easily avoid by waiting until picture is locked before beginning the whole process.

As you get serious about your sound, you will begin to add a large number of audio tracks to your project. Professional sound editors will put each character's dialogue on a separate track, in addition to allocating a few tracks for ambiances, a few more for specific sound effects, and a few more for music. These quickly add up, and editing a scene while carrying around dozens or even scores of audio tracks will really slow you down.

Traditionally, sound editing was done by a different person and on a different system than picture editing. Although this method of working is disappearing, it had many benefits. Sound editing is a specialized art and, in many ways, a totally different type of skill than picture (or story) editing. This may seem surprising. Picture editors are constantly making changes to the sound tracks, so aren't they inherently good sound editors? While picture editing is about taking things away—"eliminating the bad bits," as famed film and sound editor Walter Murch calls it—sound editing is all about adding things back in.

Sound editors layer dozens of discrete sounds to create a single effect, and they do this for every moment of every scene. Effectively matching sounds to pictures is not always an obvious process. It takes a special talent to look at a shot of a person getting stabbed and think of the sound of slicing watermelons, or to match images of tornadoes with sloweddown lion roars. Sound editors are constantly recording things, adding to their libraries. In fact, in the sound world, editors boast about the size of their effects collections, or about the most bizarre sounds they've recorded. Picture editors are storytellers. Sound editors are designers.

Sound editing is usually broken into six stages. First, the dialogue is cleaned up and optimized; then ambiances are made for each scene; sound effects are then added; sound design elements are built and added; music is added; and finally, all of the elements are pulled together in a final mix.

Editing Dialogue

Almost all movies contain human voices. The voice communicates information, emotion, and can elicit an almost unlimited variety of responses in the listener. Our ears are specially tuned to hear and understand human speech, and we are very susceptible to barely perceptible changes in pacing, timbre, or volume. This incredible sensitivity translates into a special challenge for editors seeking to keep viewers caught up in the story and not distracted by tiny audio mistakes created by poor sound recording or editing.

Fortunately, there are many tools designed to improve the quality of recorded voices. Final Cut Pro includes one audio filter solely designed to remove unwanted pops that can occur when a microphone is placed too close to the speaker's mouth (Vocal DePopper), and another to remove excessive sibilance (the Sssss-sound) that can occur during recording (Vocal DeEsser).

Soundtrack Pro features a variety of other dialogue-oriented tools, including sophisticated equalization, a variety of reverbs to help match a voice to an environment, and a filter that can speed up or slow down the delivery of a line without generating a give-away pitch change. Countless third-party audio tools and plug-ins are available that can improve the quality of recorded voices depending on the problem you are facing.

Even so, don't rely on your ability to "fix it in post." If the microphone was too far away from the subject, or the background noise level was too high during recording, there is often nothing you can do to salvage the audio. In those cases (and they happen all the time, even on professional shows), the audio has to be re-recorded in a studio.

Like other lessons in this book, this one uses a dramatic scene as an example, but the concepts and techniques are just as applicable to nonfiction works. Documentaries need just as much sound design and finessing as narrative films.

1   Open **SoundDesign**.

    A sequence called *Showdown Sequence* is already open that contains a completed edit of the Friends of the Family project.

2   Play through the sequence.

    When you finished Lesson 3, you left this sequence in need of some serious sound work. Now you'll have the chance to finish that job.

Organizing Your Tracks

Dialogue editors make a point of isolating each character's voice onto its own track. This is because traditional sound mixing equipment can give each track its own equalization and filters. So, all of a character's lines can have the same sound settings and, if you want to modify those settings, you only need to make adjustments once. While Final Cut Pro doesn't have this ability internally, separating the clips this way still helps for organizational purposes. Plus, Soundtrack Pro does have track-level filtering and track bussing, so for projects that will be mixed in Soundtrack Pro, doing this work saves time down the road.

Fortunately, in this project, you previously chopped up most of the dialogue lines into their own clips, so separating them will be easy. Since Pedro has more lines than Andy, leave Pedro's lines on tracks 1 and 2 and put Andy's on tracks 3 and 4.

At around 28 seconds, Pedro says his first line, "So what's up?" At 29:18 Andy says, "We gonna do this?"

3 Zoom into that section of the Timeline.

4 Option-click the audio for **MCU Andy OTS Pedro_02** to select it.

5 Shift-drag the clips to tracks 3 and 4.

Pressing Shift constrains the horizontal movement so the clips will remain in sync with the picture.

6 Skip to the next lines at around 42 seconds.

The first line is Andy's, so you'll move it to tracks 3 and 4.

7 Option-click the audio for **G2 MS OTS Group1_02** to select it.

8 Shift-drag the clips to tracks 3 and 4.

NOTE ▶ Be sure to release the Option key or you might accidentally copy the clip instead of moving it.

The next line is Pedro's so you can leave it alone. After that, they each have a line, but those lines are part of the same clip.

9 Press B to select the Blade tool.

10 Press Option and click to add an audio-only edit after Andy says, "All right, let's go," at about 45:23.

11 Option-click again to add another audio-only edit after Pedro says, "Let's go," at 46:15.

12 Press A to select the Selection tool and Option-click the audio of Andy's line (the first part) and drag it to tracks 3 and 4.

You've successfully separated Andy's lines and moved them to tracks 3 and 4; but it's hard to locate Pedro's lines because all the other audio clips are still on tracks 1 and 2.

13 Press Shift-Z to fit the whole sequence into the window, and Option-drag a marquee around the audio for all the clips from the head of the sequence up until the first shot containing Pedro's line.

It's easy to find Pedro's first line, because it's the first clip before Andy's line on tracks 3 and 4.

14 Shift-drag the selected audio clips down to the space below tracks 3 and 4.

New tracks automatically appear to accommodate the clips.

15 Option-drag a marquee around the audio for all the clips between "Si, mon" at 31:21 and "Hey, man, I'm out of formula" at 42:11.

16 Shift-drag the selected audio clips down to tracks 5 and 6.

17 Option-click the audio from the end of the last clip (**Overhead LS tilt to walk away_01**).

18 Shift-drag the clip to tracks 5 and 6.

Softening the Edges

Audio clips with abrupt beginnings or endings are undesirable. At worst, they can cause pops or distortions. At best, they create subtle shifts in the tone of the soundtrack that are potentially distracting and unwanted.

Every single piece of audio should be faded in and faded out, even if the fades are short in duration. As part of your sound-editing pass, you should apply fades to all of your audio clips.

1 Zoom all the way in on the first line of dialogue in clip **G1 MS OTS Group2_04**—Pedro's "So what's up?"—at around 28 seconds.

2 Press Option-W to turn on clip overlays.

3   Option-click the level envelope just as the "s" from "So" becomes audible at around 28:06.

4   Option-click to add another keyframe near the head of the clip and drag it down to –inf dB to create a fade-in.

> **TIP**   Sometimes when adding or adjusting keyframes near the edges of clips your pointer may accidentally select the edge of the clip instead of the keyframe. This can be overcome by zooming in further or by using the Pen tool (P).

5   Press Down Arrow twice to move your playhead to the end of the clip.

6   Use the same technique of adding keyframes to create a fade-out.

Rather than repeating this process for every single clip, you can use a shortcut: paste attributes.

7   Select the clip (**G1 MS OTS Group2_04**) that you just faded in and out and press Command-C to copy it to the clipboard.

8   Select all of the other audio clips on tracks 1, 2, 3, and 4.

9 Choose Edit > Paste Attributes or press Option-V.

The Paste Attributes dialog opens.

10 Make sure Scale Attribute Times is selected, and select the Audio Levels checkbox, then click OK.

A similar fade-in and fade-out is applied to all the other clips. Because the Scale Attribute Times setting was active, the duration of the fades will be adjusted to the relative duration of each clip.

11 Play the sequence and check that none of the fades have accidentally cut off any words at the beginning and end of the clips.

12 If any words have been cut off, zoom in and manually fix the keyframes as needed.

Normalizing Levels

One of the most important adjustments you need to make is to ensure that the dialogue clips are all at approximately the same apparent volume level. One way to do this is to *normalize* all the clips to a similar level.

Normalization is a special type of audio level adjustment with which Final Cut Pro scans each clip and boosts or attenuates the entire clip to ensure that its loudest point (or *peak*) is set to a specified level. By normalizing a group of clips to the same value, they will all sound approximately the same volume.

1 Select all the clips on tracks 1, 2, 3, and 4.

2 Choose Modify > Audio > Apply Normalization Gain.

   The Apply Normalization Gain dialog opens.

3 Set the Normalize To slider to −12dBFS, and click OK.

   Each clip is now adjusted so that the loudest section is at exactly −12dB.

4 Play the sequence.

   The mixed volumes should seem approximately the same. But how did it work? The clips have each been changed, but the level envelopes do not seem to have been affected—they still show the fade-ins and Fade-outs you set earlier.

   Normalization in Final Cut Pro uses an audio filter to modify the clip's level.

5 Double-click the audio clip **G1 MS OTS Group2_04**.

   The clip opens into the Viewer.

6   Click the Filters tab.

A Gain filter has been applied and set to −7.11. That value was determined automatically to achieve the normalization value you specified in step 3.

7   Double-click the audio clip **MCU Andy OTS Pedro_02**.

The clip is opened into the Viewer, and automatically opened to the Filters tab. This clip has a different gain setting: −10.84 because the source clip had a louder peak than the previous clip.

One great advantage to this method is that you can still use the regular audio level setting for fades or other relative modifications.

One disadvantage to normalization is that, because it works only by examining a clip's peak level, it may not give perfect results every time. An audio clip might have only one very loud sound and the rest of it remains very quiet. Normalization also doesn't account for the difference in *perceived* volumes that different clips may exhibit. Often, higher pitched sounds *seem* louder than lower pitched ones—even at the same measured levels.

This effect is compounded by your audience's listening environment. Someone watching a film on a computer screen with $15 headphones is going to have a very different listening experience from someone watching it in a movie theater with 1000-watt speakers. It's important for you to consider such matters when determining your intended audio levels. For more information on perceived audio levels and how to accommodate different viewing environments, see Lesson 11, "Audio Finishing."

Filtering Dialogue

No matter how well the dialogue was recorded, a little bit of equalization, compression, or noise reduction can do wonders to make it sound punchier and clearer. This is often referred to as *sweetening*.

1 Navigate to Pedro's first line in **G1 MS OTS Group2_04** at 28 seconds and park the playhead anywhere within the clip.

2 Turn off Auto Select for track V1 and press X to mark the audio clip.

3 Choose View > Loop Playback or press Control-L.

Now, when you play from In to Out, the sequence will loop continuously around this clip. This is perfect for adjusting audio filters.

4 Choose Effects > Audio Filters > Final Cut Pro > Parametric Equalizer.

5 Double-click the audio clip to open it into the Viewer, then click the Filters tab to access the controls for the Equalizer filter.

Equalizers are filters that allow you change the level of specific *bands* (frequencies or frequency ranges). For example, you can turn up the volume on the high-pitched sounds without changing the level of the rest of the audio track. The result doesn't sound louder, but it changes the overall tone of the clip.

In general, you should use equalizing filters to attenuate (lower) the bands you want to eliminate rather than *boost* (raise) the parts you want to accentuate. Raising levels, even of specific bands, can cause distortion or clipping, especially when multiple tracks are mixed together.

6   Press Shift-\ (backslash) to begin the looping In to Out playback.

Listen to the clip and try to identify how it might be improved. As is typical of dialogue recording, the mids are pretty strong, but there is very little strength in the low frequencies and not much crispness to the highs. The right way to address this is to lower the mids so that the highs and lows stand out more clearly.

The parametric equalizer works by selecting a frequency, identifying "softness" using the Q slider to control how many nearby frequencies are included in the effect (the effective bandwidth), and then adjusting the gain for that frequency range.

7   While the clip continues to loop, drag the Gain slider all the way to its maximum.

This will allow you to hear which frequencies you are selecting.

8   Drag the Frequency slider down to about 100 Hz, and then very slowly drag it up to about 3000 Hz and back down again.

This is the range (100 Hz–3 KHz) that contains most of the frequencies common in human speech. Male voices typically contain more of the lower frequencies, and females more of the higher frequencies, though naturally there is wide variation among individual speakers. Also, human voices, like most sounds, simultaneously exist at many frequencies.

As you adjust the Frequency slider, you are listening for the frequency where the maximum effect is heard. This is the area where the bulk of the voice resides. In this clip, it's around 535 Hz. When the slider is set there, the voice is almost entirely unintelligible. Of course, your goal is to make the voice more intelligible, not less; so now that you've found the spot, you need to lower the Gain slider.

9   Drag the Gain slider down all the way to –20 dB.

Now you have attenuated the midrange of the voice dramatically.

10 Drag the Gain slider back toward 0 dB, listening carefully until the voice sounds both warm (meaning there is enough upper bass) and crisp (meaning there is enough treble).

In this case, a setting of about −7 should work.

You should try to limit most audio adjustments to a maximum of 5 to 10 dB in either direction. Adjustments beyond that range usually distort the sound in an entirely unnatural way.

Last, you can adjust the Q slider to affect how wide a range of frequencies is affected by the filter.

11 Drag the Q slider all the way to 20.

This limits the effect of the Gain slider to a very narrow range of frequencies around 535 Hz.

12 Slowly drag the Q slider to the left to about 5.

The lower the number, the wider the bandwidth of frequencies. A higher number will create a more focused, dramatic effect. A lower number will create softer, subtler effects because it affects a wider range of bands, tapering off the effect as it moves away from the target frequency.

13 If you want to hear a more dramatic example of the effect of the Q slider, move the Gain slider all the way up or down, and then adjust the Q again.

Be sure to return the Gain to −5 to −10 and the Q to 5 once you've finished experimenting.

14 Deselect the checkbox next to the filter name to hear what your clip sounds like without the filter.

This will automatically stop playback.

15 Press Shift-\ (backslash) to begin the loop again.

16 Select the checkbox again to turn the filter back on and play from In to Out.

You may want to add additional parametric EQ filters to isolate and attenuate other frequencies. The overall effect of the EQ process should be subtle, but attenuating the mids results in an apparent boosting of the lows and highs, which makes the clip appear both warmer and brighter without getting muddy.

There are other common EQ filters such as High- or Low-Pass filters that can further enhance your audio. A Low-Pass filter eliminates bands above a designated frequency, letting the lows "pass" through the filter. A High-Pass filter "passes" frequencies higher than a designated frequency. Frequently, there are unwanted rumblings in the low frequencies and unwanted hissing in the highs that can be eliminated with these filters.

Compressing Dialogue Dynamics

Next, you will apply a Compression filter. Human speech typically has a fairly wide *dynamic range*, meaning there is a big difference between the very quiet sounds and very loud sounds. The problem is that if you raise the overall level so the quiet parts can be heard, the loud parts can be too loud, which is undesirable as it may lead to distortion or *clipping* (chopping off the top part of the waveform).

Compressors reduce the dynamic range of a clip by lowering the loud parts (anything above a certain *threshold* dB). This allows you to increase the overall audio level. Typically, compressors permit you to optionally "preserve the volume," maintaining the impact of the loud parts while keeping the quiet parts well within an audible range.

Compressing the dynamic range results in an audio track that seems to have more "presence." Because the relative volume is more uniform, it seems to stand out more from other elements in the audio mix. Of course, you don't want to compress too much, or the voice may seem unnaturally disconnected from the rest of the sound environment. Typically, sound editors apply just a tiny bit of compression to dramatic dialogue and apply compression more generously to interviews and narrations.

1 Choose Effects > Audio Filters > Final Cut Pro > Compressor/Limiter.

   This filter is applied to the clip, after the Parametric EQ.

   The Threshold slider sets the decibel level above which attenuation is applied, and the ratio determines how much attenuation is applied. At a ratio of 1, the filter has no effect.

2 Press Shift-\ to begin the looping playback.

3 Increase Ratio to 2 and select Preserve Volume.

4 Raise Threshold all the way to 0.

With the threshold that high, the filter has no effect.

5 Slowly lower Threshold until the apparent volume seems to increase, but the *noise floor* doesn't seem to get any louder (around –12).

6 Press the Spacebar to stop the looped playback.

The noise floor is the background noise audible beneath the sound level of the words. You want this to remain as quiet as possible. If you compress the clip so much that this noise gets louder, you are probably causing more harm than good.

Once you have the filters the way you want them, you can apply them to the rest of Pedro's lines using the same technique you used to replicate the fade-in and fade-out effects.

7 Select **G1 MS OTS Group2_04** in the Timeline and press Command-C to copy the clip.

8 Select the rest of the clips on tracks A1 and A2 and press Option-V.

The Paste Attributes dialog opens.

9   Under Audio Attributes, select the Filters checkbox and click OK.

The filters are applied to all of Pedro's lines. However, because you previously per-formed the Normalize Gain function, a second Gain filter has been pasted, along with the Parametric EQ and Compressor filters.

10   Double-click each shot on Tracks A1 & A2 (except the first one). Click the Filters tab and delete the second copy of the Gain filter.

11   In the Timeline, press Option-X to clear the In and Out points.

12 Repeat steps 9 to 11 for Andy's dialogue.

Because their voices are different, Andy will need his own unique EQ and compression settings. While the same settings may work for each instance of a character's dialogue within a scene, you probably will need to create different settings for each scene, even for the same characters.

Creating Perspective

Although dialogue levels should be consistent across your entire program, it's also important to vary the level of the audio depending on the relative camera position. For example, when cutting from a close-up to a wide shot, there should be a subtle but perceptible attenuation in volume to reflect the new distance between audience and subject. Similarly, when cutting from a facial close-up of an actor to a shot over his shoulder, the volume of that actor's voice should be reduced slightly.

Such changes must be subtle and don't necessarily represent the volume shift that would occur in real life. For example, in a shot of a couple walking from very far away into a close-up, the level of their dialogue should be gradually increased as they approach the camera. But you don't want the beginning of the shot to sound so quiet you can't hear what they're saying (as it would be in reality), and you don't want the end of the shot to be louder than the overall dialogue in the film. Still, without this slight perspective shift, the sound would feel very flat and disconnected from the images.

Creating Ambiances

Unless you're in outer space, every location has some inherent background noise. An office building's ambient sounds might include air conditioners, elevators, or flickering fluorescent lights. An apartment's ambiance might include creaky floors from upstairs, or water pipes in the walls. A city park's ambiance might contain birds singing, wind in the trees, and light traffic from a nearby road. Public places frequently have low-level talking noise called *walla*. These combinations of sounds define each environment and are just as important to making a scene feel "real" as being sure the camera is focused.

In film, you can use ambiance as a subtle way to communicate information about a scene. When the prodigal son returns to confront his family, the house might emit a menacing low rumble (actually recorded inside a deep freezer) and, after the reconciliation, that sound may finally dissipate.

Good ambiances are a combination of appropriateness to the environment and appropriateness to the emotional tone of the scene. You probably don't want to hear birds chirping in a prison scene (even if they were doing so in the real prison location), but you can't exclude rain sounds if you can see that it's raining in the scene.

1   Listen to the current sequence from the beginning.

It may help if you close your eyes.

The first few clips seem to have no ambiance whatsoever, and then at around 20 seconds, as **G2 (POV Group1)_01** begins, some ambiance suddenly can be heard. Then, as the next clip starts, the audio makes an abrupt level change, and then each subsequent edit comes with a subtle shift in ambiance level.

You may try to smooth out these edits with cross-fades or by creating a *room tone* audio loop that covers the entire scene, but it is even easier to just delete them. In a moment you'll add your own ambiance tracks, which will provide the overall background for the scene, so why fuss trying to salvage the production sound? Obviously, you can't throw out the sections in which the guys are speaking, or any sections in which there is other useful sound (such as during the ending as they walk to the picnic); but as for the rest, get rid of it!

2   Option-drag a marquee around the audio tracks from the beginning of the sequence until the first dialogue clip begins at around 28:00.

3   Press Option (to select just audio) and Shift (to add to the current selection) and drag to select the clips between the two dialogue sections.

4   Press Delete.

There, wasn't that easy? Now the question is how to handle the dialogue sections. Because natural ambiance is present between the words, and before and after the guys speak, you can hear it kicking in and dropping out, which sounds terrible. Adding artificial ambiances will help, but that additional background noise will still be audible, and it will make the dialogue sound funny. So, you need to cover the entire section when they're speaking with a constant level of actual room tone from the location.

Using Room Tone

Most productions will record a track of room tone for every location used in the show. This is usually 30 to 60 seconds of "silence" recorded from the same microphone position used for recording the dialogue. This can be invaluable for filling holes in your track, such as the ones created in this sequence when you eliminated the duplicated lines (in Lesson 3). Even if you're adding a combination of ambiance tracks, the background noise heard while people are speaking will suddenly vanish in those holes, and that subtle change may be detectable unless the changes are bridged with bits of room tone.

It's vastly preferable to have a room tone track deliberately recorded on the set; but if you don't have one, you can try to construct one by stitching together segments of "silence" from between words in the current shots. For this lesson, we'll assume you're in that worst-case scenario.

1   Park the sequence playhead somewhere over clip **G1 MS OTS Group2_04** (between 28:00 and 29:23).

2   Press F to perform a match frame and open the master clip into the Viewer.

3   Click the Mono (a1) tab, and press Shift-Z to zoom the whole clip to fit.

    You want to find a relatively long section of "silence" that you can use to create a loop of room tone. It doesn't have to be literally silent (in fact, it probably won't be), but you want to make sure that there are no distinctive sounds, such as footsteps or a dog bark or anything else that might be identifiable in a loop.

    This clip has a section between when the director calls "Action!" and the first line of dialogue that should work perfectly.

4   Set an In about 1 second after the director calls "Action!" (around 01:57:39:00) and an
    Out about 1 second before the first line of dialogue (at 45:00).

You should always leave some extra "clean" space before the In and after the Out
because, in order to make a loop, you will need to create cross-fades that will require
additional frames and you don't want those to reveal the surrounding noises.

5   Play from In to Out.

There are some distracting noises in this section: voices and some footsteps. It's not ideal, but the level of those distracting elements is pretty low, and it's all you've got, so you need to make it work.

6   Make the Timeline active and choose Sequence > Insert Tracks.

The Insert Tracks dialog appears.

7   Enter *4* in the Audio Tracks field and click OK.

Four new tracks are added to the Timeline.

8   Untarget track V1 and set a1 and a2 to tracks A7 and A8.

9   Set an In point in the sequence a few seconds before the first line of dialogue (around 26:00) and overwrite **G1 MS OTS Group2_04** into the sequence.

10 In the Timeline, select the audio clip you just added, and Option-drag it to the right, overlapping a little of the end of the clip.

> **TIP** ▶ You must release the Option key before releasing the mouse button; otherwise you will perform an insert edit instead of an overwrite.

11 Repeat step 10, dragging copies of the clip to the right a few more times until the gap left by the second section of dialogue is also covered.

Try to overlap different amounts of the clip each time. This aids in making the room tone sound less like a loop.

12 Control-click the edit between the first two pieces of room tone and choose Add Transition 'Cross Fade (+3dB)'.

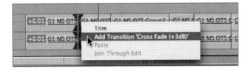

13 Repeat step 12 for each of the edits, including the beginning of the first clip and the end of the last.

The transitions at the head and tail of the section can actually be 0 dB cross-fades, since they are fading to and from silence.

14 Control-click the first transition, and choose Cross Fade (0db).

15 Repeat step 14 for the last transition.

16 Play this entire section of the sequence.

> **NOTE ▶** Because of the audio filters applied to the dialogue clips, and the number of additional tracks, you may need to render your audio before it can be played.

The room tone should successfully cover the silences left by the dialogue edits.

Increasing Real-Time Audio Tracks

By default, Final Cut Pro is set to mix eight tracks of audio in real time. If you exceed that number, you'll see a red line in the render bar. Filters and audio transitions count as multiple tracks; so, with enough filters or transitions, you can get that red render bar even with fewer than eight tracks.

However, most modern computers actually can mix quite a few more than eight tracks in real time, depending on what kind of video is being played and the speed and number of the hard disks containing the files. (Trying to simultaneously access eight different tracks from the same hard disk is challenging, even for fast hard disks.)

You can set the number of tracks you want Final Cut Pro to attempt to mix in real time in the General tab of the Final Cut Pro User Preferences window.

1   Choose Final Cut Pro > User Preferences.

2 Set Real-time Audio Mixing to 24 tracks.

If you set this to a number of tracks higher than your computer can actually manage, Final Cut Pro will stutter or drop frames during playback. Additionally, the Audio Playback Quality setting (in the same window) affects how many tracks can be played in real time. The higher this setting is, the fewer tracks that can be processed in real time.

NOTE ▶ If you encounter dropped frames or other playback problems during the remainder of this lesson, you can reset the Real-time Audio Mixing setting to a lower number of tracks.

Incorporating Prerecorded Ambiances

Once the room tone is meshing with the dialogue tracks, it's time to add some additional environmental sounds to provide atmosphere.

1 Click the FOF Sound FX bin disclosure triangle to expand it.

2 Open **Quiet Tone.aiff** from the Ambiances bin.

This is a neutral environmental tone with a little bit of distant traffic, and no birds or other natural sounds. It's perfect for the beginning of the sequence.

As you increase the number of audio tracks in your sequence, you'll want to simplify the Timeline view as much as possible and maximize the audio display area.

3 Click the Timeline Track Height button to set the Timeline tracks to their smallest size, and click the Clip Overlays button to turn off that display. Also, drag up the separator bar between the video and audio tracks as high as it will go.

4 Drag **Quiet Tone.aiff** into the Timeline and add it to tracks A9 and A10, beginning at the very head of the sequence.

5   Press Control-L to turn off looping and play the sequence from the beginning.

This tone adds some sonic continuity that ties the entire scene together. You may want to lower its level a bit, but you can save that for the final mix stage, when you have a better idea of what other sounds will be present in the scene.

Additionally, when the tone of the scene changes—after we learn that they are not going to rumble, but are going to feed babies—it makes sense to change the ambiance to reflect this. Adding some chirping birds might just do the trick.

6   From the Ambiances bin, open **Birds FX 02.aiff**.

A section of the clip has already been marked and outfitted with a slow fade-in and short fade-out.

7   Drag **Birds FX 02.aiff** to the sequence, into the area below tracks A9 and A10. Line up the clip so its Out point lines up with the end of the last clip in the sequence.

8   Play the whole sequence to hear how the birds fit.

The birds help, but they aren't enough. There needs to be more signs of life, human life, and that means walla.

9   From the Ambiances bin, open **Crowd Walla Children.aiff**.

Again, to shorten the lesson, a section of the clip already has been marked.

10   Drag **Crowd Walla Children.aiff** into the area of the sequence below tracks A11 and A12, lining up the clip so it ends with the birds clip.

11   Press Home and play the sequence back from the beginning.

You can hear how adding additional elements continues to enhance the texture of the scene.

Adding Sound Effects

The next stage in the sound design process is to add sound effects for every element in the scene that might possibly make noise. Every time someone picks up or puts down an object, takes a step, and rustles their clothes you should add a sound effect to make the show feel full and realistic. In fact, you can consider it a general rule that anytime something moves onscreen (including titles or graphics), some sort of sound should accompany the movement.

Many sounds are recorded during production and, depending on how well they were recorded and how well the actual sound matches what the audience *expects* something to sound like, you may or may not choose to replace those sounds with prerecorded sound effects or with sound effects custom-recorded for the show (called *foley*).

Even if there were sound effects recorded during production, diligent sound editors extract those sound effects and put them onto a dedicated sound effects track. This is especially important for shows that might get dubbed into other languages. In that case, the sound editor will be required to turn in an *M and E mix*, which contains the music and effects tracks but doesn't include the dialogue. If the production sound effects are only located on the dialogue tracks, they will disappear when the original dialogue tracks are removed in preparation for dubbing.

If there are sound effects that overlap lines of dialogue, you can't extract them from the dialogue tracks. While this won't be a problem for the native language mix, when creating the M and E mix, you will need to replace those sounds.

Spotting for Sound Effects

The first step in adding your sound effects is to *spot* your sequence to identify all the moments when sound effects are needed. This is identical to the process you used in Lesson 7 to mark the spots that needed B-roll.

1   Play through the show, looking for spots where sound effects are required.

Right away, you probably realize that you're going to need footstep sounds. Even if you don't need them for the opening wide shots, once you cut to a close-up of the feet, the footage is begging for some footsteps sounds.

2   Add a marker somewhere over the first feet shot (around 10:00) and name it *Footsteps*.

In actuality, you will want to add footsteps for the entire opening sequence. Once you introduce the sound, it must continue as long as you can see that the actors are still walking.

3   Continue playing the sequence, looking for areas that need sound effects.

Around 29:00, Pedro claps his hands together. There is a barely audible sound on the production track of the actual clap, but a sound effect here would emphasize the moment.

4   Add a marker there and name it *handclap*.

Then you come to all the business with the bottles coming out. There are a number of sounds that would fit here: pants rustling , the witness gasping, maybe even a tiny splash when you see the close-up of the milk.

5   Add markers for each of these moments.

You might also want to add more footsteps as the gangs walk to the picnic tables, but you can skip that for now to speed the lesson.

Adding Effects

Now that you know what sounds you need, you have to figure out the exact sounds you can use for each of these spots. Soundtrack Pro includes a huge library of sound effects, and you can purchase sound effects libraries that contain thousands of variations on every imaginable sound. Auditioning the various sounds can be fun as you listen for the nuances that make one or another sound the perfect match. But very often, professional sound designers will still record their own sounds, either synced directly to the events in the scene (foley recording) or just recorded *wild* for later integration.

1   Click the disclosure triangles to collapse the Ambiances bin and expand the Foley and Sound FX bin.

For this lesson, sound effects have been preselected for you, but in reality, you will probably have to search through hundreds of sounds to find the perfect ones for your project. That process of selecting the best sounds is actually a very important and creative endeavor, and one in which true sound artists tend to excel.

Now you're ready lay in the sound effects. The footsteps are going to be the most difficult and complex, so skip those for the moment and start with the second sound effect.

2   Control-click the Timeline ruler and choose handclap.

The playhead jumps to the moment when Pedro claps his hands.

3   From the Foley and Sound FX bin in the Browser, open **Body Hit 02.aiff**.

4   Zoom into the Timeline and find the exact frame in which Pedro's hands touch (01:00:29:02).

5   Drag **Body Hit 02.aiff** into the Timeline, to the area below the bottom tracks so it begins on that frame and adds two new tracks to the sequence.

NOTE ▶ Even though there is plenty of room to put the sound effect on tracks that already exist, it is wiser to keep your ambiances on their own tracks and your sound effects on their own tracks. This makes it easier during mixing to mute all the sound effects, or all the ambiances discretely.

6   Press \ to play around the edit.

The sound effect lines up perfectly, but it's a little too loud.

7   Select **Body Hit 02.aiff** in the Timeline and press Command-Option-L to open the Gain Adjust dialog.

Gain Adjust

Adjust gain by: ◄———————[ ]————————► [-9] dB

Make Changes: [Absolute   ▲▼]

(Cancel)   (OK)

8   In the Make Changes pop-up menu, choose Absolute, and set the Gain to –9 dB. Click OK to close the dialog.

9   Play around the edit again.

Now the hand slap is present in the scene, but not overwhelming. If you wanted to make Pedro seem more menacing, you could choose to make the hand sound even louder.

Move on to the next effect, which is the clothes rustle when the guys pull the bottles out.

10   Press Shift-M to move to the next marker.

TIP ▶   To move to the previous marker, press Option-M.

This should show Andy lifting his shirt as he grabs for his bottle.

What's needed is a nonspecific sound of clothes rustling.

11 Open **Clothes 1.aiff**.

12 In the Viewer, press Shift-Z to view the entire clip.

You can see in the waveform that there are two different takes in this clip. The first one is longer and more constant, and the second is shorter with a clear peak. Even without listening, you can guess which one will be better in this case.

13 Just to be sure, play the clip.

The sound is fine, but the level is too high.

14 Lower the level to −10.

15 Set an In point before the second sound begins (around 04:15) and set an Out after it winds down (around 07:15).

16 Drag the sound effect into the Timeline, onto tracks 15 and 16, so it begins just as Andy begins reaching for his bottle (around 01:00:32:03).

17 Play around the edit.

That works great. Now you need to add a sound for Pedro reaching into his pocket.

18 Open **Clothes 2.aiff.**

19 In the Viewer, press Shift-Z to fit the entire waveform into view, and listen to the clip.

This clip has five different takes of different lengths.

20 Mark the moment when the third rustle happens (In: 04:00, Out: 5:10).

21 Lower the level to –8.

22 Find the frame in the sequence when Pedro begins to pull the bottle out of his pocket (around 33:20).

23 Drag **Clothes 2.aiff** into the Timeline and to the area below the last track, adding two new tracks to the sequence.

24 Play around the edit.

The rustling does a great job of bringing that moment to life, except that now, when Andy finally gets the bottle out, there is no accompanying sound.

25 In the Viewer, mark the area of **Clothes 2.aiff** when the second rustle happens (In: 2:03, Out: 3:03).

26 Find the frame in the sequence when Andy actually pulls out the bottle (around 34:22) and drag **Clothes 2.aiff** onto tracks A15 and A16.

It's OK if it covers up the end of **Clothes 1.aiff**.

27 Play around the whole section.

It may be hard to hear just the sound effects with the other tracks playing at the same time. It would be ideal if you could temporarily *solo* the track you're working on, silencing everything else.

28 In the lower-left corner of the Timeline, click the Show Audio Controls button.

Mute and Solo buttons appear for each track. The Mute button (the speaker icon on the left) temporarily silences playback of that track, and the Solo button (the headphone icon) turns off the other tracks.

29 Click the Solo button for track A15. Then click the Solo button for track A16.

Now, only those two tracks will play.

30 Play around the section with the rustling.

You can hear the sound effects clearly now and judge them for timing, level, and appropriateness without the other tracks to distract you.

31 Deselect the Solo buttons for tracks 15 and 16 to turn off soloing.

There are a few more sound effects to add, but beyond this point you are beginning to venture out of ordinary sound effects editing and into sound design.

Designing the Sound

Sound design is a general term for the entire sound editing and mixing process; but it is also specifically used to refer to sound elements that are not naturally present in the scene but are used to enhance the scene. For example, you might add the sound of a heartbeat to a scene to convey someone under increasing stress. Often, the audience might construe such sounds to be in the character's head, or they might be sounds that evoke a certain emotional response. This is where sound designers contribute their creative interpretation of the scene.

Of course, you don't want to go too far. As with all editing, the goal is rarely to draw attention to the process. You might pat yourself on the back for foreshadowing a character's downfall with an ominous thunder rumble just as he shakes hands with a villain, but if the scene is taking place under sunny blue skies, it's likely to draw attention away from the scene and onto the "clever" filmmaking.

1   Open the *Sound Design* sequence.

2   If you have red areas in your render bar, press Option-R to render the sequence.

3   Play the entire sequence, paying special attention to the sound.

First of all, you can hear that the footsteps have been laid into this sequence. Footsteps are among the trickiest sound elements for a number of reasons. For one thing, different shoes sound different on different surfaces, and everyone walks with a unique gait. Second, footsteps are percussive, so they are very audible in real life. Even though we don't typically notice them, when they're absent from a scene, the scene feels strangely empty. And third, because production crews use very directional mics focused primarily on people's mouths, footsteps are rarely present in the production tracks. For all these reasons, footsteps are a sound designer's nightmare.

If footsteps are hard to work with in general, this scene might be a worst-case scenario: two parties that need to sound different from each other, and each party consisting of multiple people. To add insult to injury, the close-up shots of the feet emphasize the importance of the footsteps and, at least for that section, require that they appear in near-perfect sync with the picture.

In most cases, rather than trying to match prerecorded footfall sounds to the picture, foot-steps are recorded on a *foley stage*, where a *foley artist* watches the movie playback, and mimics the onscreen steps using the appropriate shoe and surface type.

This example shows that you can use prerecorded footstep sounds if you have to, taken here from Soundtrack Pro's extensive library. If you want to give yourself a bonus lesson, use the clips in the Footsteps bin and try to re-create the edit by yourself.

Footsteps aside, what else can you do to enhance the sequence? With all of the *practical* sounds placed (sounds that match specific actions seen onscreen), you can now turn to more metaphorical or abstract elements.

First, think about the ambiance. While the quiet tone track is sufficient background, you can do more to convey the tone of the scene.

4 Close the Foley and Sound FX bin and expand the Sound Design Elements bin.

5 Open **Wind 2.aiff**.

Adding wind noise will introduce a subtle sense of danger to the scene. If this is present at the beginning and fades out as the birds begin, it will further underscore the dramatic transition and its eventual release.

6 Set an In at the head of the sequence and set an Out a few seconds after **Birds FX 02.aiff** begins (around 40:00).

7 Control-click the track header for track A13 and choose a1 from the shortcut menu. Control-click A14 and choose a2.

8 Overwrite **Wind 2.aiff** into the sequence.

9 Control-click the ending edit of **Wind 2.aiff** and choose Add Transition 'Cross Fade (0dB)'.

10 Press Home to return to the head of the sequence and play the sequence to hear how the wind influences the scene.

The impact is subtle but effective. Wind noise is a classic sound design tool that can be used in a wide range of situations.

If you're willing to get a little more abstract, you can have some fun with sound design elements.

11 Play the part of the sequence when the guys pull out the milk bottles (starting around 34:00).

Waving a bottle in the air doesn't actually make a sound, but that doesn't mean you can't pretend it does! This is an important moment in the scene, and you have an opportunity to add dramatic tension with a sound effect.

12 Open and play **Swish 1.aiff**.

This will add emphasis to the bottle move, and as long as you keep the level relatively low, it won't sound unnatural.

13 Place the sequence playhead at 35:03 just as Andy pulls out his bottle.

14 Drag the sound effect to tracks A19 and A20, and line it up so it begins at the playhead.

15 Play around the edit to hear the effect.

You may need to adjust the timing slightly so the sound occurs in sync with Andy's arm movement. It sounds a little funny, but mainly because it's too loud.

16 Select the clip in the Timeline and choose Modify > Audio > Gain –3dB or press Control-[(left bracket) two times to lower the audio level by 6dB.

17 Play around the edit again.

By lowering the volume, the sound effect works to enhance the action in a subtle way rather than drawing attention to itself.

Alternatively, you could go over the top and use a more dramatic sound effect to play up the dueling storyline.

18 Open and play **Sword 4.aiff.**

19 Lower the level to –10.

20 Drag the clip into the sequence, lining it up with the beginning of **Swish 1.aiff** and placing it on tracks A21 and A22.

21 Play around the edit.

The unsheathing sword sound is metaphorically accurate, although obviously there's no way the bottle would make that sound, right? Well, the truth is there's no way the bottle would make the swish sound either. Depending on the overall style of your show, you may or may not be able to get away with these sorts of choices, and like all sound design, the volume of the effect determines how pronounced it is. You might be able to keep the sword sound by just lowering the level to the point where it's still audible but not drawing attention to itself.

At this point, you are also combining the sound of the swish and the sound of the sword. This may be making the overall effect too loud, but by balancing the levels of the two sounds, you may be able to create an effect that is greater than the sum of the parts.

Combining Sounds

What is the sound of a car crash? It's actually a combination of dozens of distinct sounds all happening together. There is the screeching of tires, the impact of metal on metal, the crumbling of fiberglass, the shattering of a brake light, the debris falling to the ground, and so on. Many, many distinct sounds go into that one "sound effect." And that is not the exception—it is the norm. For every sound effect you create, you will typically combine several sounds to make a full, complex, realistic-sounding effect.

But how do you combine so many sounds without creating a muddy blob of sound in which none of the elements are heard? This is the delicate art of mixing. Good sound mixing requires paying careful attention to the levels of each element, as well as to the frequencies (pitch) of the sounds you are mixing. You can easily combine the high-frequency shattering of glass with the low-frequency thud of metal colliding with metal. Also, by adjusting the timing of your sound effects so as not to precisely overlap their *attack* and *decay* periods (the build-up and wind-down of the sound), you can mix several sounds that appear to happen at the same time but each element can be detected.

1   Open and play **Low Frequency Hit FX.aiff**.

    This is a very generic bass note that could be used musically or used to add some gusto to a higher-pitched sound effect.

2   Find the moment in the sequence when Pedro slaps his hands together (around 29:00).

    Because at this point in the story the audience still thinks the guys are going to fight each other, using the bass note to add weight to this gesture makes it more threatening. But, you don't want it to be so loud that it draws attention to itself.

3   Lower the level to −8 dB.

4   Drag **Low Frequency Hit FX.aiff** to the sequence onto tracks A21 and A22, and line it up so it begins at the same frame as **Body Hit 02.aiff**.

    Professional sound designers rarely use a single sound for any effect. You don't have to use five different clips for every situation, but it is a good idea to think about how you can incorporate this technique to improve your sound design.

As usual, there's plenty more for you to do if you want to continue working on this project on your own.

5   To see a finished version, open and play **The whole shebang**.

Although music may obscure quite a bit of your sound design, don't be fooled into thinking you can skip over that design work as long as you slather on enough music at the end. The music should supplement, not replace, the sound design elements. Using music as a primary sound design element is cheating, and it cheats your audience as well. If you're relying entirely on someone's musical composition to convey the tone and emotional impact of your scene, you are giving up control of a very crucial and essential part of your job as storyteller.

Sometimes editors lay a "temp track" into a scene to provide a rhythm to cut to or an emotional tone to reinforce. This can be helpful, but once picture is locked, you should turn off the music and go through the sound-editing process described in this lesson before adding music back in. Who knows, you may find you don't need the music at all!

Editing Music

Musical soundtracks fall into two categories: *practical* or *source* music, which appears to be coming from a source within the scene, such as a radio or a live band; and *score*, which refers to music added to the film for the purpose of supplementing the scene.

Practical music will be mixed to sound like it is coming from a specific location. So when someone turns off the car, or walks out of the party, the music will end or change volume.

Score can be further divided into prerecorded songs and original music composed to go with the show. If your show contains both, only the latter is referred to as the score. There are other terms commonly used such as *stingers* and *stabs*, which are very short musical elements timed specifically to moments in the show, such as a character's entrance or a moment of suspense.

▶ **Using Commercial Music**

It is illegal to use published music in your film or video projects without obtaining rights from both the author and publisher. You may think you can get away with it, but be aware that the music industry lawyers spend all day looking for violators. They patrol film festivals, tradeshows, and even the Internet. If you are caught, you can suffer a fine and a lot of legal hassle.

In addition to libraries of royalty-free music—and all the amazing loops in Soundtrack Pro—there are thousands of musicians who are eager to help you use their music for free. You should consider using these resources instead of ripping your favorite band's latest single and throwing it into your movie. If you still feel compelled to use commercially published music, do your homework and get the rights.

You typically need two sets of rights to use music in a film. You need the publishing rights (usually held by either BMI or ASCAP), which are the permission to use the composition of the song; plus you need the performance rights (sometimes called *sync* rights), which covers the specific recording of the song you want to use. If you can get publishing rights but not sync rights, you can hire a band to *cover* the song (record their own version) and use that version in your film.

For very reasonable prices, music publishers frequently offer limited rights that allow you to show your film in festivals or similar limited engagements. If you want to begin selling your film for profit, you then need to renegotiate those rights.

Some lazy editors steal tracks from the published scores of finished films. This may be tempting, since the music was created as the soundtrack for a film in the first place. It may fit nicely in your film, but beware. Publishers almost never allow a piece of music composed specifically for a film to be reused in another film (for fairly obvious reasons).

Often you'll use just the beginning and end of a song, since most songs are at least 3 minutes long and most scenes are less than 2. Those beginnings and endings are wonderful when they reinforce the start and finish of your scene, but cutting out a chunk of the middle of the song requires music editing.

Music editing for film requires a specialized set of skills, somewhat unrelated to the skills used when editing music during its composition. You need to be able to identify the measures, rhythms, and arrangements of a song, and stitch together different sections to create a version that is exactly the right length. Sometimes you will remove a verse or double the length of a bridge. Sometimes you just find one measure and loop it three or four times to make the overall length of the song fit your scene.

1   Close the Friends Of The Family bin and expand the Art Lic Trailer bin.

This bin contains the trailer for "Artistic License" and the original music that goes along with it.

2   Open and play the **AL Trailer** sequence.

3   Open and play **Farewell to Innocence.aif**.

4   In the Viewer, press Shift-Z to fit the entire waveform into view.

It can be very helpful to look at the waveform for a song you want to use as a potential score. Typically, you will be most interested in the beginning and end of the song. However, when a song has transitions or bridges where the music makes a sudden or dramatic change, this might be a section you can use as well.

Such bridges often can be identified by looking at the waveform. Sections in which the waveform dips indicate a section of relative quiet, which means there is an upcoming ending (leading into a bridge) and beginning (starting the next section) that could be useful in your show. This clip has two such dips midway through the song.

In this case you will use the beginning of the song to begin the trailer.

5   In the Viewer, set an In point just before the music kicks in, at 05:13.

6   Play the sequence and think about the best place to begin the music.

The trailer opens with a J-cut, when the first line of dialogue begins over the title card and then the picture arrives a moment later. This is a fairly strong opening, and adding music might undermine it. Instead, try beginning the music after that beat, on the cut to the next scene.

7   Set an In point in the sequence just before Brianca says, "I'm warning you, Milken!" at 06:24.

8   Target a1 to track A3 and a2 to track A4 and overwrite the music into the sequence.

Because you didn't set an Out point in either Viewer or sequence, the music extended well past the end of the trailer video.

9   Press Shift-Z to fit the entire sequence into the view.

10   Drag the right edge of the music clip to the left until it lines up with the end of the video clip, and press Shift-Z.

11 Play the sequence.

The music works very well with the trailer. It almost seems like it needs no editing at all, until you get to the end where the music is just cut off. You could simply fade it out, but it would be far superior to use a natural musical ending to add punctuation to the end of the show.

The first, obvious place to look for an ending is at the end of the song.

12 In the Viewer, play the ending of the song.

There is a nice ending, but the song seems to have progressed to a totally different instrumentation by that point and there is no obvious way to integrate that ending with the beginning you're using. What about those bridges you identified earlier?

13 In the Viewer, play across the dip in the waveform at around 00:02:04:00.

This is an interesting section, but it doesn't really work as an ending, since it continues to build until it explodes into the next section.

There is another dip in the waveform a little earlier, around 00:01:30:00.

14 Play across the section starting at 01:30:00.

This section is more promising. The two-beat, pause, two-beat, silence, phrase could easily work as an ending for the song.

15 In the sequence, watch the ending of the trailer, starting around 56:00. Think about how you might tie those ending beats into the picture.

There are two possibilities. One idea is to line the first beats up with the shot of Brianca "crushing" David with her fingers, and the other is to line it up with the beginning of the ending credits. Start by trying out the first approach.

To do this, you can use the replace edit.

16 In the sequence, set an In point 5 or 10 seconds before the finger-crush and set an Out at the end of the sequence.

You know you're going to have to clean up the In point edit, so there's no need to make it precise.

17 Place the sequence playhead directly on the frame where the finger-crush happens (approximately 01:00:57:24).

18 In the Viewer, position the playhead precisely on the frame where the first beat (of the four ending beats) occurs (around 00:01:30:00).

It may help to zoom in on the waveform.

19 Drag **Farewell to Innocence.aif** to the Canvas and when the Canvas Edit Overlay appears, choose Replace.

A replace edit is unlike all the other edit styles that base their edit timing on the first or last frame of the marked section of the clip (the In or Out point). Instead, a replace edit lines up the playhead position in the Viewer with the playhead position in the sequence. This allows you to base an edit around a frame that occurs somewhere *between* the In and Out points. The source clip replaces the area between the In and Out markers on the target tracks in the sequence.

If no In or Out points are specified in the sequence, the boundaries of the current clip are observed instead.

20 Play around the new edit.

The timing works very well, although the music starts again after the four beats, when you really want it to go to silent.

21 Zoom in on the end of the sequence and drag the right edge of the last music clip to the left to where the visible gap in the waveform indicates the silence after the four beats (01:01:01:00).

Now you need to tackle the other side of the edit, and find some way of meshing the two parts of the song. Ideally you can find the beginning of a measure in each section and line them up, so the musical rhythm feels continuous. Unfortunately, it is very unlikely that the timing will line up perfectly, so you have to get creative.

Begin by using markers to identify the rhythm in each piece. This is similar to the marking beats exercise you did in Lesson 9; but, rather than adding a marker on every beat, just add markers on the beginning of each measure. Since this music is in 4/4 time, that means a marker every four beats.

22 Zoom back out and click the Show Audio Controls button in the lower-left corner of the Timeline.

23 Click the Solo buttons for tracks A3 and A4.

24 Select the first section of the music track on A3 and A4.

25 Move the sequence playhead to the section where the drum break occurs (around 25:00) and begin to play.

26 Each time a measure begins, press the M key to add a marker. Try to get the markers exactly on the first beat.

Now you need to add markers in the second piece of the music.

27 Press R to select the Roll tool and select the edit point between the two pieces of music. Drag it to the left about three-quarters of the way toward the beginning of the sequence.

There's no need to be precise, as this is just a temporary edit to expose more of this part of the song. It will be easier to find the beats the longer you listen to the music, so the further you drag it to the left, the easier it will be.

28 Press A to select the Selection tool, and select the second piece of the music.

29 Move the playhead to the beginning of that clip and begin to play.

30 Press the M key at the top of each measure.

About halfway through the section, it gets a little difficult to find the start of each measure because the music gets a little syncopated. If you find it too difficult to mark each measure, just mark the beginning of each phrase or section when the music changes. Ultimately, you are looking for a good place to switch from the first piece of music to the second, so those beginnings of sections are the most useful sections to spot.

31 Select the Roll tool again and roll the edit back to the right, so the edit falls about midway through the sequence.

32 Press Command-+ several times to zoom into that section of the Timeline.

33 Roll the edit so it falls directly onto one of the markers in the first piece of music.

Now you can see how many frames separate the two pieces of music. For the rhythm to sound continuous across the two pieces of music, the marker to the right needs to line up exactly with the edit point.

34 Press R twice to select the Ripple tool, and ripple the incoming clip (on the right side) until the marker lines up with the edit point.

35 Play around the edit.

The transition will still sound rough since the musical style changes abruptly, but the rhythm should remain consistent across the edit.

36 Control-click the edit and choose Add Transition 'Cross Fade (+3dB)'.

A cross-fade effect appears on the edit.

37 Control-click the transition icon and choose Duration (00:00:01:00).

A Duration dialog appears.

38 Type 5, press Enter to set the duration to five frames, and click OK.

39 Play around the edit again.

Now the transition should sound a little smoother, although depending on the marker you lined up on, it may or may not be an ideal edit. It doesn't matter, as long as the rhythm sounds continuous. You can now move the edit anywhere you want and the rhythm will remain consistent.

The trick is to find a good place to hide the edit. One of the best techniques is to look for a loud section in the main audio track that might serve to cover up the musical edit.

40 Deselect the Solo buttons for A3 and A4 to unsolo the tracks.

41 Zoom back out to show the whole sequence, then select the Roll tool and drag the transition to the right until it is underneath the area in tracks A1 and A2 where the waveform appears large (indicating a loud area), around 49:15.

Using the Roll tool on a transition moves the transition without affecting its duration or other settings.

Use snapping to line the edit up precisely with the markers, so the transition still occurs at the head of a measure.

42 Press Home and listen to the whole sequence play.

The edit isn't completely invisible, but it isn't drawing too much attention to itself, either. You can experiment with placing it elsewhere in the sequence if you like.

The rippling you did earlier moved the four beats at the end of the scene a little bit to the left. This can be remedied in one of two ways. You can move both pieces of music to the right to make up for the frames you trimmed, which means the music at the head of the show will begin a few frames later, or you can live with the whole piece ending a few frames earlier. It's up to you to select the compromise you prefer.

The bigger remaining problem is that the music level is competing with the dialogue in the first half of the trailer.

Using the Mixer

Although you can use the clip overlays to do simple audio fades, when you want to control an audio track's level over a longer period of time, it's far more efficient to use the Audio Mixer. Lesson 11 covers the Audio Mixer in more detail, but this exercise gives you a short preview.

1 Choose Tools > Audio Mixer or press Option-6.

The Audio Mixer window appears.

2 Press Home to move the playhead to the beginning of the sequence.

3 Play through the sequence once, just watching the Audio Mixer window.

Tracks 3 and 4 begin at -inf, and then jump up to 0dB at the point where the track begins.

You should be thinking about what changes you'd like to make. The music starts off fine, but after the first line of dialogue, it begins to seem too loud. Then, around the time when Brianca screams "Milken!" the volume no longer seems excessive. In fact, it propels the energy of the scene.

4 In the button bar of the Audio Mixer, click the Record Audio Keyframes button.

With this setting activated, you can drag the audio sliders and control the clip levels dynamically while the scene plays. It does take a bit of practice to get good at this, but just like trimming edits, it is preferable to make changes as the sequence is playing and you can hear everything in context than it is to drag around keyframes when the playhead is stopped.

If you make a mistake, you can always clear the changes you make, or there's always Undo.

5 Press Home to move the playhead to the beginning of the sequence.

You're going to concentrate entirely on tracks 3 and 4, which are linked together (because they are a stereo pair). So, you just need to drag the slider for one of them.

Remember your goal: You want to lower the audio after the first line of dialogue ("I'm warning you, Milken!") and then bring it back up when she screams, "Milken!" That's only two moves; the rest of the time, you can leave the slider alone.

6 Press the Spacebar to begin playback.

7 As soon as the sliders for tracks 3 and 4 jump up to 0 dB, grab one of them and smoothly drag it down to about −7.

8 Hold it there until you hear Brianca scream "Milken!" and then smoothly drag it back up to 0 dB. Press the Spacebar to stop playback.

That's it! Your level changes appear in the clip as keyframes.

9 Play back the sequence and listen to your work.

If you don't like the results, you can reset the keyframes and try again.

10 Double-click the first instance of **Farewell to Innocence.aif** in the Timeline.

The clip is opened into the Viewer.

11 In the Viewer, click the Reset button.

All audio keyframes are eliminated.

12 Press Option-6 to bring the Audio Mixer window to the front.

13 Repeat steps 5 through 9.

If you're still unhappy with the mix you can repeat steps 10 through 12 ad infinitum.

Lesson Review

1. Identify the six stages of sound editing.
2. How are audio filters best used?
3. What does a compressor filter do?
4. What makes a good ambiance?
5. How do you manually create room tone?
6. Identify the four ways to control a clip's level.
7. How do you navigate to markers in a sequence?
8. How can you effectively combine sounds?
9. How do you stitch together pieces of music with different timing?
10. What advantage does the Audio Mixer window offer?

Answers

1. Dialogue, ambiances, sound effects, sound design, music, and the final mix.
2. By looping playback and adjusting sliders until satisfied.
3. A compressor reduces a clip's dynamic range by attenuating loud sections of a clip.
4. Appropriateness to location and appropriateness to theme.
5. Select a section of "silence" from a dialogue clip and duplicate it, then stitch the duplicates together with short cross-fades.
6. Using the level slider in the Viewer, the clip overlays in the Timeline, the Levels dialog, or with a gain filter (often applied automatically using the Apply Normalization Gain command).

7. Pressing Shift-M moves to the next marker; pressing Option-M moves to the previous marker. Also, you can right-click the Timeline ruler or Current Timecode field and choose the name of a marker from the shortcut menu.

8. Choose sounds with differing pitch, timing, and levels.

9. Use markers to identify the beginnings of measures or phrases, roll and ripple to line up the markers in the two clips, and then apply a short cross-fade effect. Finally, roll the edit to a place where it can be well hidden.

10. It allows you to automate clip levels dynamically while playing.

11

Lesson 11
Audio Finishing

Have you ever heard the expression "Video is two-thirds audio?" Well, it's true. The ear is more sensitive than the eye, and viewers are much more tolerant of mediocre picture quality than they are of less-than-perfect audio. Look no further than the infamous *Blair Witch Project*. Despite being photographed to deliberately look like it was shot by frightened kids with a $200 camcorder, it was given a million-dollar sound mix before being released into theaters.

Happily, there's no reason why your audio should ever turn a viewer (or *listener*) away, because creating a quality audio mix can be a simple process. In this lesson, you will use a reference tone to correctly configure the level of your sequence's audio. Then, you'll learn how to set the level of audio clips, use Final Cut Pro's Audio Mixer, and automate audio tracks in real time.

Preparing the Sequence

Movies are all about suspending your disbelief—losing yourself in the magic of the story and forgetting reality, if only for a moment. So in the finest cinematic tradition, suspend your disbelief by pretending you're not a video editor, and put on the hat of an audio engineer.

1   Open **AudioMix**.

The *Pencil Scene* sequence should open, with six tracks of audio.

2   Choose Final Cut Pro > User Preferences (Option-Q), and in the Editing tab make sure that the Record Audio Keyframes box is deselected.

3   Click OK.

Muting and Soloing Audio Tracks

The secret to good audio is getting the dialogue right. More than any other sound in your video, it is the dialogue that commands your viewer's attention. In the following exercises, you're going to focusing your attention on the sequence's dialogue alone. So you should temporarily disable the audio tracks that do not contain dialogue. In Final Cut Pro, there are three ways to do this:

▶   Disable the audio track by clicking its green Audible button. (These buttons are often called Track Visibility buttons—even on audio tracks—but this book refers to them as the Audible buttons.) If the Audible button is disabled, the audio track's sound does not play.

▶   Mute the audio track. A muted track does not play.

▶   Solo the dialogue audio tracks. Soloing a track turns off the sound of all the other audio tracks in a sequence (except for other soloed tracks, which continue to play).

1   In the Timeline, move the playhead to the beginning of the sequence and press the Spacebar to begin playback. (Do not clear the In and Out marks.)

2   On track A5 and track A6, click the Audible buttons to turn the tracks off (disable them).

Clicking the Audible button is a good way to turn off the track's sound, as long as you remember the following: Disabling the Audible button not only turns the track off, but it also excludes it from the rendered or output version of your movie—this includes movies exported to QuickTime, Print to Video, Edit to Tape, and so on.

A less permanent way to turn off a track's sound involves using the Mute buttons. Muted tracks are still included in the sequence's sound when you export it to a QuickTime movie or print to tape.

Before you can mute a track, you need to show the audio controls in the Timeline.

3   In the lower-left corner of the Timeline, click the Audio Controls button.

Mute and Solo buttons appear at the far left of each track.

Muting and soloing audio tracks affect the sequence only while you edit it. When it comes time to output the sequence, the Mute and Solo button choices are overridden, so all muted or soloed tracks are included in your final renders.

Disabling audio tracks with the Audible button has one distinct advantage over using the Mute and Solo buttons: It removes the strain the audio track places on your computer's CPU. Muted tracks, on the other hand, still consume CPU cycles, because you can instantly turn these tracks back on by unmuting them.

If your sequence drops frames as it plays, click the Audible button to disable audio tracks you don't need to hear, and save those CPU cycles for more important parts of your project (like adding more effects to the other tracks).

4   On track A3 and track A4, select the Mute button.

The Mute button has a black speaker on it. Selecting it turns the speaker yellow and temporarily turns off a track's sound. Consequently, track A3 and track A4 can no longer be heard.

5   Deselect the Mute buttons to unmute track A3 and track A4, and then re-enable track A5 and track A6 by selecting their Audible buttons.

All audio tracks are now playing together.

6   On track A1 and track A2, select the Solo buttons.

Track A1 and track A2 are soloed. All the sequence's other tracks are automatically muted so you can't hear them. That's great, because for the next few exercises you are going to concentrate on getting your dialogue right, so it's fine to have the other audio tracks temporarily silenced. You'll turn track A1 and track A2 back on a little later, but leave them soloed for now and continue to the next exercises.

Understanding Dialogue Levels

Imagine you're channel surfing in your living room. As you switch through the programs, you pay the most attention to the dialogue, which is the main way a program delivers aural information to you. The music and background sounds all slip into a supporting role, and your ears focuses on the spoken words. You'll also notice that the sound of dialogue across all television channels is more or less uniform and always reaches your ears at the same volume level. In other words, the average volume of the dialogue purposefully has been configured to be consistent across all broadcast programs. This allows a more pleasant viewing experience, because you can confidently flip between programs without having to jump for the remote control's volume buttons to raise or lower the television's sound.

To keep the level of dialogue constant, broadcast television uses an average level of dialogue that corresponds to approximately –12 dB on Final Cut Pro's digital level meter. For example, if you were to take a video sequence from Final Cut Pro in which the average dialogue level was set to –12 dB, use DVD Studio Pro to turn it into a DVD-Video, and then play that DVD on your TV, your dialogue would sound at exactly the same level as the dialogue on a television broadcast. Consequently, if you want your sequence to play at the same volume as broadcast television programs, it's a good idea to ensure that the average level of your sequence's dialogue is between –15 dB and –12 dB as you edit in Final Cut Pro.

Comparing Peak and Average Levels

One of the most important audio concepts to understand is the difference between peak and average audio levels.

Peak level is represented by spikes in the waveform. These spikes represent short bursts in volume that last only a fraction of a second. In music, the peaks usually correspond to rhythmic elements in the song, such as kick drums and cymbal crashes. In dialogue, peaks typically fall on the "plosive" sounds, or hard consonant sounds such as *p*, *t*, and *k*. In fact, if you say the word *peak,* you can even hear how your own voice sounds louder and more pronounced during the "p" and "k" portions of the word, while it's quieter during the "ea."

A waveform's average volume level is represented by the maximum edge of the waveform's solid body. Notice the peaks in the waveform, and then look closely at the more solid part of the waveform—its body. If you shaved off the peaks of the waveform, you'd be left with a flat, smooth wave. This smooth wave approximates the waveform's average level.

As you listen to an audio stream, you are much more sensitive to the stream's average level than you are to its peaks, and if the audio sounds too loud or too quiet, it's very likely the average level that you are noticing, not the peak level.

Dialogue: Common Average and Peak Levels

Delivery Format	Average Volume	Peak Volume
Broadcast television	–12 dB	–6 dB
DVD	–12 dB	–3 dB
Theatrical Dolby Digital	–20 dB	–3 dB

Exploring Dynamic Range

Dynamic range is the difference between your audio stream's loudest and quietest portions, and it's important to take dynamic range into consideration when you determine how loud your sequence's dialogue should be. For example, film soundtracks are often mixed using a wide dynamic range. They are meant to play on the big screen, with big sound systems that are very efficient and accurately reproduce a wide difference between loud and quiet sounds. In a movie, you want to hear the lovers' whisper, and you want to be shocked by the exploding car. You want big sound, and consequently a big dynamic range is required. For this reason, movies typically mix in dialogue at between –20 dB and –31 dB. At first glance this may seem surprisingly low on the level meter, but it's all relative; add an explosion that peaks at –6 dB, and you've got a very dynamic—and dramatic—soundtrack.

Television, on the other hand, has different concerns. Most televisions are not equipped with efficient speakers, and the mono 3-inch driver on the front of a typical budget television has a hard time just reproducing sound, let alone blasting the full dynamic range of a film score. Consequently, audio destined for TV uses a severely reduced dynamic range.

The following chart lists the dynamic range commonly employed in different exhibition formats:

Dynamic Range vs. Program Delivery Format

Delivery Format	Dynamic Range
Internet	3–6 dB
Broadcast television	6 dB
HD television	12 dB
DVD	12–18 dB
Theatrical Dolby Digital	20–30 dB

Using the Audio Meter

In Final Cut Pro, –12 dB is a very significant number because it makes a good reference level to use for video destined for viewing on a television. When you output your sequence to analog tape formats, such as Betacam SP, you should adjust your tape recorder so that –12 dB on Final Cut Pro's level meter is 0 dB on your tape recorder's analog, or volume unit (VU) level meter. (On an analog audio meter, 0 dB is often referred to as *unity gain*.)

Tape recorder
VU meter

Final Cut Pro
Audio Meter

Digital videotape recorders such as DV, HDCAM, DVCPRO, and Digital Betacam receive digital audio straight from Final Cut Pro and will record audio at levels identical to those you see on your Final Cut Pro Audio Meter.

1   In the *Pencil Scene* sequence, press Shift-\ (backslash) to play from In to Out.

Right now, tracks A1 and A2 are soloed, so all you hear is the production sound. This marked section contains a continuous section of talking.

2   Look at Final Cut Pro's Audio Meter, and note the peak levels compared with the average levels.

As the sequence plays, the Audio Meter pulses between a high and a low value. The high value represents the sequence's peak level, and the low value approximates the average level. The difference between these two levels determines the audio stream's dynamic range.

Peak levels

Average levels

The Audio Meter helps you determine peak values by temporarily holding a yellow line in position at audio peaks. (This is called a peak and hold display.) The average volume level, on the other hand, takes a bit of practice to work out. As you watch the Audio Meter pulse between its high and low levels, notice that some green is almost always displayed in the Audio Meter, and the volume level very rarely drops to silence. Pay careful attention to the lowest level of the green in the display. For all intents and purposes, this is the average level of the audio stream. In this example, the average level of the dialogue is approximately −18 dB.

3   Press the Spacebar to stop playback, and look at the Audio Meter.

Even though the sequence has stopped playing, the Audio Meter continues to show the level of the frame the playhead is currently parked on.

Choosing a Reference Level

So, you've examined a lot of the theory involved in audio—now it's time to start mixing! The first step to creating a great mix is calibrating your speakers using a reference tone. A *reference tone* is a steady 1 kHz sine wave that sounds like a long, sustained note. It's important because this reference tone helps you set a comfortable monitoring level and provides a volume reference to use as you set the levels of your sequence's dialogue.

The reference level is used for two purposes. First, if you are outputting your sequence to tape in preparation for broadcast or replication, you should always include one full minute of video bars and audio test tone at the beginning of the sequence. This test tone plays at the same average level as the dialogue in your sequence, and it allows the broadcaster or duplicator to calibrate her equipment to play your audio at the correct level. The test tone also provides a steady signal you can use to calibrate your audio signals to an appropriate listening level, and that's the purpose you'll put it to in the next few steps.

For the purpose of this exercise, initially assume you want your video to play at the same level as standard broadcast television. To achieve this, you'll use a reference level of –12 dB and then calibrate your speakers to an appropriate listening level for mixing.

1   In the Viewer's Video tab, click the Generators button.

The Generators pop-up menu opens.

2   Choose Bars and Tone > Bars and Tone (NTSC).

The Bars and Tone Generator opens into the Viewer.

3   Click the Viewer's Play button.

A 1 kHz test tone plays. Notice that Final Cut Pro's Audio Meter holds steady at −12 dB while the test tone plays. This is an appropriate reference level for broadcast television.

However, if you intended to mix your sequence with more dynamic range than is required for television, you would need to lower the level of the test tone from its default −12 dB, as demonstrated in the following steps.

4   Click the Viewer's Stereo (a1a2) tab to display the test tone.

You'll notice the Level slider is set at −12 dB. This, of course, is exactly the same value displayed on Final Cut Pro's Audio Meter.

5   Move the Level slider down to −20, and check out Final Cut Pro's Audio Meter. (If the test tone is not playing, click the Play button to start playback once again.)

The Audio Meter now displays a level of −20 dB.

If you continued with this more dynamic reference level, you would mix in the dialogue at approximately the same volume level as this lower test tone, which, in turn, would give you more *headroom*, or more room above the dialogue level to mix in effects such as explosions or music.

6   Set the Level slider back to −12 to ensure that the test tone plays at −12 dB.

7   Play the −12 dB test tone, and adjust your speakers so the tone sounds neither too loud nor too quiet.

The test tone should be loud enough so that you can hear it clearly, but not so loud that it tires your ears. Once set, don't change the volume of your speakers as you mix your audio in Final Cut Pro. Maintaining a consistent playback level lets you get used to the volume you're working at, which, in turn, gives you a good feel for how your audio sounds. When it comes to volume, consistency is the key!

NOTE ▶ Adjusting speaker volume is very different from adjusting the Viewer's Level slider. You can adjust the speaker volume by increasing or decreasing the output volume of your computer using the speaker keys at the top of the keyboard's keypad or turning a physical dial on your speakers.

▶ **Audio Monitoring**

It is critical that you perform your final mix in an environment that matches the environment of your intended audience. Room acoustics and speaker types have a huge impact on the way your audio sounds. If you create your final mix in a perfectly soundproof environment and you're making a safety video for airplane passengers, or you're mixing in your bedroom with tiny speakers and planning to project the finished film in a cavernous theater, you're in for unpleasant surprises.

If you don't have the flexibility to create your mix in the intended environment, at least make a preliminary cut and schedule a preliminary screening in your target location. Then, having heard the results, go back and tweak your EQ and dynamic range settings to accommodate those acoustical conditions.

Furthermore, if you're fantasizing that your film is going to be screened exclusively in movie theaters and you build a mix with 18–20 dB of dynamic range, but instead the vast majority of viewers watch it on DVDs on their laptop computers, neither you nor the audience are going to be happy with the results. You're far better off planning for a narrower dynamic range, or even making multiple versions like feature film sound engineers commonly do.

Setting a Dialogue Level

Now that you've decided upon a reference level and have properly configured your speakers, it's time to tackle the sequence's audio. The first step in this process is to set the dialogue so its average level is approximately the same as the level of your reference tone.

In Lesson 10, you applied normalization gain to help give your clips a more uniform level. But normalization sets the peak level, which may or may not accurately align the various clips' average levels.

If you take care to set your dialogue's average level to the same level as the reference tone, all of your sequence's other sounds fall naturally into place. For the purpose of this lesson, you'll stay with the broadcast-compatible reference tone of –12 dB.

NOTE ▶ You also must pay attention to your sequence's peak level. For broadcast, audio that uses a reference level of –12 dB should never peak above –6 dB on Final Cut Pro's Audio Meter.

1   Play the sequence again and determine the average level of the dialogue.

Right now the average level of the dialogue is approximately –18 dB. Furthermore, this level is consistent across the entire sequence. Your reference tone is at –12 dB, so you need to raise the level of each audio clip by 6 dB. You could progress clip by clip through the sequence, grabbing the pink level overlay line, and raising the level of each clip by hand. But that would be a slow and arduous task. Instead, use the following trick to boost the level of all the clips at once.

2   With the Selection tool, drag a selection range around all of the audio clips in track A1 and track A2.

All of the clips in track A1 and track A2 are selected.

3   Choose Modify > Levels (Command-Option-L).

The Gain Adjust window opens.

This window lets you simultaneously adjust the level of several audio clips. It's simple to use; just grab the slider and set an amount to adjust the gain by. Positive values increase the level of the selected clips; negative values decrease it.

However, there is one important setting in this window, and that's Make Changes. This setting has two different values: Absolute and Relative.

▶   *Absolute*: Each selected audio clip is moved to the exact value indicated on the "Adjust gain by" slider. If the clip contains keyframes, the keyframes are erased.

▶ *Relative*: This is the default setting. All gain adjustments look at the current level of each individual clip, and then adjust the clip by the amount specified in the "Adjust gain by" slider. If the clip contains keyframes, each individual keyframe is adjusted by the amount specified in the "Adjust gain by" slider.

NOTE ▶ The Gain Adjust window modifies clips' actual level settings, not the gain filter used by the Normalize Gain control.

4   Leave the Make Changes setting at Relative, set the "Adjust gain by" slider to 6, and click OK.

The level of each clip increases by 6 dB.

5   Play the sequence again and watch the Audio Meter.

Now the average level of the dialogue is approximately –12 dB. Perfect!

With the dialogue set to the correct level, it's time to adjust the level of the sequence's other audio tracks. You'll do that in the following exercises using Final Cut Pro's Audio Mixer.

Exploring the Audio Mixer

Final Cut Pro's Audio Mixer is a great component in your audio editing arsenal. With a fader (level slider), a Pan slider, and Mute and Solo buttons for every audio track in your project, the Audio Mixer mimics the functionality of a hardware audio mixing console.

Using the Audio Mixer

Open the Audio Mixer and take a look around.

1   Choose Tools > Audio Mixer (Option-6).

A Tool Bench window opens containing the Audio Mixer.

This window is dominated by a central section that contains a dedicated level fader for each track in your project. At the top of each track's fader is a Pan slider, a Mute (speaker) button, and a Solo (headphones) button. The Mute and Solo buttons in the

Audio Mixer provide exactly the same function as the Mute and Solo buttons in the Timeline.

A quick glance at these buttons shows that track A1 and track A2 are currently soloed. This means tracks A3 through A6 cannot be heard.

2 On track A1 and track A2, click the Solo button to turn soloing off for those two tracks.

3 Press Home to go to the head of the sequence, then play the sequence.

Watch the track faders. In Final Cut Pro, levels are assigned to the individual clips rather than to the track as a whole. Consequently, as the sequence plays you will often see the level faders jump up and down to reflect the level of each individual clip. Areas of the Timeline that do not have an audio clip are silent, and the track faders obligingly drop to –inf (infinity) when these blank spaces are encountered.

4   While the audio is playing, drag A2's Pan slider to the left.

A2's audio is now heard completely in the left speaker.

5   Option-click A2's Pan slider.

The Pan slider jumps back to the center. Option-clicking a fader is a quick way to reset the fader to its default setting, and it works on each track's level fader as well.

TIP▶   To gear down a fader's movement and make it more precise, hold the Command key as you drag the fader. This works with all sliders in Final Cut Pro.

6   Drag the Master fader slider (on the right side of the window) down to the bottom.

The Master fader controls the level of the entire mix, so lowering the Master fader causes the entire mix to drop in level.

TIP▶   If you are using a mouse with a scroll wheel, you can position the pointer over a fader and use the scroll wheel to move it up and down. This is often easier and more precise than dragging.

The scale used for the Master fader can be a bit confusing at first. By default, the Master fader sits at 0, but does not indicate whether the 0 refers to unity gain or −12 dB on the digital scale. In fact, the 0 setting here indicates that no boost or attenuation has been applied to the level of the sequence as a whole. You can use it to apply up to 12 dB of boost to the entire mix, or attenuate the mix until it is silent.

7   Option-click the Master fader.

The Master fader returns to 0.

8   Raise or lower the faders on tracks A3 through A6 to set the level of these audio tracks.

Listen closely to the dialogue as you adjust these faders, and set the level so that the dialogue in track A1 and track A2 is still clearly present and easily heard above the other elements of the mix.

Working with Views

This sequence has only 6 audio tracks, which is a very manageable number. Indeed, on most monitors, all 6 tracks easily fit in the Audio Mixer. But what happens if you have 24 audio tracks, or 64? Or even the maximum number of 99 audio tracks available in Final Cut Pro? In those situations, your Audio Mixer would become very crowded. Fortunately, the Audio Mixer lets you hide audio tracks, which allows you to focus only on the audio tracks you currently need to adjust.

Even better, Final Cut Pro gives you access to four different views, or custom track configurations, in the Audio Mixer. For example, you can create one view for dialogue tracks, one for ambiances, one for sound effects, and one for music. When it comes time to adjust the dialogue, just enable the view that contains your dialogue tracks, and only those dialogue tracks will appear in the Audio window.

1   In the Track Selection pane on the left edge of the Audio Mixer, deselect track A6.

The dot beside track A6 turns from black to an outline. Track A6 is hidden, and its track strip disappears from the Audio Mixer.

2   In the Track Selection pane, deselect tracks A3, A4, and A5 to hide them.

Track strips for A1 and A2 are the only ones that remain visible in the Audio Mixer.

3   If the sequence is not playing, play it now.

Although tracks A3 through A6 are hidden in the Audio Mixer, you can still hear them. This demonstrates an important point: Hidden audio tracks are not turned off—they continue to play.

4   In the top-left corner of the Audio Mixer, click View button 2.

All of the audio tracks are once again visible in the Audio Mixer.

5   Deselect track A1 and track A2 to hide them.

You've just created a second view that contains only the music and ambiances. Now, if you wish to adjust the dialogue, click View button 1. If you need to adjust the background audio, click View button 2.

6   Switch back and forth between View 1 and View 2 by clicking the View 1 and 2 buttons.

Resizing the Audio Mixer

Views go a long way to helping you deal with sequences that use many audio tracks. There will, however, be times when you need to adjust several audio tracks at the same time. In these situations, it helps to resize the Tool Bench window that holds the Audio Mixer tab so that all the tracks are visible.

Resizing the window with the Audio Mixer has another distinct advantage: If you are attempting to make very subtle level adjustments, the Audio Mixer's faders might seem a bit short, and not exact enough in their movement. You can increase the resolution of these faders by dragging the bottom of the mixer toward the bottom of your screen. This makes the Audio Mixer nice and tall, which gives you more precise control over fader movements.

1   Drag the Tool Bench window to the left (by its title bar).

Notice that the Tool Bench is actually its own window and not part of the Viewer. When you opened the Tool Bench, it completely covered the Viewer, but it's actually an independent window that you can open, resize, and close, as needed.

2   Drag the bottom-right corner of the Tool Bench window down toward the bottom of the screen.

The Tool Bench window becomes taller—and so do its faders! You now have more precise control over your fader settings.

On the other hand, the Audio Mixer is now obstructing a lot of your valuable screen real estate. Final Cut Pro contains a window arrangement that is tailored for audio mixing.

3   Choose Window > Arrange > Audio Mixing.

The Tool Bench window opens in the top-right corner of the screen, displaying the Audio Mixer in a tab.

Using Real-Time Keyframing

Real-time keyframing is arguably the coolest audio feature in Final Cut Pro, because you can record level, pan, and audio effects changes in real time simply by moving a fader or slider. Real-time keyframing really shines if you need to do quick edits like *ducking* (temporarily lowering) background music so it doesn't drown out a section of dialogue, or when creating custom level fades.

1   Make sure the Audio Mixer is set to View 2.

2   In the top-right corner of the Audio Mixer, click the Record Audio Keyframes button (Shift-Command-K).

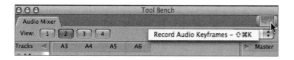

You can now record keyframes in real time, as the sequence plays.

NOTE ▶ You can also enable and disable audio keyframe recording by opening the User Preferences window and selecting the Record Audio Keyframes box.

3   Open User Preferences by choosing Final Cut Pro > User Preferences or pressing
Option-Q. Click the Editing tab.

4   In the Record Audio Keyframes pop-up menu, choose All and click OK.

5   In the Timeline, press Option-X to clear the In and Out points.

6   Press Home to move the playhead to the beginning of the sequence, then press the
Spacebar to start playback.

7   In the Audio Mixer, drag the fader up and down for track A5 as the sequence plays.

Track A5 and track A6 are a stereo pair, so as you move the fader for track A5, the
fader for track A6 comes along for the ride.

8   After you've made a few changes to the fade, stop playback.

In the Timeline, notice that your fader movements have been recorded as keyframes
in the **PencilMusic.aif** clip overlay.

With the Record Audio Keyframes option set to All, Final Cut Pro records keyframes
for every fader movement. This is precise, but it also means that over the course of
the sequence, there are many tiny abrupt adjustments. Often a curve will be smoother
(and easier to modify later) if it consists of fewer points.

9   Choose Final Cut Pro > User Preferences and click the Editing tab.

10 Choose Record Audio Keyframes > Peaks Only. Click OK.

11 Press Home to return to the top of the sequence and play it again.

12 While the sequence plays, drag the fader up and down for track A5 in the Audio Mixer.

13 After a few movements, stop playback.

First of all, notice that the keyframes for the tracks have been entirely replaced. Each time you make changes, it erases the previous keyframes.

Because you changed the setting to Peaks Only, far fewer keyframes are recorded this time.

14 Deselect the Record Audio Keyframes button in the Audio Mixer button bar to disable real-time keyframing.

WARNING ▶ When you're done recording real-time keyframes, always disable this option! If you don't, adjustments you make to Level and Pan sliders in the Viewer and Timeline will automatically be recorded as keyframes, which may not be desirable.

Resetting a Clip's Keyframes

If you record keyframes, either intentionally or accidentally, and then decide you don't want them, you can reset the clip and delete all keyframes using the following technique.

1 In the Timeline, double-click the **PencilMusic.aif** audio clip in track A5 to open it in the Viewer.

2 In the Viewer Audio tab, click the Reset button.

3 All of the clip's Level keyframes are deleted, and its overlay is set back to its default value of 0 dB of boost/attenuation.

Lesson Review

1. Do peak levels or average levels best indicate the apparent volume of a clip?
2. How is dynamic range measured?
3. What is a reference tone used for?
4. How many views are contained in the Audio Mixer?
5. Is a muted track included when you export an AIF?
6. Is a disabled track included when you export an AIF?
7. How do you reset a slider in the Audio Mixer?
8. In Final Cut Pro's Master fader, what does 0 (zero) mean?

Answers

1. While peak levels show the absolute highest levels a track reaches, average levels are a better indication of the overall volume of a clip.
2. In decibels (dB), measuring the difference between the quietest and loudest levels in a program.
3. A reference tone indicates the average level of the dialogue in your program. It informs exhibitors, broadcasters, or duplicators at what level they should set their equipment in order to reproduce the sound the way you intended.
4. The Audio Mixer contains four views, each of which can contain a subset of tracks from your entire program.
5. Muted tracks are included in all exported and output files.
6. Disabled tracks are not included in any exported or output file.
7. Option-click a slider to reset it. You can also Control-click and choose Reset from the shortcut menu.
8. In Final Cut Pro's Master fader, 0 (zero) means no boost or attenuation. It is not an indication of decibels (dB).

The Big Picture

12

Lesson Files	Lesson Files > Lesson 12 > BigPicture
Media	Media > FBI Guys
Time	This lesson takes approximately 30 minutes to complete.
Goals	Construct a master sequence
	Examine a rough cut to identify common problems
	Replace a nested sequence with its component clips
	Re-nest clips into a subsequence
	Rearrange scenes in a master sequence
	Add transition effects between sequences

Putting It All Together

There is nothing more exhilarating—or more disappointing—than finishing your rough cut and watching it for the first time. At long last, you get to see the whole show assembled and hear the story told from beginning to end. But that first viewing also exposes the inadequacies or deficiencies of your show, and inevitably there will be some.

The show will be too long. There will be scenes and sequences that are redundant and repetitive. Transitions between sequences will feel clunky or inorganic. Bits won't work. And—borne from Nature's cruelest sense of irony—these will be the bits that you and your team love the most. In essence, everything about the show will feel wrong.

Relax. Everyone feels exactly the same way at this stage.

Organizing a Master Sequence

Final Cut Pro allows you to nest sequences inside one another, which is a great way to organize a show as you complete it, allowing you to cut individual scenes (or sometimes a small group of scenes that make up a single event) in their own sequences. This technique has numerous benefits: It allows you to work on a scene in the middle of your show without worrying about how much space to leave before or after it; it keeps your Timelines relatively short and easily viewed at once; and it allows you to move or rearrange sequences as whole objects, which can be invaluable during the post-roughcut phase.

When your scenes are nearly complete, you can throw them all into a master sequence to watch the show as a whole. This doesn't preclude you from continuing to tweak and modify the scenes. On the contrary, it makes it easier for you to focus on one scene at a time without worrying about adversely affecting other sections of the show.

1   Open **BigPicture**.

This project contains several sequences that are intended to demonstrate a few of the common tools used at this point in the editing process. However, for obvious reasons, it cannot include a full rough cut for you to experiment with. At this point in your studies, you ideally have your own full-length projects in which to implement the important concepts described in this lesson.

2   Open *Master Sequence* into the Canvas and Timeline.

This sequence contains two items, each of which is an entire sequence on its own.

3 From the Finished Sequences bin, drag *Scene 41 Pepper Spray* directly into the Timeline, lining it up with the end of Scene 43.

NOTE ▸ You may need to enable snapping (N) to ensure that the sequences line up without leaving a gap.

Nested sequences can be modified easily.

4 Double-click *Scene 43 Boardroom* in the *Master Sequence*.

The sequence opens into its own tab.

5 Play the sequence.

At the end of this sequence, a bit of "dead air" is present as the door shuts behind the departing agents.

6 Shorten the last clip by 5 seconds, so that the scene ends just as the agents go through the doorway.

7 Switch tabs, returning to the *Master Sequence*.

8 Play around the end of Scene 43.

You'll see that the nested sequence has been trimmed automatically. Play across the edit between Scene 29 and Scene 43.

The end of Scene 29 seems to be cut off.

9 Try to ripple the outgoing edge of Scene 29 in the *Master Sequence*.

A Media Limit tooltip appears: There are no additional frames in the nested sequence.

10 Double-click *Scene 29 Pencil Throw*.

The sequence opens into another tab in the Timeline.

11 Extend the last clip by 6 seconds.

12 Return to the *Master Sequence.*

The change is automatically updated in the master sequence.

You can also rearrange scenes within your master sequence just as you would individual clips.

13 Drag *Scene 41 Pepper Spray* to the left until it snaps to the beginning of *Scene 43 Boardroom.* Before releasing the mouse button, press Option to activate the Swap pointer, then release the mouse button to perform a swap edit.

The scene order is successfully reversed.

Making It Shorter

It's very common, and even healthy, for a first rough cut to be more than twice as long as the final show will become. In fact, if you're editing a 90- to 100-minute feature, and your first cut is only 120 minutes long, you may be in trouble. By the time you tighten it up, remove redundancies, and streamline sequences, you're likely to end up with a scant 75 minutes. This is very true for narrative fiction films, and it's doubly true for documentaries.

The longer the show, the more likely you are to find common problems such as sequences that drag on too long, scenes that reiterate the same emotional or factual point, or even story beats that repeat within scenes. Very often, sections will feel muddy or convoluted, and some scenes won't quite move the story forward.

No matter how you look at it, your show is probably too long. While it is possible to cut a movie too aggressively, sucking all of the air out of it, that is the exception to the rule. Most editors tend to leave some fat around the edges, iteratively trimming off a little with each editorial pass. Here are three basic approaches for shedding those extra pounds:

Tightening Scenes

Before you try to solve your show's excessive length by eliminating whole scenes, search for ways to tighten existing scenes. It is likely that pauses can be eliminated, "ums" and "ahs" can be extracted from interviews, dialogue exchanges can be overlapped, and reaction shots can be shortened.

If you have been cutting to temp music, now is the time to turn off the music and watch the scene for its own content. When matching the pacing and flow of a music track, it's a common mistake to let some shots linger on too long. Your music should be serving your picture, not the other way around.

Often, through simple tightening, you can remove 10 percent of the overall show length without sacrificing one frame of your story. Remember that the overall goal of a film is to use the power of story to convey a theme. As long as the theme remains clearly communicated, cut with impunity.

Eliminating Redundancy

To elaborate on that point, almost every show of any type will suffer from redundancy that doesn't serve the story or the theme. A certain amount of repetition can be artful—such as the techniques described in Lesson 5 for cutting comedy—but you'll invariably find superfluous scenes or shots that convolute your story and undermine your theme.

Even the best writers will deliberately build redundancy into their scripts, to ensure that the audience understands a character's motivations or a plot's intricate cause and effect. However, an actor might evoke an emotion with a single expression that renders a two-minute speech unnecessary, or a clever framing through a window might obviate the need for the scene going on inside.

Similarly, audiences are very astute at keeping track of details in a film, often unconsciously. If an element (such as a particular prop, car, location, or character) appears even twice, we assume it holds major significance. If it turns out that it doesn't, you evoke disappointment and confusion, which is generally antithetical to your goal of engaging and controlling the viewers' point of focus. It's up to you to pay careful attention to identifying such redundancies.

Removing Whole Scenes

Eventually, you may have to consider removing an entire scene or sequence from your show. A documentary may have too many ideas competing for attention, resulting in an overall lack of focus. A drama may have a subplot that is stealing too much energy or doesn't support the main plot. Sometimes you get lucky, and a sequence can literally be extracted from the master sequence leaving the surrounding scenes neatly stitched together. More often though, removing one scene means shifting other scenes around, or removing other scenes from the same subplot. This is delicate surgery that can result in making things worse before they get better.

When removing scenes, always remember to experiment on duplicates of your sequences, so that you can quickly retrace your steps and return to an earlier cut. You'll do that in the following exercise.

1   In the Browser, right-click *Master Sequence* and choose Duplicate.

A new sequence is added at the same bin level as the original.

2   Rename the duplicate sequence with an incremental number or a descriptive name such as *Master without Breakin Subplot*.

3   Double-click the new sequence and make your changes to that sequence.

It's very easy to forget to do this last step. If you do, you will wind up making your changes to the currently-open sequence, and removing the "breakin subplot" from the *Master Sequence*. Meanwhile, the *Master Sequence without Breakin Subplot* becomes the one that actually contains the whole, original show.

While you may think you can keep track of such confusing names in your head, a few days from now you will invariably get tripped up; and, if you are working in a collaborative environment, you will certainly make a mess for your fellow editors.

If you do get really lost, you can check the last modified date of a particular sequence.

4   Scroll the Browser all the way to the right to view the Last Modified column.

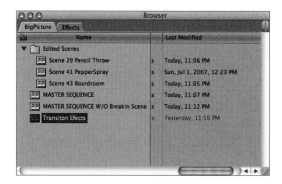

5   Click that column header to sort by most recent.

Now the sequences can be identified based on the last time you made changes to them.

Intercutting Scenes

Sometimes you may seek a compromise between keeping or cutting a whole scene. In some instances, a single essential moment of a scene can remain, while all of the buildup or wind-down can be eliminated.

If multiple scenes take place at the same time in the story, or are otherwise redundant, you may wish to choose individual sections of each and cut between them. This is called *intercutting*. Intercutting techniques were described in more detail in Lesson 3; but, at this stage in the edit, each of your scenes is represented by a single object in the Timeline, so intercutting them is more difficult.

Rather than intercutting the two nested sequences as if they were clips, it may be more advantageous to replace the nested sequences with their contents.

1   In the Timeline, make sure the *Master Sequence* tab is selected.

2   From the Browser, drag the *Scene 41 Pepper Spray* sequence to the Timeline and line it up directly at the beginning of the identical clip in the Timeline. Don't release the mouse button.

NOTE ▶ You may need to zoom in and/or turn on snapping to ensure that the objects line up precisely.

3 Before releasing the mouse button, press the Command key.

You'll see the outlines of the individual clips that comprise the sequence.

4 With the Command key held down, verify that the pointer indicates an overwrite edit (a downward facing arrow) and release the mouse button.

The subsequence is replaced by its contents.

By following this procedure for two or more nested sequences, you could intercut them to your liking. After you have constructed the new section, you can easily return it into a single subsequence object using the Nest Items command.

NOTE ► For this lesson, rather than actually intercutting two sequences, you will just take the same clips from that scene and re-nest them.

5   Using the Selection tool (A), drag a marquee around all of the clips between the Scene 29 and Scene 43 sequence clips.

6   Choose Sequence > Nest Item(s), or press Option-C.

The Nest Items dialog appears.

7   Name the new sequence *Recut Scene 41*, leave the rest of the settings at their defaults, and click OK.

The clips are replaced in the Timeline by a single, nested sequence.

Transitioning Between Scenes

Another pervasive dilemma that arises at the rough cut stage is the challenge of transitioning from one sequence to the next. While each scene may be a complete and tidy package, there seems to be no connective tissue to string them together. In instructional or documentary projects, switching between subjects or segments can feel clumsy and inelegant. In fact, developing smooth and transparent bridges between scenes and sequences is an art unto itself.

Some transitions will be conceived during production: One scene is shot to end with a certain framing that will match the beginning of the next. One of the most common examples is when someone exits frame left at the end of one scene and enters frame right at the start of the next.

However, when you don't have such organic or well-planned connections, you'll have to invent your own. Fortunately, this is when you can employ those thousands of seemingly unusable transition effects included in Final Cut Pro.

1   Open and play the *Transition Effects* sequence.

This is a slightly altered version of the documentary footage you edited in Lessons 6 and 7. The sections have been grouped into subsequences that are nested into a new master sequence.

2   Position your playhead at the edit between *Crew* and *Crew2*.

3   Choose Effects > Video Transitions > 3D Simulation > Spin 3D.

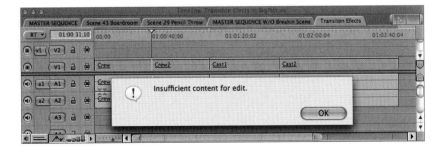

An error occurs because there are no additional frames available in either sequence to accommodate the transition effect.

4   Select the Ripple tool (R) and drag the outgoing edge of *Crew* to the left by approximately 15 frames.

NOTE ▸ You may have to zoom in and/or disable snapping to accurately trim by this amount.

5   Ripple the Incoming edge of *Crew2* to the right by about 15 frames.

Now there are adequate frames to permit a transition effect of up to 1 second.

6   With the edit still selected, choose Effects > Video Transitions > 3D Simulation > Spin 3D.

The transition effect is applied. Because of the unusual footage format, you will have to render the transition effect to see it play.

7   Press Command-R to render the effect.

8   Press \ (backslash) to play around the edit and see the effect.

While such unnatural effects have no place in the middle of a scene, using them for transitions between sections can be effective and fun.

9   Experiment with different transition effects for the remaining edits.

Killing Your Darlings

Inevitably, there will be some element of your edited show that just doesn't work. It could be an elaborate camera move or special effect shot, it could be a genius scene transition idea, or maybe it is your one celebrity interview. The element is something that, until this point, everyone believed was essential—if not downright fundamental—to the essence of the show; and now, it's something that you must cut.

One of the few absolute requirements in order to excel as an editor is the ruthless ability to kill your darlings for the sake of the show. The director and producers may fight you, clinging to that element that is now distracting or undermining the rest of the program. You may even be in love with it yourself, but it's up to you to summon the strength to cut it.

Playing a Game of Inches

Sailboat racing is often described as a game of inches; not because the winning boat will pass the finish line mere finger lengths before the competition, but because, in a tight race, boats can maneuver mere inches apart, nearly colliding and damaging one another. Also, the stiffer the sail, the more precisely you can control the wind, and pulling the main sheet three inches tighter will make a measurable difference that could determine whether you win or lose the race.

In many ways, editing is also a game of inches. Tiny changes can have a dramatic impact on the overall show. An edit point that's off by three or four frames can make a transition look terrible and pull the viewers out of an otherwise emotional scene. Eliminating or replacing one shot that doesn't fit perfectly will change the entire dynamic of a sequence— and one slow sequence can make the whole show seem too long.

Be careful not to oversteer. Make very small changes and see how they impact the whole before you do something drastic. In the end, remember that filmmaking—indeed, all storytelling—is a collaborative endeavor, and ultimately the collaboration is between the creators and the audience. Show your project to an audience and gauge their interest. When do they shift in their seats, or cough, or fall asleep? There is nothing more helpful than a brutally honest test screening. After all, whether your film is intended to earn a buck, change a mind, enlighten a soul, or sell a product, ultimately your audience and its response to your work defines your skill as an editor.

Lesson Review

1. How can you create a master sequence to view your rough cut?
2. What are three common problems that appear when the rough cut is complete?
3. Can you trim a nested sequence directly in the master sequence?
4. What happens to the master sequence when subsequences are modified?
5. Can you apply a transition between two subsequences?
6. How do you replace a sequence with its contents?
7. How do you re-nest loose clips into a sequence?

Answers

1. Place the sequences for each scene or section into a master sequence.
2. The show feels too long or drags; redundant or repetitive elements need to be eliminated; transitions between sequences seem clunky and inorganic.
3. You can shorten a nested sequence, but lengthening it requires opening the sequence into its own Timeline.
4. The master sequence will automatically ripple to accommodate any duration changes in the sequences nested within it.
5. Only if frames exist beyond the In and Out points of the sequences (just like ordinary clips).
6. Drag the sequence from the Browser to the Timeline and press Command before releasing the mouse button.
7. Select the clips and choose Sequence > Nest Item(s).

Index

Final Cut Pro Tools and Features: Look-up Guide

If you're looking for specific Final Cut Pro tools and features, we've put together this cross-referenced list directing you to relevant pages.

Editing

Trimming

Commands

Interface Elements

Timecode

The Apple Pro Training Series

The official curriculum of the Apple Pro Training and Certification Program, the Apple Pro Training books are comprehensive, self-paced courses written by acknowledged experts in the field. Focused lessons take you step by-step through the process of creating real-world digital video or audio projects, while lesson files on the companion DVD and ample illustrations help you master techniques fast. In addition, lesson goals and time estimates help you plan your time, while chapter review questions summarize what you've learned.

Final Cut Pro 6
0-321-50265-5

Cut a scene from the USA Network television series *Monk*, create a promo for Seaworld's *Belief* documentary, master filters and effects as you edit a segment of BBC's *Living Color*. In this best-selling guide, Diana Weynand starts with basic video editing techniques and takes you all the way through Final Cut Pro's powerful advanced features. You'll learn to mark and edit clips, mix sound, add titles, create transitions, apply filters, and more.

Final Cut Pro 6: Beyond the Basics
0-321-50912-9

Director and editor Michael Wohl shows how to master advanced trimming techniques, make polished transitions, work with nested sequences, edit multi-camera projects, create fantastic effects, color-correct your video, and composite like a pro. Also covers Soundtrack Pro, and managing clips and media.

The Craft of Editing with Final Cut Pro
0-321-52036-X

Superbly fitted to a semester-length course, this is the ideal curriculum for a hands-on exploration of advanced editing. Director and editor Michael Wohl shares must-know techniques for cutting dialogue scenes, action scenes, fight and chase scenes, documentaries, comedy, music videos, multi-camera projects, and more. Two DVD-9s of professional footage and project files give students the chance to work with every genre as they learn.

Motion Graphics and Effects in Final Cut Studio 2
0-321-50940-4

This practical approach focuses on just the parts of Final Cut Studio that editors and designers need to create motion graphics in their daily work.

Motion 3
0-321-50910-2

Top commercial artists show you how to harness Motion's behavior-based animations, particles, filters, effects, tracking, and 3D capabilities.

Soundtrack Pro 2
0-321-50266-3

Audio producer Martin Sitter is your guide to the only professional audio post application designed specifically for the Final Cut editor.

DVD Studio Pro 4, Second Edition
0-321-50189-6

Learn to author professional DVDs with this best-selling guide. Build three complete DVDs, including the DVD for the Oscar-nominated *Born into Brothels* documentary.

Color
0-321-50911-0

This guide to Apple's masterful new color grading software starts with the basics of color correction and moves on to the fine points of secondary grading, tracking, and advanced effects.

Apple Pro Training Series: Logic Pro 7 and Logic Express 7
0-321-25614-X

Create, mix, and polish your musical creations using Apple's pro audio software.

Apple Pro Training Series: Advanced Logic Pro 7
0-321-25607-7

Comprehensive guide takes you through Logic's powerful advanced features.

Apple Pro Training Series: Shake 4
0-321-25609-3

Apple-certified guide uses stunning real world sequences to reveal the wizardry of Shake 4.

Encyclopedia of Visual Effects
0-321-30334-2

Ultimate recipe book for visual effects artists working in Shake, Motion and Adobe After Effects.

Encyclopedia of Color Correction
0-321-43231-2

Comprehensive training in the real-world color correction and management skills editing pros use every day in the field.

Aperture 1.5
0-321-49662-0

The best way to learn Aperture's powerful photo-editing, image-retouching, proofing, publishing, and archiving features.

Final Cut Express 2
0-321-25615-8

The only Apple-authorized guide to Final Cut Express 2 has you making movie magic in no time..

Optimizing Your Final Cut Pro System
0-321-26871-7

The ultimate guide for installing, configuring, optimizing, and trouble-shooting Final Cut Pro in real-world post-production environments.

Final Cut Pro for Avid Editors, Third Edition
0-321-51539-0

This comprehensive "translation course" is designed for professional video and film editors who already know their way around Avid nonlinear systems.

Final Cut Pro 6 for Sports and News Quick-Reference Guide
0-321-51423-8

This easy look-up guide provides essential techniques for broadcast studios using Final Cut Pro to edit news and sports.

Shake 4 Quick Reference Guide
0-321-38246-3

This compact reference guide to Apple's leading compositing software offers a concise explanation of the Shake interface, workspace, and tools..

Compressor 3 Quick-Reference Guide
0-321-51422-X

Learn essential techniques for audio and video compression, batch-encoding, test-clip workflows, exporting podcasts, and more.

QuickTime Pro Quick-Reference Guide
0-321-44248-2

An invaluable guide to capturing, encoding, editing, streaming, and exporting media.

Final Cut Server Quick-Reference Guide
0-321-51024-0

Final Cut Server delivers intuitive media asset management, review and approval tools, and workflow automation.

Xsan Quick-Reference Guide, Second Edition
0-321-43232-0

Apple's exciting new enterprise-class file system offers high-speed access to centralized shared data.

The Apple Training Series

Apple Training Series: Mac OS X Support Essentials
0-321-33547-3

Apple Training Series: Mac OS X Server Essentials
0-321-35758-2

Apple Training Series: Desktop and Portable Systems, Third Edition
0-321-33546-5

Apple Training Series: Mac OS X System Administration Guide, Volume 1
0-321-36984-X

Apple Training Series: Mac OS X System Administration Guide, Volume 2
0-321-42315-1

Apple Training Series: iLife '06
0-321-42164-7

Apple Training Series: GarageBand 3
0-321-42165-5

Apple Training Series: iWork 06 with iLife 06
0-321-44225-3